How do citizens and leaders in democratic nations communicate about their problems and prospects for the future? What can be learned from other nations about how to communicate in more effective and satisfying ways? These are important questions in an age of instant electronic communication in which the populations of the world's industrial democracies are wired for all manner of input. The irony, or perhaps the result, of communication in this Digital Age is that the quality of political ideas in many nations has deteriorated into simplistic sloganeering and angry rhetoric with little perceptible improvement in the human political condition.

Democracy and the Marketplace of Ideas explores the institutional links between society and government that shape political communication. These regulators of national communication include parties and electoral representation systems, interest group processes, campaign finance mechanisms, and the media – factors that are familiar to anyone who follows politics yet that may not be recognized for their combined effects on the quality of political discourse. Erik Åsard and W. Lance Bennett show how these core elements of political systems affect the ways in which people communicate and how effective that communication is at defining public problems and identifying workable solutions.

Democracy and the
Marketplace of Ideas

Democracy and the Marketplace of Ideas

Communication and Government in Sweden and the United States

Erik Åsard
Uppsala University

W. Lance Bennett
University of Washington

CAMBRIDGE
UNIVERSITY PRESS

CAMBRIDGE
UNIVERSITY PRESS

32 Avenue of the Americas, New York NY 10013-2473, USA

Cambridge University Press is part of the University of Cambridge.

It furthers the University's mission by disseminating knowledge in the pursuit of education, learning and research at the highest international levels of excellence.

www.cambridge.org
Information on this title: www.cambridge.org/9780521565257

First published 1997

A catalogue record for this publication is available from the British Library

Library of Congress Cataloguing in Publication data
Åsard, Erik.
  Democracy and the marketplace of ideas: communication and government in Sweden and the United States / Erik Åsard, W. Lance Bennett.
    p.   cm.
  Includes bibliographical references.
    ISBN 0-521-56336-4 (hc). — ISBN 0-521-56525-1 (pb)
    1. Communication in politics—United States. 2. Democracy—United States. 3. Communication in politics—Sweden. 4. Democracy—Sweden.   I. Bennett, W. Lance.   II. Title.
JA85.2.U6B46   1997
324'.014—dc20

ISBN 978-0-521-56336-9 Hardback
ISBN 978-0-521-56525-7 Paperback

Contents

Preface

How do citizens and leaders in democratic nations communicate about their problems and prospects for the future? What can be learned from other nations about how to communicate in more effective and satisfying ways? These are important questions in an age of instant electronic communication in which the populations of the world's industrial democracies are wired for all manner of input. The irony, or perhaps the result, of communication in this Digital Age is that the quality of political ideas in many nations has deteriorated into simplistic sloganeering and angry rhetoric with little perceptible improvement in the human political condition. This book explores the institutional links between society and government that shape political communication. These regulators of national communication include parties and electoral representation systems, interest group processes, campaign finance mechanisms, and the media – factors that are familiar to anyone who follows politics, yet that may not be recognized for their combined effects on the quality of political discourse. We propose to explore how these core elements of political systems affect the ways in which people communicate and how effective that communication is at defining public problems and identifying workable solutions.

Our main argument is that fundamental changes have occurred in the way that most democratic nations conduct their public discourse – how publics and leaders, in effect, define themselves in the contemporary world. The link between rhetoric and the workings (and breakdowns) of government has never been more apparent. We are witnessing rebellious voters and renegade candidates the world over taking often misguided aim at institutions of power. We take a more systematic look at how institutions forged in earlier eras may limit the terms of national debate. At the same time, it is clear that not all nations face the same institutional limitations, making the study of national differences as important as the concern about common trends. The political marketplace in many Western democracies has been transformed from being a forum for heated debate and a comparatively lively exchange of ideas into one dominated by only a few substantive issues and a lot of quite streamlined rhetoric that is more likely to be the product of political marketing research than of inspired leadership. What today's public seems to get, in political systems as diverse as those of the United States and Sweden, are increasingly similar ideas marketed in increasingly similar ways to increasingly smaller audiences. Publics in most of these nations have recognized the marketing and emotionalism of this discourse for what it is: political hype that only accentuates the lack of ideas and the reluctance of parties and leaders to engage in searching national debates. This shrinking range of ideas exchanged among parties, candidates, and publics in the political marketplace is the *leitmotif* of our analysis. This condition results in the spiraling discontent of publics and the fragmentation of traditional forms of governing institutions from disciplined, broad-based parties to stable alliances of interests.

With power fragmented and political language placed increasingly in the service of short-term tactical (opinion and media management) ends, publics come to regard hypocrisy as the political norm. Citizens, too, become corrupted by these experiences and lose the sense that common visions and moral guidance can come from civic life. The rhetoric of candidates and parties alike often encourages people to seek private gain from government rather than common good. The imagined communities that we call societies become pockets of isolated and often suspicious groups easily led by the languages of nationalism, racial animosity, personal economic interest, and suspicion of others. These failures of the political imagination further undermine the possibility for broad visions of society that might promote identification across groups and mobilize support for enduring agendas of political action. Levels of distress caused by these developments are evident in many forms, including the loss of confidence in politicians and governments reported in countless opinion polls, attacks on government itself by candidates and elected leaders, and the accompanying loss of governmental stability. At the personal level, we note chronic increases in drug and alcohol abuse (among other problems) in many nations, along with other lifestyle disruptions caused by rising levels of underemployment in allegedly recovering economies. At such historical moments, it becomes important to investigate the ways different governmental systems respond to the demands for political guidance that loom so large in the minds of their citizens.

THE POLITICS OF IDEAS

The solutions for these dilemmas are not so simple as just thinking about society anew – although that is not a bad place to start. Ideas are not free-floating entities: their origins, publicity, popular comprehension, nurturance, and implementation depend on institutional conditions that give political life (or death) to the human imagination. Even the most brilliant or workable ideas can be stifled by the overbearing institutions of government when those same institutions select and promote often absurd or demonstrably failed policies instead. Our primary interest is to understand how governing ideas are produced in different political systems. More important, in light of the trends noted, we are interested in how different systems respond to the decline of ideas and to the growing disjunctures among parties, leaders, publics, political ideas, and the agendas of governments. Our goal is to place this contemporary democratic disarray – along with signs of promising changes – in comparative and historical perspective.

The comparative framework developed in this book – and tempered by the analysis of two very different national cases – is intended to apply to any advanced industrial democracy that has evolved relatively stable arrangements for party government, interest aggregation and expression, political finance, and mass political communication. Differences between nations become, from this perspective, opportunities to compare and learn. In particular, our approach clarifies how key institutional differences between nations affect the production of political ideas and how those ideas are incorporated into the governing process.

Our most sweeping contribution in this book is to point out the inseparability of institutions and ideas. The popular notion of "empty rhetoric" may reflect less the failure of human imagination or the mysterious dearth of inspired leaders than the propensity of particular institutional habits to actively block the consideration of new ideas. Rather than continue deploying these same institutional routines (only to discover that the rhetoric remains empty), it may make more sense to think about institutional reforms as the first step toward opening up the national dialogue to new ideas. This is a lesson that cannot be learned from just one nation alone but requires study of the ways various polities engage with similar problems and issues. Today's world has provided us with a set of laboratory conditions ripe for exploring different democracies that are going through remarkably similar experiences. In the spirit of breaking down barriers to thinking about how nations can better address their difficulties, we invite the reader to join us on an exploration of political rhetoric and governance in two interesting political systems. For the people of these two systems who may read this book, we encourage the attitude that this is not just a book about ourselves but a book about each other.

A TALE OF TWO NATIONS

In developing this framework, we have concentrated on two nations in particular, Sweden and the United States. These countries are very different in terms of size, party and election systems, communication institutions, interest processes, and political cultures – particularly in traditional citizen expectations about the nature and responsibilities of government. Like many scholars before us, we were drawn to these contrasts as challenges to the construction of more general and durable frameworks of comparative analysis. In particular, we were drawn to the comparison for several other reasons. First, these two different political systems are suffering some startlingly similar political patterns and problems. Second, the ways in which leaders and voters are trying to sort these problems out reflect some interesting similarities and differences that invite generalizations beyond any that could be supported by a study of either nation alone. Finally, as has been noted, two such different countries present interesting challenges for theory and comparison. If we can say something useful about cases as different as these, then we may have something to say about general problems of democratic institutions and their capacity to help people address and resolve new conditions and problems in society.

The United States and Sweden today find themselves in similar states of democratic disarray. In both countries confidence in governments, leaders, and parties has declined sharply in the post–World War II period. Traditional forms of communication between leaders and citizens have given way to short-term emotional media campaigns aimed at mobilizing public support for policies and votes for candidates. These battles for public opinion have undermined stable political coalitions based on earlier and more enduring governing visions. Publics increasingly view politicians with suspicion, and politicians approach publics warily with an eye to polls and news management. Citizens reinforce this vicious spiral by abandoning party loyalties and adopting centrist and increasingly personalized political outlooks. Parties scramble to stay in power by fitting their ideas to these shifting trends in opinion, trying to capture blocs of opinion and votes for narrow, strategic political ends.

The paradox is that as mass communication grows more sophisticated, the media are used to transmit ever more personalized political messages to ever more isolated and carefully marketed networks of information consumers. As the electronics frontier expands into the realm of virtual reality, citizen disconnection from social and civic institutions may be replaced by growing participation in imaginary electronic communities. The resulting fragmentation of publics and the targeting of specialized groups with personalized messages suggest the parallel development of a virtual democracy. As political leaders increasingly rely on coteries of pollsters and media consultants to manage their communication with citizens, the hope for spontaneous, two-way exchanges of ideas becomes ever more remote, as does the hope for developing more sustainable, long-term ideas for governing. Hence, the irony is that as communication technologies become more sophisticated and individuals are more easily brought on-line, the hope for greater public autonomy and input becomes more remote.

The problem lies with political communication strategies aimed at shoring up power in institutions that are products of an earlier political era – institutions that are, in the largely prescient view of publics, inhibiting creative solutions for the problems of the present day and age. The core breakdowns in these electronic democracies result from communication techniques that effectively prevent, defuse, or deflect unmanageable citizen input, thereby creating a "democracy without citizens," in the words of communication scholar Robert Entman. Despite the considerable institutional and cultural differences in our two national cases, we note that the institutional power arrangements from which enduring governing agendas emerge have become fragmented and unstable. An important result of the present institutional disarray, we believe, is the failure of governments and democratic politicians to communicate with the electorate about the causes of current national troubles and to hold forth a guiding vision for a brighter future. At the same time, this failure of ideas further undermines the stability of governments.

EXTERNAL PROBLEMS, INTERNAL SOLUTIONS

The causes of democracy's contemporary dilemmas may be external to nations in important respects. The collapse of communism has left an ideological void throughout the Western world, leaving both the left and the right frustrated and disoriented. The restructuring of world economic production and money markets, and the resulting dislocations in national economies, have increased citizen demands on government institutions forged by earlier – and very different – political and economic conditions. As governments have let the regulation of multinational corporations slip their grasp, the nation–state has increasingly become hostage to private international business and economic regimes. Pressures to yield national powers to international governing entities have witnessed the United States joining the North American Free Trade Agreement (NAFTA) and Sweden struggling over the loss of sovereignty implied by membership in the European Union, and both nations supporting the rollback of tariff barriers and labor protections in the latest round of the General Agreement on Tariffs and Trade (GATT).

At the same time, these external forces rocking the contemporary world are surely no greater than the global depression of the 1930s that witnessed dramatic rebirths of the political imagination and the rise of new governing visions within many nations. In that earlier era the diffusion of Keynesianism and often sweeping transformations of national institutions were inspired by changing definitions of government itself. Yet today's debates about similarly momentous changes are conducted as media spectacles, generating little sense of where this world system is going or how to protect the needs of national citizens affected by these changes. One of the issues that we explore at some length is what permitted grand governing visions to sweep into national politics following this earlier period of international transformation, while nations today continue to trade on those spent ideas of *l'ancien régime*.

Equally important to understand about the contemporary rhetoric of many nations, including those of our two cases, is the overwhelming tendency of politicians to win elections and mobilize short-term support through misguided symbolic policy initiatives such as crime crackdowns, moral crusades over abortion and religious freedoms, and restrictions on immigration and immigrants. Such policy concerns may actually divert public attention from more important underlying national issues and undermine the capacity of nations to invent workable social and economic policy agendas based on stable systems of political ideas.

These circumstances underscore the importance of language in politics and the relations between language use and the institutions of power and communication that have evolved in particular political systems. Whether the language of politics is high-minded and effective or base and misguided, it shapes policies and political actions. Following the work of Murray

Edelman, we are reminded that language is a form of political action that shapes human sensibilities, directs public attention and concern, and ultimately directs the course of national policy. It is conceivable that dysfunctions in national communication about society's problems actually lead to policies that worsen underlying conditions. As conditions worsen and citizen psychology becomes more volatile, the opportunities for reasoned discourse about institutional reforms become more difficult to create through routine political channels such as voting or the exchange of ideas in the daily news.

Even if constructive solutions for pressing problems exist in the writing of theorists or in the experiences of leaders, they may be hard to sell and even harder to implement as a result of various breakdowns in national institutions. Both the rhetoric and the resolve of politicians are undermined and destabilized as parties lose their bases of mass support, as interest groups pull against the grain of common social values, as campaign finance practices permit a powerful few to set the tone of election discourse, and as the electronic media publicize dramatized, short-term visions of society over more thoughtful and educated exchanges between citizens and their governors. In these ways, governing ideas have fallen prey to communication marketplaces that are either poorly regulated or, worse yet, that are regulated by political brokers to maintain aging institutions and power arrangements that are no longer responsive to contemporary national realities.

THE MARKETPLACE OF IDEAS

This analysis of political language, institutions, and citizen responses in two democracies is based on the idea of a marketplace. In the simplest sense, election campaigns, interest group conflicts, and policy battles involve exchanges of political language for political support. As they become realized in this process, ideas – no matter how uninspired their origins – can alter the shape of policy and the course of government. The rhetoric of such dynamic exchanges can be understood variously as political promises, attacks on opponents, arousal of fears, explanations of programs, exhortations to support parties, and so forth. However, the important point is that these exchanges are shaped by the institutions and power arrangements through which the following are accomplished:

- Candidates are nominated and financed.
- Parties gain representation and power in government.
- Organized interests are expressed.
- Mass communication media inform publics about candidates, interest group activities, and public policy debates.

This perspective offers a new approach to the often ignored intersection of language, institutions, and mass political communication. We propose to look squarely at the impact of such institutional and power arrangements on the production and public valuation of ideas in policy debates and elections. This focus includes not just social, economic, and political theories but the everyday rhetoric used to sell those theories to the masses. As great ideas become worn down by historical and institutional changes, it may be the everyday rhetoric of politics that carries most of the intellectual load. And this load is supported poorly by forms of political communication that have made the term *empty* almost synonymous with the term *rhetoric* in contemporary politics. Yet the sweep of political history tells us of times within many polities when rhetoric inspired people, forged alliances, explained complex ideas in compelling ways, and brought the creative human potential of politics into the governing process.

Whatever the intellectual status of the rhetoric that links citizens to leaders and leaders to government, it is important to understand the institutional forces and constraints that shape that rhetoric. It is equally important to understand that, whether grandiloquent or superficial, the language of politics is not only the simple invention of candidates and their personal advisors but also the product of the institutions and systemic constraints within which those politicians make their calculations about what to tell the people and how to put it symbolically.

OVERVIEW OF THE BOOK

Part I provides a broad overview of democracy, communication, and the marketplace of ideas. Chapter 1 explores in more detail the problems of democracy mentioned in the foregoing section, providing an overview of the ways in which institutions and power arrangements affect political communication in contemporary democracies. In Chapter 2, we identify the mechanisms of the idea market that define the rhetorical capacities of nations: party and election systems, interest group processes, campaign finance practices, and mass media organizations.

Part II traces the rise and fall of the last great governing ideas to dominate the politics of our two nations: the New Deal in the United States (Chapter 3) and the remarkably parallel idea of the *folkhem* that introduced the vision of government as the "people's home" in Sweden (Chapter 4). These grand ideas have had an impact on elections, public policy, and the accompanying rhetoric in both countries for much of this century, serving in such capacities as (1) a focus for political mobilization and opposition in society, (2) intellectual guidance for policy processes, (3) easy-to-grasp public explanations for the actual policy results, and (4) rhetorical targets for opponents.

The institutional differences in our two cases illustrate the different capacities of our two nations to respond creatively to policy and leadership challenges, as explored in the case studies of policy processes and elections in Part III. Chapter 5 analyzes the interplay of institutions and ideas in the policy process involving tax reforms in the United States (1986) and Sweden (1990). Although both cases display remarkably similar political origins, the inability of the decision makers in the U.S. system to control either direct interest group pressure or the impact of campaign finance on party discipline ultimately admitted a high volume of noise into the communication process and undermined the coherence of the tax policy itself. Candidate–party rhetoric in recent national elections in both countries is analyzed in Chapter 6, where the key question is: How do leaders and parties adjust their political messages to new political circumstances such as the declining loyalty of voters and the abandonment of traditional party positions on issues?

Part IV contains the concluding discussion in Chapter 7, which reviews the comparisons introduced in the book, beginning with the rise and fall of dominant governing ideas and proceeding to how the decline of those ideas has created problems in contemporary public policy making and the electoral configuration of government itself. This summary draws out the similarities and differences in the idea markets of the two nations, emphasizing the dilemmas encountered in mobilizing stable public support in systems driven increasingly by short-term emotional rhetoric. A more detailed overview is found at the end of Chapter 1.

In general, we note how the market mechanisms identified in both nations (election and party systems, interest arrangements, political financing, and the mass media) have grown unwieldy, and often work against each other in ways that inhibit the revitalization of governing ideas. However, differences in these institutional arrangements in each nation also matter in important respects for the production of policies and the rhetoric that links them to citizens. The comparative complexity of American institutions and the decentralized relations among them make it difficult for leaders to lead, parties to govern, and citizens to maintain loyalty to broad governing agendas. In a sense, the more centralized and interconnected Swedish institutions may make it easier to govern even when the rhetorics that connect publics to policies are in disarray. The Swedish experience suggests that new ideas are relatively easier to introduce into the political forum. Moreover, even when those ideas are eventually rejected as models for national renewal (as has been the case with various "new idea" parties and coalitions entering Parliament and government in recent years), the activities of government are less likely to be destabilized in the process. Understanding the effects of these different institutional and power arrangements enables us to conclude by identifying possible reforms that might create more responsive governments and more public consensus about national problems and priorities. The book closes with a look at what we have learned that can be applied to the political discontents of democracies in the contemporary world.

Acknowledgments

Many people and organizations have contributed encouragement, questions, funding, and, yes, ideas to this project. In Sweden, the project gained focus through the lively exchanges with the review panel for the *Riksbankens Jubileumsfond,* which provided generous funding for the research. We also acknowledge the support of the Swedish Institute for North American Studies at Uppsala University, the Fulbright Commission, and the University of Washington.

While we labored in Sweden, our work prospered from the comments and stimulating questions of Kurt Johannesson, whose grasp of political communication spans Gustavus Adolphus and Ronald Reagan. Olle Josephson and Alexander Davidson also contributed to our thinking on important issues. And in a memorable late evening session near the end of the writing, Rolf Lundén offered helpful counsel on our conclusions.

In the United States, the project benefited from the reading and insightful suggestions of Murray Edelman. We were also encouraged by comments from Bruce Gronbeck and Ben Page that our approach contributed something to both political science and communication studies. Susan Herbst both encouraged the comparative perspective and suggested that we show a draft of the manuscript to Alex Holzman, who proved to be the perfect editor for the project. The three reviews contributed by Robert Entman, Susan Herbst, and Jerry Manheim were among the most helpful and critically constructive in the memory of either author. Thanks also go to Jay Blumler and David Swanson for their comments on late drafts of the manuscript.

We also acknowledge the valuable support we have had in researching and preparing this book. In Sweden, Liisa Melton and Pia Karlsson assisted with the production of preliminary reports and drafts of various chapters. In addition, Paula Blomqvist, Pia Karlsson, and Dorothea Schweizer assisted with the research on Swedish historical materials. In the United States, research assistance was provided by Naomi Stacy, Tod Haggard, Susan Holmberg, and John Klockner. The merging of often dramatically different word processing files was handled smoothly by Ann Buscherfeld, who was present at every step of the way.

Portions of Chapter 5 appeared in *Polity* (Fall 1995), and portions of Chapter 6 appeared in *Political Studies* (vol. XLIII, no. 4, 1995) and are reprinted here with permission of those journals. We thank the editors and anonymous reviewers of these journals for the useful feedback they provided at earlier stages of the project.

These generous colleagues have all greatly improved the quality of our ideas.

PART I

THE MARKETPLACE OF IDEAS

1

Democracies in Disarray

Opinion surveys taken in many countries around the world have been reporting a
common finding: Majorities of record or near-record proportions expressing
dissatisfaction with or pessimism about their countries' political and economic
performance and their own personal prospects.... [These] high levels of public
dissatisfaction are also being found in that most prosperous, free, and stable group
of countries, the advanced industrial democracies. The reports coming out of them
read as though each is experiencing a unique national malaise, but taken together
these reports tell a remarkably similar story.
                                                              – Everett C. Ladd

After the fall of the Berlin Wall and the collapse of Soviet-style communism, the old bipolar world system suddenly disappeared and the West
basked in triumph. To some observers this was by no means a foregone conclusion. For example, Samuel Huntington argued as late as the mid-1980s
that "the likelihood of democratic development in Eastern Europe is virtually nil" (Huntington 1984: 217). To others, most notably Francis Fukuyama, the momentous events signaled the "triumph of the West, of the Western *idea*." What we may be witnessing, he wrote, "is not just the end of the
Cold War, or the passing of a particular period of postwar history, but the
end of history as such: that is, the end point of mankind's ideological evolution and the universalization of Western liberal democracy as the final
form of human government."[1]

These sentiments proved to be rather short-lived, however. Western tri-
umphalism quickly came to an end as a bloody civil war erupted in Yugoslavia
and a prolonged economic recession put millions of people out of work in the
industrial world. Unemployment trends put the number of jobless Europeans
alone at 20 million by 1995, about a quarter of them young people between 18
and 25.[2] An Organization for Economic Cooperation and Development

3

(OECD) report released in 1995 projected unacceptably high unemployment levels to continue in Europe beyond the year 2000.[3] Social unrest, ethnic strife, and rampant nationalism have spread while political leaders, often beset by scandals and corruption, seem helpless and devoid of ideas about how to confront – and much less solve – today's pressing problems.

Voter dissatisfaction meanwhile has reached previously unheard-of levels in many Western democracies. There is nothing new about governments being unpopular in times of economic hardships, but the level of discontent registered in Western Europe and the United States has few if any parallels. Neither incumbents nor opposition parties have been spared the wrath of increasingly independent and inattentive electorates.[4] Even more startling, the signs of political disarray persisted in nations such as the United States in which strong economic recoveries were proclaimed by the economists but ignored by voters whose behavior dashed some of the most reliable economic voting models of political scientists. In Canada, which has been on the verge of a constitutional breakdown for years, the ruling Conservative Party was virtually obliterated in the October 1993 elections. Kim Campbell, who succeeded the unpopular Brian Mulroney as prime minister in June, was unable to hold her own seat in Parliament and announced her resignation in December, only six months after she had been elected party leader.[5] Similar voter disgust has been evident in other developed nations, resulting in record-low job approval ratings for governments and a decline of traditional party systems.

Individual politicians and parties are not the only targets of citizen disaffection. Government itself has become a negative symbol, representing distant, uncaring, and often corrupt power – power that has somehow been removed from the grasp of the helpless citizen. Election contests in the United States are as remarkable for the absence of party rhetoric and ideological conflict as for the efforts of candidates to convince voters that the candidates are politically independent, antigovernment outsiders. In countries such as Italy and Japan, the whole political system has been called into question, leading in turn to the overthrow of old established parties and governments. The forty-year rule of the Japanese liberal Democratic Party was ended in 1993, only to be followed by a period of political drift in which participation rates plummeted to historic lows and a nation of party loyalists was transformed rapidly into a majority of skeptical political independents.[6] The 1995 election for the upper house of Parliament produced a historic low turnout of 44.5 percent. The largest single block of seats went to an upstart party with the name of New Frontier.

Even in Germany, long regarded as a pillar of stability and economic growth, the *Wirtschaftswunder* (economic miracle) of the past gave way to a gloomy "bust" mentality that quickly dampened the celebration of unification. Just a few years after the country was united, the prestige of German politicians sank to the lowest recorded levels of the modern era. Asked in a 1993 poll whether they thought that "the right people are in leading positions in Germany today," two thirds of respondents said no. (The popular term for this condition in post-unification Germany is *Politikverdrossenheit:* disenchantment with politics.) In the election of 1994, voters returned the Christian Democrats and Chancellor Helmut Kohl to power on a thin margin in Parliament, where one vote decided the formation of the government. Summarizing these cross-national trends, former French President Valery Giscard d'Estaing said they were nothing less than "a crisis of representative democracy."[7]

Consider a sampling of surveys taken by leading survey firms in various industrial powers during this turbulent era. On variously phrased questions about satisfaction with the way things were going at that time, the percentages answering "dissatisfied," "worse," or "wrong track" were as follows: United States (71%), Canada (70%), Great Britain (63%), France (61%), and Japan (44%). On the more specific question of satisfaction with government performance, the levels of dissatisfaction reported in the early to mid-1990s were: United States (69%), Canada (56%), France (57%), Italy (76%), and Japan (84%).[8]

It is not surprising that such angry voters are out of synch with traditional parties and politicians or that they have few reservations about switching loyalties, splitting tickets, and throwing ruling parties and politicians out of power. Surveys in the United States following the much heralded Republican landslide of 1994 revealed that a decidedly mixed set of signals had been exchanged between citizens and their representatives. For example, a *Time* magazine–CNN poll showed that 60 percent of those who voted regarded the election as a repudiation of the Democrats, and only one in six called it an affirmation of the Republican agenda. Although the Republican "Contract With America" may have been a brilliant strategy to nationalize the ordinarily local midterm campaign, a *Times Mirror* survey showed that the overwhelming majority of voters had neither heard of the Republican "contract" nor had relied on any of its provisions in making their choices. Finally, after a brief two-year bout with single-party control of both the White House and Congress (the first in forty years), 58 percent of respondents in a *Wall Street Journal*–NBC News postelection poll registered positive feelings that the nation had returned to divided government.[9]

THE CRISIS OF POLITICAL CONFIDENCE:
A COMPARATIVE PERSPECTIVE

Just a few decades ago, things were quite different in the industrial democracies. Consider, for example, the cases of Sweden and the United States, two very different political systems that find themselves in, and have responded to, similar states of democratic disarray. In both countries confidence in governments, leaders, and parties has declined sharply in the post–World War II period (Lipset & Schneider 1983; Miller & Listhaug 1990: 357–386). Traditional forms of ideological and party-cued communication between leaders and citizens have given way to short-term emotional media campaigns aimed at mobilizing public support for policies and votes for candidates. Such calculated battles for public opinion have undermined stable political coalitions based on more enduring governing visions. Publics increasingly view politicians with suspicion, and politicians approach publics warily with an eye to polls and news management.

Citizens reinforce this vicious cycle by abandoning party loyalties and adopting centrist, pragmatic, and increasingly personalized political outlooks. Parties scramble to stay in power by fitting their ideas to these shifting trends in the opinion market, trying to capture blocs of opinion and votes for narrow, strategic political ends (Ginsberg 1986). In both nations, despite their considerable institutional differences, the ideas from which stable, popular governing agendas emerge have become fragmented and unstable. In many cases, policies are affected adversely by the breakdowns in governing consensus. And even when politicians act responsibly to represent available opinion, negative communication about government from talk shows, news reports, and aspiring candidates often undermines public support for policies. We are concerned with the ways such different political systems have produced these similar governing crises and whether their institutional differences offer any comparative advantages in resolving crises.

The thesis developed in the book is that the problems of democracy experienced by nations as different as Sweden and the United States at this critical historical moment are not easily attributed to faulty representation or to inordinate levels of government waste, corruption, and insensitivity – as many politicians have convinced voters. Rather, the recent period of profound global economic and political change has led to the withering of citizen identification with domestic social and political organizations such as parties, unions, and other institutions that once served as mechanisms for explaining the world ideologically – or at least thematically – to citizens. Even governments that commanded loyalty through the physical and psychological security they provided against external threats can no longer define the world in simple thematic terms of good and evil. The contemporary crisis of democracy is thus one of the failure of political ideas born of an old era, exacerbated by the rather uncertain process of constructing new meanings.

Other scholars have shown that the forms of political communication profoundly affect the democratic experience, from language use as a tool for empowerment or marginalization (Edelman 1964, 1977), to the spectator role and anonymity of ordinary citizens in media representations of politics (Edelman 1988; Entman 1989), to the isolation of individuals and the decline of face-to-face publics owing to the ways in which opinion polls are conducted and reported (Herbst 1993). We extend this tradition by exploring the institutional bases of both the grand governing ideas and the everyday rhetorics that enable (or disable) concerted political action and productive evaluation of the results of government.

Understanding the origins and life cycles of governing ideas and rhetorical patterns in political systems may seem initially to be a daunting and elusive quest that is more appropriate to intellectual history than to political analysis. Although the authorship and sociology of intellectual trends complements our enterprise, we trace patterns of rhetoric and conventional political wisdom to everyday institutional channels that serve as gatekeepers in the flow of communication between citizens and their representatives. Among other things, this approach implies that difficulty in constructing new political ideas is not simply a failure of human imagination – although the present era seems populated more by polemicists than by towering intellectuals (see, for example, Jaccoby 1987). More important, ideas are anchored in social and political institutions that disseminate them to large groups, which in turn use their common worldviews to formulate actions and evaluate the results. The dilemma of the present democratic moment is that bygone historical conditions produced the institutions that constitute and regulate the market for the production, distribution, and valuation of ideas within nations. In some cases these institutions that link citizens, ideas, and governments together are insensitive to new ideas, and in other cases they are openly resistant to political invention.

In exploring the workings of different national idea markets, we propose to trace the ways in which familiar political and social institutions, including parties and electoral representation rules, interest organizations, and the mass media have contributed both to the wearing away of old political understandings and to the often fitful attempts to introduce new thinking and direction into public discourse. To these familiar institutions of the democratic society we also add an often overlooked but crucial element in an idea market: the means by which parties and candidates are financed and through which their ideas are placed into political circulation (see, for example, Ferguson 1995). Chapter 2 explains in more detail why these familiar institutional arrangements are not just means of concentrating political power but at the same time serve as the generators, filters, and amplifiers for communication in democracies.

Getting Down to Cases: The Elements of a Comparative Approach

A moment in history in which guiding political ideas have clearly been overthrown by significant numbers of the world's democratic citizens is ripe for study. The kind of study required is not the armchair multination overview that easily falls prey to speculation and overgeneralization. We propose a comparative study of political communication that uses the perspectives of both political science and communication research. From the communication field, we acknowledge the core question posed originally by Blumler and Gurevitch in their early call for comparative analysis: "How does the articulation of a country's mass media institutions to its political institutions affect the processing of political communication content on the orientations to politics of audience members?" (1975: 169). However, we expand this perspective to recognize what political scientists have learned from studies of agendas and politics: Before the media disseminate ideas to audiences, other social and political institutions have often prepared the governmental scripts, so to speak, selecting among the ideas of parties, interest organizations, and the influential backers who support them (Kelman 1988; Kingdon 1984). Thus, our framework neither privileges the media-centered perspective of communication research nor the institutional approach favored by political scientists who study the flow of ideas in government. Rather, we explore the interactions among key institutions involved with the production and distribution of ideas in the democratic marketplace: from the crucial entry point of the finance arrangements that constitute investments in ideas – to the parties and interests that promote particular ideas, reject others, and move a select few onto the agendas of government – to the media organizations that provide for the ultimate distribution of those ideas to the consumer.

The selecting of two very different cases in the United States and Sweden assures a rigorous exploration of our framework for analyzing national communication and yields new insights about the rise and fall of ideas in political systems. At a minimum, as Gurevitch and Blumler note, the analysis of contrasting cases guards against the two original sins of scientific inquiry: naive universalism and unwitting parochialism (1990: 308–309). For example, they point out that single-case approaches such as Ranney's (1983) look at news coverage of American elections can lead to conclusions – in this case, claims about extraordinary levels of information transmitted to voters – that are absolutist and ultimately impossible to evaluate. By contrast, comparative studies such as Semetko and Barkin's (1986) analysis of British and American election coverage can produce more reliable and often surprising insights – in this case, the conclusion that by British standards, information about American elections carried in the news is rather anemic.

In addition, the selection of sharply contrasting cases improves what Gurevitch and Blumler refer to as "the capacity to render the invisible visible" (1990: 309). For example, the extent of noise introduced into American political discourse through interest group processes – often regarded by American political scientists as being focusing elements in the U.S. system – is illustrated by the comparison of Swedish and American tax reforms in Chapter 5. To cite another example, the combined effects of two-party politics, a fragmented interest group system, and a corporate-dominated political finance process have rendered the Democratic Party in the United States something of a catchall for poorly organized ideas. The collapse of liberal ideas in the United States is brought into sharp relief by the historical comparison in Chapters 3 and 4 of the rise and fall of twentieth-century responses to conservatism in two such different nations. In the Swedish case, the increasingly personalized and confrontational news coverage of elections is easier to grasp when viewed in conjunction with the advent of commercial television and electoral communication strategies that are readily comparable to American varieties.

We recognize that caution must be used in comparing two systems and cultures as different as those of the United States and Sweden. The countries differ considerably in terms of prevailing values, rhetorical traditions, and political institutions. In Sweden many people still embrace the notion of a welfare state, with a strong labor movement and a large public sector. The United States, by contrast, is an unambiguously capitalist society where "welfare" is a dirty word and the values of individualism, opportunity, and free enterprise reign supreme. Whereas Sweden is small, relatively homogeneous (although less today than before), and unitary, the United States is vast, heterogeneous, and federal. In Chapter 2, we explore both the differences and the role of culture in our analysis, but suffice it to say here that the two political cultures are notably different. Not only are there fundamental differences in the social and rhetorical emphases on individual freedom and choice versus social and economic equality, but personal values reflect important contrasts as well. Swedes tend to rank "true friendship" and "mature love" as high personal goals, whereas Americans put more emphasis on "salvation," "self-respect," and "a sense of accomplishment" (Granberg & Holmberg 1988: 5–7).

These and other differences notwithstanding, we are reminded that comparative analysis requires variation and contrast in order to produce generalizations. Differences that appear to be worlds apart at a purely descriptive level can become the fruits of theory and explanation when given the right conceptual organization (Hague & Harrop 1982: 6–14). Indeed, we draw inspiration from the long-established tradition of U.S.–Swedish comparisons that have used the differences between the two nations to sharpen our theoretical understandings of interest group processes, party systems, participation patterns, policy processes, and democratic state structures in capitalist societies (Granberg & Holmberg, 1988; Heclo & Madsen 1987; Kelman 1981; Lundquist 1980; Miller & Listhaug 1990; Steinmo 1989; Weir & Skocpol 1985). The comparative dimensions that we have selected for our analysis (as outlined earlier and defined more completely in Chapter 2) are more general and powerful theoretically for holding them accountable to two such different cases. Ultimately, the strength of our analysis is in the ability to learn from how two such different nations communicate about and attempt to reach popular understandings of remarkably similar sets of political problems.

Different Nations, Similar Problems

Our opening overview of similar problems in various democratic nations holds true upon closer inspection of the United States and Sweden. In the United States, public trust in key institutions reached its peak in the early

1960s. In those days, only 25 percent of the public concurred with the statement that the government was being run for the benefit of business and a few special interests. In the beginning of the 1990s, a whopping 77 percent shared that view (Bennett 1992: 9). The cultural revolution of the 1960s, coupled with the traumas of civil rights struggles, Vietnam, and Watergate, undermined many Americans' faith in parties and government. As a consequence, voting in presidential elections has gone down over 20 percent since 1960 (30 percent outside the South), most drastically among younger people. Summarizing the trends over the 1972 to 1988 period, one writer concluded: "Most citizens under forty-five have withdrawn from politics and, indeed, never entered that realm of American life" (Greider 1992: 315).

There were some promising signs of a participation rebound in the 1992 election, with voting turnout up a few points overall, and up nearly 20 percent among young voters between the ages of 18 and 24. However, the strength of these trends must be reevaluated in 1996 and 2000 and weighed against the third candidacy of Ross Perot in 1992. Perot's party-less candidacy clearly stimulated voter interest, including that of younger voters. As one would expect in a three-way race, Perot also stimulated greater degrees of issue differentiation among the candidates and of voter satisfaction with the discourse on campaign issues. However, neither Perot nor the majority of his supporters felt the need to institutionalize their movement with a party apparatus in 1992, and had troubles with party-building in 1996, raising doubts about the stability of these trends. Moreover, other features of recent elections suggest the persistence of chronic problems, as indicated by high percentages of victory by incumbents in congressional races that remained near 90 percent in 1992 and 1994 despite public approval levels of Congress that ranged from a record low of 19 percent around the 1992 election to a less-than-inspiring 30 percent at the time of the 1994 campaign (Bennett & Lawrence 1995).

Another sign of an increasingly dysfunctional political system is the spiraling cost of campaigning in the United States. Much of the money that pours into American politics is spent to communicate with voters. However, there are few signs that the barrage of carefully designed and personalized political messages have increased voter knowledge or their sense of identification with candidates or the electoral process. A better case can be made for an inverse relationship between the costs and methods of communication and the production of stable, positive ideas that resonate with large numbers of voters.

New records continue to be set in campaign spending for races at all levels. The spending spiral reached dizzying heights in 1994 when Republican challengers narrowed the spending gap between themselves and the incumbents in hotly contested House and Senate races, including a California Senate race that topped $40 million (more than twice the amount spent in the Swedish *national* elections in the same year for all parties and lists of candidates for all offices). Symptomatic of these electoral strains, the large freshman congressional class of 1992 (created by many retirements from the ranks of incumbents) turned out, despite campaign rhetoric to the contrary, to be little more interested in sweeping electoral reform than were their elders. Echoing the same obligatory political line was the 1994 Republican promise for political finance reform, yet the newly elected Republican majority backed away from the issue as quickly as did their Democratic predecessors.

The 1996 presidential American presidential election was presaged with a televised encounter between Bill Clinton and Newt Gingrich in mid-1995, in which both shook hands on a promise to clean up the monetary arrangements that have corrupted political communication. Following that compact, both politicians promptly set about their respective strategies to raise record sums for the 1996 contests. Gingrich and Clinton are quintessential modern politicians: outsiders whose parties either coalesce around or flee from them depending on their personal media fortunes – fortunes that rise and fall with the skill of their hired pollsters, image consultants, marketers, and spin doctors. Such leaders understand the deceits required by the harsh realities of communication in an era of weak parties and independent voters: Clinton's victory in 1992 was due to the support of just 24 percent of the eligible electorate, and the Gingrich-engineered Republican landslide of 1994 was produced by a mere 21 percent of those eligible to participate in the core ritual of democracy. In an age of 21 percent landslides, the communication link between people and their elected governors is both fragile and expensive to maintain.

Similarly in Sweden, voter distrust of parties and politicians has increased steadily over the years. From 1968 to 1991, the proportion of the electorate that agreed with the statement, "The decision makers in Parliament do not care much what ordinary people think" went up from 46 to 70 percent. Party allegiance also dropped sharply (from 65 percent in 1968 to 48 percent in 1991), and the traditional five-party system, once among the world's most stable, has recently been challenged by the emergence of new parties and movements (Elliot 1993: 11–22; Gilljam & Holmberg 1993: 169–184).

Turnout has remained relatively high, but voters are increasingly uneasy about their choices and ready to switch parties if elected politicians do not deliver on their promises. For instance, the Conservative-led coalition that came into power in 1991 was ousted just three years later after having lost much of its initial momentum in the wake of rising unemployment and growing voter dissatisfaction with its market-oriented policies.

Meanwhile, the new Swedish parties have been unable to sustain their populist appeal, either because the traditional parties have stolen their thunder by adopting some of their rhetoric and policies (as in the case of the Greens) or because voters get wary when these maverick parties, once they have made it into Parliament, do not live up to expectations and start disintegrating as soon as they are forced to make tough decisions. For example, the New Democracy Party thundered onto the scene with an impressive first showing of 6.7 percent of the vote in 1991 and dropped just as quickly out of approval by the 1994 contest. The Social Democrats were restored to power in 1994 only to face rapid losses in public approval when they began to address severe budget deficits by cutting various social welfare programs.

It would seem that the rhetorical exchanges between candidates and voters in both countries may be more effective in terms of registering short-term citizen discontent than in building voter consensus and party commitment to the agenda of government. To put it another way, the ideas exchanged in the political marketplace these days in nations as different as Sweden and the United States may be better suited to getting politicians elected than to helping them form the coalitions and maintain the public support necessary to govern.

GLOBAL CHANGE AND NATIONAL POLITICS

Why are modern democracies such as Sweden and the United States in such disarray and their citizens so disaffected? What are the underlying causes of the current malaise? Part of the answer lies in the global economic recession of the early 1990s and in the growing inability of governments to control their national economies. Perhaps the most important economic transformation of the past two decades has been the virtual erasure of national boundaries to the flow of capital and the location of manufacturing and service industries. Managers of large corporations can now move their plants almost anywhere in the world if they are not content with the investment or political climate in their countries.[10] Left of center or right of center, governments have found it increasingly difficult to deal with the problems and effects of economic dislocation. If leaders try to impose tougher labor, safety, or environmental regulations, they risk an exodus of factories and jobs crucial to the well-being of their economies (and to their own reelection chances as well). Because voters still hold politicians responsible for what happens to their nations' economies – at least on the down side – candidates must find communication strategies to hide their failures.[11]

Despite the political difficulties created by global change, the diminished capacities of political systems to respond cannot be explained simply as their having lost control of national sovereignty. Trade and monetary agreements have introduced important controls on the disruptive effects of multinational corporations. More to the point, the grand worldwide economic upheaval of the 1930s presented even greater political challenges, yet there was a flowering of grand political ideas within nations, as noted in our analyses of the Swedish and American responses to the Great Depression in Chapters 3 and 4.

Why, then, do so many of today's democracies seem unable to respond to the call for new governing visions? Perhaps there is some inherent inertia of leadership and mass psychology that favors the brittle ideas of the past long after they have failed and lost favor with large numbers of citizens. Yet the wholesale abandonment of socialist and egalitarian ideologies by politicians and parties of the left – even at the risk of being left with *no* ideas – would suggest a much more knowing calculus of communication linking institutions, voters, and the politicians who make rhetorical choices aimed at remaining in government. In part, the symptoms of democratic disarray noted previously may be attributed to the calculating failure of politicians to place the larger interests of democracy or large groups in society above the promotion of their own power. This possibility points toward institutional power arrangements as explanations for patterns of political communication choices made by politicians. Moreover, as our comparative perspective will show, differences in these institutions also account for the greater capacities of politicians and voters in some systems to correct (or at least to minimize the extent of) their communication breakdowns.

At its core, the crisis of confidence in contemporary democracy has both a broadly common source and a range of potentially different national solutions. At the common core, most national democratic systems, Sweden and the United States among them, continue to be defined by power arrangements (e.g., parties, interests, and the political financing that sustains them) formed during an earlier era of economic development. As a result, the institutional structures of contemporary politics present a profound dilemma for creative political communication:

- *Either* politicians must reinvent the modern state and its representative mechanisms – a prospect that risks destroying the very institutional arrangements that bestow those politicians with power.
- *Or* politicians must continue to live (and die) politically through short-term rhetorical artifice that keeps them at best one step ahead of the angry citizenry.

We live in a political age shaped by this dilemma. It is consequently an age in which political promises and the subsequent uses of political power are often profoundly at odds. Indeed, political rhetoric is so commonly referred to as "empty" that one could easily assume this to be a defining property of the term and something that has always characterized public discourse. The uneasy resolution of this communication dilemma in many nations has been to turn to merchants of meaning – the pollsters, marketers, and image consultants who negotiate the precarious tensions between publics demanding new ideas and the politicians who recognize the threat to their own power if those new ideas ever transformed the party and interest mechanisms on which politicians' personal power rests. The resulting corruptions of democratic communication vary from one political system to another. The pioneering and arguably the most extreme interventions of strategic communication in idea markets have occurred in the United States, where a core tenet of the conventional wisdom among political communication professionals was pronounced by David Gergen, whose ministerings to both Democratic and Republican presidents earned him the title *Sultan of Spin* from the press corps: "[I]t has come to be held that what sort of person a politician actually is and what he actually does are not important. What is important is the perceived image of what he is and what he does. Politics is not about objective reality, but virtual reality" (Kelly 1993: 64).

DEMOCRACY, POWER, AND COMMUNICATION

Promises that are made and broken as openly as those regarding campaign finance reform in the United States or the preservation of the welfare state in Sweden at once signal the crisis of contemporary political communication and an important underlying cause: Power in this age of electronic democracy depends overwhelmingly on strategic or managed communication. We are not talking about communication as an adjunct to politics – a means of conveying information between politicians and publics – but communication increasingly as the central concern of politics – a means of strategically constructing information that at once *creates* publics and protects politicians from undesirable public reactions to their acts.

It is debatable whether communication has become more central in modern politics or whether it has always been important since Machiavelli advised the prince on the wiles of public relations. What is more commonly accepted among communication scholars, however, is that the nature of political communication has changed in the recent period into an increasingly professionalized, scientific, *strategic* process (Manheim 1991) aimed at moving publics in short-term support of candidates and rationalizing any subsequent failures candidates may display in governing between elections. Noting this trend, Kavanagh (1995) cites two of the advertising consultants who engineered negative communication campaigns in recent British elections:

Voters will follow their instincts and discount a party's claims about its achievements. You have to address voters' fears.

People are so disillusioned with politicians that you can't convince them of your good points. But they are prepared to believe that the other lot are worse.... People are so fed up with politics that you are now pushing at an open door. If they have doubts about the other side you have to make people hold them even more strongly.

Such communication is a day-to-day, election-to-election proposition that preys on citizen fear, insecurity, and cynicism. At the same time, it contributes to those same public dispositions by enabling political rhetoric to become disconnected from the policies and results of government without forcing politicians to suffer punishment in the electoral arena. In effect, the universal application of strategic communication techniques drives governing ideas out of public discourse. For purposes of this preliminary discussion, *we define governing ideas as broad thematic agendas that guide government policies and attract stable alignments of voters who can use those ideas to evaluate and discipline policies.* A key question for the future of democracy thus becomes: Given the forms of communication that have replaced (and contributed to the decline of) more traditional party and ideological discourse, will the future ever again witness anything resembling the twentieth-century configurations of mass parties with loyal followers joined in commonly understood purpose?

The Fall of Governing Ideas and the Rise of Strategic Communication

The proximate cause of the present "democratic distemper,"[12] in our view, is *the chronic failure of politicians to communicate in ways that empower electorates with common guiding visions for government.* Distant causes of this failure may well include the reorganization of the world economy and the collapse of communism, forces that have frustrated and disoriented both the left and the right. The right has lost its most potent enemy, the threat of Soviet communism, and the left has abandoned its belief in central government planning. Commentators and pundits have decried the stunning absence of governing ideas capable of giving direction to the voters in a new, complex, and bewildering era. This rhetorical vacuum in many countries has been filled with polarizing populist politicians who evoke public outrage about crime, immigration, ethnic differences, affronts to nationalism, and the evils of government itself.

This is not the first time in recent history that people have complained about the exhaustion of political ideas. In the mid-1950s, a group of distinguished international scholars – foremost among them Raymond Aron, Daniel Bell, Seymour Martin Lipset, T. H. Marshall, and Herbert Tingsten – proclaimed that "the end of ideology" had been reached. Writing in an age that combined growing material affluence with lingering Cold War sentiments, these scholars argued that the grand old political ideologies derived from the eighteenth and nineteenth centuries were exhausted and that the class divisions of the past had greatly diminished in the developed Western democracies. Democracy – not liberalism, socialism, or conservatism – had become the dominant ideology, rendering old differences between left and right more or less obsolete. What characterized the middle to late twentieth century, according to these analysts, was a gradual development from politics to administration, from principles to pragmatism. Where impassioned rhetoric and competing utopias once reigned, consensus and banal rhetoric now ruled.[13]

We are not interested in examining the validity of the "endism" debates. Neither the "end of history" argument nor the "end of ideology" thesis helps us understand why governments today are in such disrepute or why so many voters feel left out of the political process. Our objective is not to establish that history or ideology may have triumphed or ended but, rather, to argue that something has fundamentally changed in the way that politicians and citizens within nations define themselves in the contemporary world. Although it may be equally hazardous to propose an "end of rhetoric" thesis, it is worth considering that the political marketplace in many Western democracies has changed from being a forum for heated debate and a comparatively lively exchange of ideas into one dominated by few substantive issues and quite streamlined rhetoric that is more likely to be the product of political marketing research than inspired leadership and solidary parties committed to educating publics and rallying support for new, if risky, theories of political economy and society. What the public seems to get, in polities as diverse as those of Sweden and the United States, are increasingly similar ideas marketed in increasingly similar ways to increasingly smaller audiences. This shrinking range of ideas between parties and candidates in the political marketplace is one of the *leitmotifs* of our analysis. Rather than focus on distant ideological – and ultimately metaphysical – explanations for this state of communication, we propose to ask the more pragmatic question: Why have national markets of ideas not adjusted to produce new governing visions capable of attracting sustained popular support and producing new streams of government policies? Our comparative framework is aimed at discovering common breakdowns in communication while locating differences in national capabilities to fix communication problems.

Characteristics of a New Political Communication

Traditional governing visions and ideological discourse in many nations are being replaced (in some cases, rapidly) by profoundly negative and personalized political rhetoric developed through scientific techniques of market research, polling, and focus groups. This strategic communication encourages people to turn away from government even as (one is tempted to say, because) they elect the merchants of that rhetoric to represent them in government. The breakdown in governing ideas is thus fostered and accompanied by a general trend of depolitization, which seems to appear in four principal forms of communication.

First, we have *the personalization of politics*. The decline of parties and party systems has been followed, particularly in the United States, by an even greater focus on the individual candidate, his or her character, personality, or family life, and a much diminished focus on what the candidate has accomplished in the political and legislative arena. Candidates increasingly choose to operate as individual entrepreneurs, rendering party labels obsolete and contributing to a further fragmentation of the political system. Examples of this abound, especially in the United States (Loomis 1990; Wattenberg 1991). The same trend is also evident in Sweden, where a constitutional change may open up possibilities for a more candidate-oriented system.

Second, over the last decade we have witnessed a *moralization of politics*, visible most of all in the "hot button" issues that are being publicly discussed. Candidates are often being asked about patriotism, religion, ethics and, in light of the personalization trend, moral issues involving their personal problems, finances, marriages, or love affairs. The Gary Hart debacle in the 1988 U.S. presidential campaign was instrumental in this regard. The senator from Colorado, who some predicted to be a front-runner in the race, was forced to withdraw after some members of the press staked out his Washington house and exposed his affair with a model (cf. Sabato 1991). In the 1992 presidential campaign and later as president, Bill Clinton was repeatedly haunted by stories about his personal life. The issues involving ethics, and corruption in the 1988 Swedish election campaign provide an example of the same trend.

Third, we have likewise seen an *avoidance of complex, controversial issues* by both the mass media in general and candidates and parties in particular. For example, in Sweden the issue of whether the country should join the European Union (EU) was thoroughly discarded in crucial election campaigns. The Social Democrats, who for more than thirty years had argued against Swedish membership, made a sudden about-face in late 1990 and decided, without any public debate, that now was the time to join the EU. The public reaction, not surprisingly, was one of uncertainty and confusion (Stråth 1992: 23–27, 227–242). In the United States, debates over budget deficits invariably degenerate into simplistic arguments about big government and cutting out waste, and concerns about economic decline are as likely to trigger patriotic rhetoric as discussions of labor markets and industrial policies.

Fourth, we now see a global trend for voters to increasingly turn their backs on old-style, professional politicians and register their exasperation by supporting fresh, new candidates with clean fingers and no previous experience in politics. Examples of this *rise of the amateur politician* abound: Ross

Perot and Steve Forbes in the United States, Vladimir Zhirinovsky in Russia,
Ian Wachtmeister and Bert Karlsson in Sweden, Silvio Berlusconi and
Umberto Bossi in Italy, and Alberto Fujimori in Peru, among others.[14] The
attractiveness of these politicians is partly that they are perceived as being
nonpolitical (Vaclav Havel in the Czech Republic is a good example of this).
But it is also a question of rhetoric and style. Ross Perot's greatest asset in the
1992 U.S. presidential campaign, apart from his wealth, was his claim that
he was not "one of them," that he was running against the flawed, inside-the-
Beltway gang of politicians who had turned their backs on ordinary Americans and made a mess of the U.S. economy. This rhetoric was carried to its
naked extreme in 1994 by multimillionaire California Senate candidate
Michael Huffington, who summed up his entire vision for government in a
rare press interview with *Time* magazine in which he issued the breathtaking
dictum: "I want a government that does nothing."[15] This combination of
antigovernment and "I'm just an ordinary guy" rhetoric was effectively used
by the New Democracy Party in the 1991 Swedish election. Neither institutional stability nor stable patterns of participation and opinion would seem
to follow from this emergence of the populist businessman as a curious sort
of folk hero on the political landscape.

The implications of these developments for representative democracy
could be far-reaching. The breakdown of governing ideas threatens an *individualized democracy* in which public opinion becomes a socially isolating private process, not a socially cohesive and stabilizing public one. Government
institutions as socially inclusive political structures may ultimately collapse
with the withering of a competitive idea market. The potential for a vicious
spiral emerges, because coherent election programs and party platforms are
less likely to emerge in an age of independent politicians who preach negative, antigovernment rhetoric while offering "trust me" as their rallying cry.
If public institutions are not perceived to embody motivating, socially cohesive ideas, the ties that bring people into the political system may weaken.
Even if a resulting retreat from public life appears to be what most people
want, should a democracy satisfy such dubious and ultimately antidemocratic individual preferences? (Particularly when those preferences are constructed by manipulative communication processes?) In short, we are concerned that the corruption of communication may endanger the future of
democracy. We subscribe to the standard that a healthy democracy rests on
competitive parties and candidates as well as a vibrant public deliberation

and dialogue about the important ideas and issues of the day (Fishkin 1991). To understand the status of public communication in different polities, we need a better set of analytical tools than has hitherto been provided either by scholars of rhetoric and political communication or by political scientists.

Understanding How Political Systems Respond to Communication Problems

Our primary interest is to understand how governing ideas and the rhetoric used to present them to publics are produced in different political systems. More important, in light of the trends already noted, we are interested in how different systems respond to the decline of ideas and to the growing disjunctures among parties, leaders, publics, political ideas, and the agendas of governments. In short, how are particular systems responding to the problems of political vision that seem to loom so large in the minds of their citizens?

This set of concerns invites us to take a new approach to the often ignored intersection of institutions and political communication. We propose to look squarely at the impact of institutional arrangements on the production and public valuation of ideas in public policy debates and elections. This focus includes not just grand social, economic, and political theories but the everyday rhetoric used to sell those theories to the masses. Indeed, as great ideas become worn down by historical and institutional changes, it may be the short-term rhetoric of politics that carries most of the intellectual load. The trends we have noted suggest that this load may be increasingly light, with little enduring substance for voters or the officials they elect to govern for them. This same personalized, short-term rhetoric also disrupts the policy process by evading the responsibilities of educating the public about complex and difficult issues – responsibilities that arguably go with leadership in democracy.

Yet whatever the intellectual status of the rhetoric that links citizens to leaders and leaders to government, it is important to understand the institutional constraints that shape that rhetoric. It is equally important to understand that whether grandiloquent or superficial the language of politics is not only the simple invention of candidates and their personal advisers but also the product of the institutions and systemic constraints within which those politicians make their calculations about what to tell the people and how to put it symbolically.

To grasp the qualities of present-day communication, it is necessary to trace its evolution from the past. In this sense, we are also interested in the historical sweep – the rise and fall – of the great governing ideas in our two cases, beginning in the modern era with the rise of the American New Deal and the parallel case of the Swedish *folkhem* during the last great period of political upheaval associated with the Great Depression. It is instructive to see how the changing institutional arrangements in both systems have affected the viability of these grand visions (as well as their conservative counterparts) and the sorts of replacement ideas that have emerged in their demise. The replacement of grand governing visions with short-term strategic rhetoric may make it difficult for citizens to evaluate the outcomes of government or even to appreciate the role of government in their lives. The result may well be a disjuncture between how well governments represent broad public preferences and how publics perceive the quality of that representation. In the extreme case, we may find a contradiction between democratic governments that represent public preferences fairly well, while political communication renders those same publics incapable of developing realistic expectations about representation and the role of government in their lives.

A DEMOCRATIC PUZZLE:
REPRESENTATION VS. SATISFACTION

The foregoing discussion suggests the possibility that the performance of some governments may be better than their failure to win citizen support would at first glance suggest. In the case of the United States, for example, Page and Shapiro's (1992) sweeping review of polls and policies over the period from World War II to the present time indicates a remarkable correspondence between public preferences and government policy responses to those preferences. How do we reconcile the apparent contradiction that a democracy that appears to be doing a reasonable job of interest representation has also suffered major losses of public confidence and support?

There is some debate about how much of this linkage is "bottom up" (in the sense of public pressure shaping the political agendas of government elites) and how much is "top down" (in the sense of elites setting policy agendas and then propagandizing public support – preparing public opinion – to accept emerging policies) (Margolis & Mauser 1989). However, no matter which way the causal arrow between opinion and policy runs, the larger puzzle about public confidence and cynicism remains. That is, whether elites convince publics to support government decisions or publics pressure elites to accede to their wishes a good deal of the time, it would seem that levels of public support for institutions, parties, leaders, and election processes should be higher.

We suspect that at least part of the puzzle involves the ways the decisions of government are represented symbolically during the interest, election, and decision processes that convert public demands into policies. These symbolic processes may not produce satisfying or stable understanding of government actions even when the outcomes of government are defensible by more distant empirical measures, suggesting that idea markets are not perfect exchanges of information between voters and representatives about policies. We argue that the design of political institutions affects the exchange of ideas, distorting the communication process in systematic ways. In some cases, people may fail to agree with the actions of government or with the gains or losses of others because governments fail to produce a compelling vision of their common interests in society. For example, the rhetoric of a personalized politics may stir up an unhealthy measure of ill will no matter how governments act. The remainder of the book explores these institutional arrangements that shape the exchange and valuation of ideas in political systems.

OVERVIEW OF THE BOOK

The idea of a marketplace that is sketched only briefly in this chapter is developed in more detail in Chapter 2. Our proposed framework for comparing the forms of communication in different political systems is explained and expanded in the context of the discussion of how institutions regulate the introduction and evolution of political ideas. In the process we address basic differences in Swedish and American political cultures and show how it is both possible and useful to compare two such different nations.

The analysis of Swedish and American political communication patterns begins in earnest in Part II, with two chapters (3 and 4) on the history of the rise and fall of the grand governing ideas of the twentieth century that have had such an impact on public policy and the accompanying rhetoric in both countries: the New Deal and its legacy of activist government in the United States and the *folkhem* metaphor in Sweden. These governing ideas operate in at least two ways to structure political processes (or, when they become poorly articulated through institutional regulatory mechanisms, to promote political disarray in those processes):

1. These grand visions provide focus for the mobilization of voter support. In the United States, as explained in Chapter 3, the Republican rhetoric for most of the post–New Deal period was aimed squarely at the activist government, with the promise to restore traditional principles of small government, free and unregulated enterprise, and individual initiative and volunteerism. In Sweden, the opposition parties of the right also introduced rhetoric of less government intervention and market economics, which contributed to the occasional electoral defeats of the Social Democrats (SAP), as explained in Chapters 4 and 6.

2. The governing ideas and the rhetorical counterpoint of the opposition can provide both intellectual guidance for policy processes and easy-to-grasp public explanations of the results.

In both cases, we explore the factors that have led to the decline of these grand visions of government, along with the reasons new political ideas have not emerged rapidly to replace them.

The third part of the book examines the interplay of institutions and ideas in more focused election and policy processes. Chapter 5 explores the cases of tax reform in both Sweden and the United States during the 1980s, showing how both the intellectual guidance and the public information functions of rhetoric became disconnected from grand visions and party programs. This disconnection resulted from the corrosive processes of short-term voter appeals, magnified by interest group and campaign finance pressures. In addition, media strategies aimed at controlling political damage in the short term created confusion and rhetorical drift in the long run. Driven by election strategies and interest pressures, the remarkably similar income tax reforms passed in the United States in 1986 and in Sweden in 1990 left parties on both sides of the issue sounding remarkably alike in their public pronouncements, resulting in considerable confusion and loss of support surrounding the actual policies (and, ironically, little impact on voter support despite rhetorics designed with short-term election strategies in mind). The troubling implications of the grinding down of public discourse by core political institutions is that policies themselves begin to suffer. Party leaders and theorists in both countries became distressed by the breakdown of ideological and economic principles guiding policy and by the degree to which strategic political communication shaped and ultimately corrupted the outcomes of important policy deliberations. This case also points up important differences in the capacities of leaders in the two systems to control communication strategies that begin to produce undesirable effects.

The electoral arena provides what is perhaps the clearest illustration of how the great twentieth-century political ideas have lost their capacity to guide both policy and credible public debate. Chapter 6 explores patterns of candidate–voter communication in recent Swedish and American national elections. Elections are arguably the place for fine-tuning the governing ideas of parties or regimes to the evolving preferences of voters and the problems of changing societies. However, what we find increasingly is the mechanical or ritualistic pronouncement of party positions and promises, while the work of attracting voters is increasingly done by short-term images created by marketing research on voter moods. The result is a vicious cycle of voter cynicism in which elections fail to clarify the guiding principles that bind voters to parties or parties to programs, resulting in voters who are increasingly suspicious of parties, candidates, and their promises.

Thus, we have several different kinds of case studies, each illustrating how governing ideas and the rhetorics used to present them are affected by comparable political institutions in different political systems. To varying degrees, the core institutional mechanisms for mobilizing power in both nations seem to be working against the revitalization of governing ideas. However, the different institutional arrangements in the two nations do matter in important respects for the production of the everyday rhetorics that link governments, policies, and leaders to citizens. The complexity of American institutions and the decentralized relations among the regulatory mechanisms make it much more difficult for leaders to lead, parties to govern, and citizens to maintain loyalty to broad governing agendas. In a sense, the more centralized and interconnected Swedish institutions make it easier to govern, even when the rhetorics that connect publics to policies are in disarray. In fact, as the tax analysis in Chapter 5 shows, when rhetoric fails, the Swedish corporatist institutional structure more easily permits party leaders to close the market of ideas to stop the erosion of public support and the defection of members of policy coalitions. On the other hand, the tendency of Swedish parties to replace ideological appeals with short-term media strategies has undermined the capacity of voters in a multiparty system to discipline public discourse.

What we ultimately hope to accomplish is to reestablish the importance of language and rhetoric in the study of institutions and public policy in modern democracies. Scholars belonging to the "new institutionalist" school in political science may overlook the effects of rhetorical practices on policy formation. Students of rhetoric do not seem to appreciate (or even recognize) the connection between language choices on the one hand and the parameters set by institutional structures on the other. Actors do have language choices, and why they choose one communication strategy over another is frequently the result of institutional constraints operating in the marketplace of ideas. By highlighting the connection between language and institutions, we hope to move the analysis of political rhetoric closer to the traditional methods of political science, while placing the importance of communication more squarely on the agenda of political science.

2

The Idea of a Marketplace

Downs's *An Economic Theory of Democracy* misspecifies the basic market in which
political parties operate. Not voters but investors constitute their major constituency.
— Thomas Ferguson

Although Ferguson (1995: 37) may err toward another extreme by pointing
out the extraordinary impact of party finance on the selection and framing of
political issues, his corrective is a useful reminder that the exchange of ideas
in democracies is not just an idealistic and rarefied dialogue between citizens
and leaders. Parties do not listen to voters only; they must also bend to the
will of those who support them or risk losing their competitive place in elections. Thus, party finance mechanisms become important considerations for
understanding the patterns of communication in polities. As we shall see, by
contrast the public financing of Swedish parties opened up a broad spectrum
of debate about issues as varied as the future of the welfare state and the evolution of a national energy policy based on environmental protection. Moreover, Swedish parties that suffer catastrophic misfortune with ideas that suddenly prove unpopular — as was the case of the Communists after the end of
the Cold War — are given a cushion of time in which to develop new ideas
(and even change their name). The protections of Swedish public finance saw
the popularity of the newly named Left Party rebound to stunning levels in
the polls within five years of its sudden fall from grace.

In the United States, the combination of institutional factors that act upon
the formulation of political programs often have more of a wearing than a
building effect. The Democrats, for example, have suffered an idea slump of
such magnitude that party conferences to invent a new "story" to present to
the voters have become as regular as they have proved uneventful. In a poll

taken by the Wirthlin Group on the eve of the 1996 election campaign, for example, voters gave their hearts to the Democrats but credited the Republicans with being the party with the clear vision. In response to the question "Which party do you believe is best described by" the phrase "Has a clear vision as to where to lead the country," the Democrats scored a lowly 29 percent to the Republican rating of 48 percent. Yet the party of fewer ideas was rated higher on a Wirthlin Group survey of 1,001 adults, using the measure of "Is concerned with people like me" by a margin of 47 to 38 percent over the Republicans.[1] It would seem that if the Democrats could align their hearts and minds, they might have an easier time of it with the voters. Chapter 3 explains what happened to the governing ideas of the Democrats between 1932 and today, and the present chapter explores the larger institutional factors, campaign finance among them, that make the production and sale of new ideas more than a simple act of the political imagination.

IDEAS AND DEMOCRACY

Ideas have figured prominently in political and economic theories as diverse as those of Adam Smith, Karl Marx, and John Maynard Keynes. Keynes wrote: "The ideas of economists and political philosophers, both when they are right and when they are wrong, are more powerful than is commonly understood.... I am sure that the power of vested interests is vastly exaggerated compared with the gradual encroachment of ideas" (Keynes 1964: 383–384). Liberal political theorists point to the free exchange, or *marketplace*, of ideas as a defining condition of liberal democracy itself (e.g., Jefferson 1939; Locke 1960; Mill 1966). Thomas Jefferson once claimed that newspapers were more important than government itself, and John Stuart Mill proposed rethinking geographical and majoritarian representation schemes in favor of plans that enhanced the diversity of ideas in government (Mill 1977: 448–466).

Renewed attention to the politics of reform has rekindled interest in the importance of ideas in the policy process (Hadenius 1986; Heclo & Madsen 1987; Kelman 1988; Kingdon 1984; Stone 1988; Weir & Skocpol, 1985). For example, the force of ideas played a key role in both the Swedish and American tax reforms of the 1980s. In their analysis of the U.S. case, Beam, Conlan, and Wrightson (1990) cite the irresistible pull of public symbols in moving unlikely coalition partners into agreement behind a reform package that leading experts on tax policy had dismissed from the realm of possibility prior to its passage with comments like that of Witte: "There is nothing, absolutely nothing in the history of politics of the income tax that indicates that any of these schemes has the slightest hope of being enacted in the forms proposed" (Witte 1985: 380). Reforms in both nations began with grand rhetoric of fairness and ended in interest group propaganda campaigns and melodramatic news reports that threatened public support for the resulting proposals. However, important differences in the Swedish institutional structure through which communication is regulated enabled party leaders to maintain higher levels of acceptance for their accomplishment, as explained in Chapter 5.

Despite the long flirtation with the importance of ideas in political processes, the analytical precision of the concept remains weak. As Weir and Skocpol note in response to Keynes's 1964 statement, "to assert that ideas are powerful is not to reveal how policy-relevant ideas emerge and how they may be variously influential" (1985: 116). Their argument about state structures as idea filters is persuasive, and we agree with their attention to the importance of parties and interest processes in the exchange and implementation of ideas. However, the generality of the state concept, along with vast national differences in state structures, discourages precise and systematic analysis of routine (i.e., nonhistoric or course-changing) public policy debates, electoral discourse, and other everyday political situations of the sort that interest policy analysts. Although we are uneasy with the analytical slipperiness of the state concept, we fully agree that the failure to adopt a clear analytical framework results in weak explanations that allude to the sheer force of ideas on policy makers (Hall 1989), a view that one critic complains ignores the "intensely competitive market for ideas, in which policy makers buy with a discerning sense of fit, quality, and need" (Rogowski 1991: 1000). It is this marketplace of ideas as it intersects key institutions of states and societies that we propose to explore.

COMPARING THE RHETORIC OF NATIONS

Since liberal philosophers first proposed that the health of a polity depends on its marketplace of ideas (Mill 1966), societies have grown more complex, and idea markets have become more highly regulated and driven by the standardizing forces of mass communication and opinion polling (Ginsberg 1986; Hallin 1985). Publics in these modern democracies have been described as quiescent (Edelman 1964) and even dependent on political propaganda to soothe their powerlessness and alienation (Ellul 1965). Critics of modern democracy argue that the political marketplace is heavily brokered by elites who hold sway over the formation of interests, the definition of problems, and the production of solutions. Ideas in this managerial state are largely offered to publics to produce compliance with core policies. Only in areas in which elite interests are not adversely affected by public intervention (e.g., race, immigration, morality, drugs, and other symbolically volatile discourses) are "bottom up" ideas frequently encountered.

Despite the limiting tendencies in the exchange of ideas in the modern democratic marketplace, there still appear to be substantial differences in the production of ideas and the formation of political agendas from one polity to another. Equally intriguing are the variations in the flow of ideas from one issue area to another within a given society. These market variations within and between societies include the competitiveness of varying ideological viewpoints in the marketplace, the degree of two-way flow (or exchange) of ideas between groups and between elites and mass publics, the likelihood of innovative responses to crises and chronic social problems, and resulting levels of popular support for institutions, policies, and leadership.

Identifying the market mechanisms and dynamics that regulate communication in polities provides a useful point of departure for understanding the patterns of debate about national issues, the intensity of political participation, and ultimately the structure of power in society. In short, the marketplace of ideas, as we propose to define it, is a useful way of analyzing and comparing political systems without placing undue emphasis on single factors such as institutions, behavior, or culture. By providing a bridge among such reductionistic approaches to political analysis, the idea market model highlights the integrating properties of political language and communication. In this perspective, political rhetoric becomes the currency of the public realm – the creative political capital that lends power its institutional vocabulary, its cultural acceptability, and its humanly inventive possibilities.

Defining Key Concepts

We address the evolution and uses of political ideas at two levels of analysis in this book. First are the grand visions, or *governing ideas*, that guide national policy agendas and political alignments for generations. These ideas are the source material for everyday political discourse, yet they may not be invoked directly very often in the communication of election campaigns or policy battles. The grand visions of twentieth-century American politics are broadly identified here as conservatism and the alternative vision of activist government that has its origins in New Deal liberalism. The modern Swedish political experience is framed by the grand image of an activist and caring government evoked by the idea of the *folkhem,* or people's home, countered by an undercurrent of conservative opposition. From these grand visions, the rhetoric of everyday politics emerges. By the term *rhetoric* we mean here the strategic uses of language and mental images to persuade publics to take positions on policies about particular issues or to make judgments about parties and candidates in elections. This second, everyday level of political language encompasses the gamut of ordinary persuasive political communication, from political campaigns and policy discourses to soundbites in the news.

In its simplest conception, the political marketplace is defined by the institutional arrangements through which political language is produced, circulated, granted status or value by authorities and publics, and ultimately exchanged for political support. Promises are traded for votes. Legislative language is amended in exchange for coalition partners. Trial balloons are launched in the media to test public responses to controversial actions. In these and other ways, rhetorical boundaries are constantly pushed and pulled around the host of governmental actions that ultimately affect the quality of peoples' lives. This constantly shifting rhetoric is valued or devalued against the hard standard of political support. If idea markets are dynamic, popular support can be reallocated with measurable effect when policies fall short of rhetorically aroused expectations. By contrast, markets stagnate when shifts in political support are punished, propagandized, or merely ignored by those in power. The exchange of rhetoric for political support is intended merely as a rough opening statement about the workings of idea markets. Our later case studies show how communication can also directly alter political agendas and shape the course of policies as well, often with quite unintended results.

It is clear that no society exhibits a pure or "ideal" market in which language and support are traded directly with no restrictions, no consumer protections, and no elite hedges against the fluctuations of unpredictable public passions. Such an idealized market would be a direct democracy in which shifting public moods dictated the terms of political debate and citizens would become vulnerable to the suasions of demagogues with few protections beyond the empty warning, *caveat emptor*. In contrast to this ideal type of market, most polities achieve some degree of market stability through various regulatory mechanisms, formal and informal, that limit the exchange of ideas (Mill 1977: 581–613, 648–653).

Linking Language to Institutions

Much has been written about patterns of mass communication and propaganda that arise to protect the competitive political advantages of some groups over others. Gramsci (1987) described the methods through which ruling groups achieve hegemony, or ideological domination, of the public sphere of ideas. Lippmann (1922) wrote about the ways in which elites protect their prerogatives by representing situations in stereotypical terms likely to generate popular responses based on prejudice rather than on critical appraisal. Lasswell (1960) explored the emotional imagery that reduces political discourse to a vocabulary of security symbolism. Edelman (1988) has portrayed an impoverished public space dominated by grand political spectacles that dazzle citizen-spectators while deadening political debate. Ellul (1965) doubted the capacity of any modern state, democratic or not, to survive without keeping an addictive supply of propaganda flowing to the masses. And Habermas (1975) has argued that power in liberal society is maintained less through coercion than by restricting access to political communication channels.

Various political and economic structures have been identified as supporting these systematic communicational advantages of elites in the democratic marketplace. For example, Bagdikian and Herman describe the corporate ownership of the media in the United States as a growing monopoly that keeps the content of news and public affairs in line with state power interests at the expense of broader conceptions of the public interest (Bagdikian 1985, 1987; Herman 1985). In Sweden the electronic media have been undergoing a fundamental change since the early 1990s with the advent of commercial radio and television. New channels are being auctioned off to the highest bidder, with the result that one media tycoon now owns a substantial part of the country's radio and television networks (Hadenius & Anderberg 1994). Dramatized news coverage and increasingly simplified media-oriented campaign rhetoric in recent Swedish elections have added to fears that increasingly commercialized and monopolized media are undermining the diversity and richness of public debate.

However, the propaganda, manipulation, and elite interest perspectives on political communication have failed to identify the extent of market differences between countries, just as they have not accounted very well for within-country differences in the openness of political debate from one issue area to another. Granting that propaganda, hegemonic forces, and patterns of elite consensus may exist, the question is how these tendencies are played out within the particular institutions and cultures that define and distinguish polities. Perhaps most important, critical communication scholars fail to account for the palpable chaos and symbolic disarray that have emerged in so many of the world's democratic regimes.

Relatively little has been written about how political institutions, mass communication systems, and cultural codes work together to regulate the marketplace of ideas and, in many cases, how these regulatory processes break down to create unstable communication environments. We feel that these regulatory processes may account for variations in idea markets that hegemony and propaganda theories fail to explain. Moreover, regulatory mechanisms constitute the contexts within which the uses and effects (along with the abuses and defects) of propaganda begin to make sense. In short, we agree that all mass societies experience distorted political communication, but we also contend that such distortion is inevitable and, in the right forms, even desirable. The fundamental question is: How do regulatory mechanisms affect idea markets on different issues in different polities? Once we begin to answer this question, it will be easier to talk about the predations of propaganda, the distribution of power, and the resistance of different democratic systems to manipulation and control of political agendas by elites.

The following analysis addresses two analytical questions that flow from the foregoing concerns. First, what are the most obvious market mechanisms operating to regulate the flow of rhetoric in democratic societies? Second, how do these mechanisms work in different combinations in different polities? We explore these questions by outlining a framework for comparing the marketplace of ideas. This framework is applied to case studies of Sweden and the United States, beginning with the rise and decline of the great political ideas of this century in both nations and focusing on more recent tax reforms in both nations, and political rhetoric in national elections. These case studies illuminate similarities and differences in the idea markets of the two polities, while suggesting possibilities for more general comparative analysis. A key concern is to assess the capacity of these different systems to respond to their respective crises of democracy with new, effective, and popular governing ideas.

Regulatory Mechanisms in the Marketplace

To begin, consider the possibility that political systems evolve through the creation of charters, institutions, and reforms aimed as much at the regulation of ideas as at the distribution of power. For example, the fearful idea of overly dominant rulers led the designers of the American constitution to limit the powers of the chief executive, leaving future presidents with little more than what one observer described as the "power to persuade" (Neustadt 1990: 29). Tulis (1987) argues that modern presidents have turned this deficit into an advantage by developing rhetorical skills and using the mass media to mobilize public support for their political initiatives.

More generally, the institutions and rules that flow from charters and reforms end up regulating group conflicts by regulating the flow of ideas. Again in the American case, Madison outlined in Federalist No. 10 a defense of proposed constitutional arrangements designed to check the effects of faction. The enduring result of that Constitution has been a representative system with a circuitous, highly mediated set of accountability relations between rulers and publics. One result of this governmental design is the singular difficulty of sustaining coherent, programmatic ideological debate in the political marketplace. As our cases show, the emergence of various latter-day market mechanisms from interest group processes to campaign finance procedures has pushed this fragile system into chronic instability in patterns of public debate about critical issues.

Sweden, too, has a written constitution, but its effects on rhetorical practices are much more vague and uncertain. The idea of a constitution guiding the conduct of public policy is not nearly as salient in Sweden as in the United States. Instead, the deep structuring principle underlying policy debates in the modern era (including the post-1994 coalition) is traceable to the legacy of the long-ruling Social Democrats, who were successful in promoting party discipline based on the idea of the state as a *folkhem*, or "people's home," to which everybody, regardless of status or income, belongs. This rhetorical foundation – something of an ideological regime that rivaled the sanctity of a constitutional order – contributed to the success of the so-called Swedish model, a system characterized by policy consensus and moderation in which competing parties seldom challenged the notion of a welfare state even as significant ideological differences swirled around this common political ground.

The successful bureaucratic institutionalization of welfare policies may have figured into the Social Democratic loss in the 1991 election, a contest in which the opposition parties carefully avoided direct debates about the incumbent party's greatest achievement. This left the Social Democrats (SAP) badly positioned rhetorically during a period of economic decline and voter disaffection. On the one hand, the party vigorously defended a "unique" Sweden (a rhetorical code for the various benefits of the welfare state) against no visible attackers. On the other hand, the SAP gave up traditional rhetorical positions on taxes and economic regulation and downplayed traditional values of justice and equality to stay competitive with an increasingly united chorus of opposition. The result was a loss of ideological market share compounded by a drop in public confidence about both the meaning and the reliability of the party's message (Gilljam & Holmberg 1993). Even after the SAP rebounded with its victory in the 1994 election, their support was not stable. Cutbacks in government services sent opinion polls swinging in the direction of the Left Party (the newly reinvented Communists) with its promise to maintain broad public services despite the widely acknowledged budget problems that the SAP had pledged to address. As noted in Chapter 6, the decline of party loyalty clearly makes it more tempting for leaders to disconnect campaign promises from government actions as much as possible. The resulting use of advertising, marketing, and news management strategies in electoral communication feeds the mistrust of parties, politicians, and their promises, creating poor conditions for new ideas to emerge within parties or among electorates.

Although constitutions or ideological regimes may set the parameters within which public discourse is constructed, it is equally clear that communication dynamics of the sort we have described can be discussed more comfortably at the level of parties and media. Moreover, differences of constitution and ideological regime, although suggestive, are too idiosyncratic to make for good comparisons. If constitutions or regimes can set limits and provide rhetorical frameworks within which debates are played out, the more important issues become *What specific institutional factors shape the outcomes of particular political situations?* and *What factors vary measurably across political systems to permit comparative analysis?* Our project is to identify constraints on the flow of ideas that enable us to talk about systematic differences and similarities between polities. Although there are many possible candidates for market regulatory mechanisms, the goal of parsimony encourages us to identify the smallest number of such mechanisms that have the largest potential impact on political debates and at the same time make sense from a comparative perspective.

The most obvious mechanism affecting the articulation of ideas in democratic societies is the mode of representation through which popular preferences are aggregated and channeled into the policy process. In all democracies, representation involves political parties and the electoral rules for apportioning political offices based on votes (i.e., winner take all vs. a variety of proportional representation schemes). Thus, the *party and election systems* constrained by the representation rules of a given polity are the first element of our framework for comparing idea markets (Ferguson 1995; Ferguson & Rogers 1986; Ginsberg & Shefter 1990; Schattschneider 1960).

We recognize, however, that the competitiveness and representativeness of parties cannot be described purely in terms of the electoral laws within which they operate. To function effectively, parties need resources. The methods available for obtaining funding (bribery, interest group financing, private donations, public financing) can impose limits on the rhetorical positions taken by party candidates, thereby rendering parties more or less open to articulating popular views. In other words, the political financing practices in a polity may limit the receptiveness of parties to certain ideas before the competition for votes ever begins. Other financing arrangements, by contrast, may open party competition to the broadest range of social viewpoints. Thus, the next regulatory mechanism we encounter is the type of *political financing* operating in a political system.

Beyond the core of party competition and finance, most societies also develop some other means of interest articulation to raise issues that escape electoral debate, to keep pressure on politicians between elections, and to refine policy priorities and language beyond the often crude and ambiguous discourse of campaigns. These political dialogue processes generally involve *interest group systems* that take different forms in different polities. In Sweden, interest organizations participate in public discourse and try to influence policymaking through a variety of channels. Particular to Sweden is the public commission system (also called the remiss system) in which the parties and established interest groups are assigned institutional roles in formulating government policies in different areas. The remiss system is discussed further on page 41. In the United States, with the rare exceptions of public commissions, the group dialogue is organized less systematically, with interest groups becoming involved in issues on an openly competitive basis, sometimes resulting in broad policy input and sometimes overrepresenting the views of narrow factions. In either case, pressure groups can play a direct role in defining, sharpening, or blunting the rhetoric of political conflicts.

Surrounding the core exchange of ideas established by party and election systems, political financing, and group pressure processes, the *mass media* amplify some political ideas, downplay others, and generally set the agenda of political discourse in society (Bennett 1996b; Entman 1989; Iyengar 1992; Iyengar & Kinder 1987; Lippman 1922). Depending on factors like ownership structure and journalistic norms, the media may privilege some voices and ideas in national dialogues, ignore others, challenge the accountability of politicians, or leave the political system to police itself. In any event, the media select and emphasize the rhetorical exchanges among the various players in public debates (Asp 1986; Bagdikian 1985; Bennett 1989, 1990; Hadenius & Weibull 1989; Herman 1985; Petersson & Carlberg 1990). Moreover, as mass media fragment into ever more personalized channels, marketing increasingly drives political information (O'Shaughnessy 1990).

These four regulatory mechanisms are not exhaustive, but they may be *the minimum conditions necessary* to understand patterns in the flow of democratic ideas. Other possible regulatory mechanisms may come to mind; public opinion, courts, and constitutions are obvious examples. However, we submit that these and other possibilities are eliminated for one of several reasons: (1) they are as much the products as the producers of ideas and therefore are often subordinate to the mechanisms we cite (public opinion being an example of this); (2) they are divisible into more manageable component parts (for example, constitutions are better broken down into their implications for parties and elections, interest group dynamics, and even the role of the media); (3) they are distributed so unevenly across democratic polities that they are of little use for comparisons (both courts and constitutions fall into this category). Arguing from a pragmatic vantage, we submit that the four regulatory mechanisms identified here have universal comparative potential in the liberal democracies (at least) and that their ultimate merit lies in analyses like those that follow. We are also encouraged that our framework is similar to that derived independently by Blumler, Kavanagh, and Nossiter (1996) in their analysis of modern political communication patterns in Britain.[2] Prior to applying our framework to the case studies in Chapters 3 through 6, a brief description of each mechanism will help to clarify how they compare in the Swedish and American contexts.

PARTIES AND ELECTORAL REPRESENTATION

The most obvious difference between the United States and Sweden is the contrast between a two-party, winner-take-all system of representation and a multiparty proportional representation system. A two-party framework often makes it more difficult for small ideological viewpoints to be heard nationally in the American context. However, third-party movements have occurred throughout American history for the expressed purpose of raising marginalized ideas to national consciousness. The problem with such movements has generally been their lack of staying power and their inability to translate party platforms into policies, although movements such as the Populists and the Progressives that failed to attain much power at the national level left significant marks on state and local governments.

In Sweden, by contrast, a multiparty system has given voice to a range of social interests at the national level, even making way for popular issue movements of the kind that saw the Green Party gain national representation in the 1988 election and the New Democracy Party bring its rhetoric of individual enterprise and coded racial nationalism into Parliament in 1991. However, the dominant role played by the Social Democratic Party, supported by a strong union movement, has in some ways limited the vitality of the system. Although there is considerable room for debate in the national forum, policies have tended to narrow around labor positions, partly because of the dominance of the Social Democrats and partly because of the inability of the opposition parties to articulate a coherent and credible political alternative. However, we cannot look to party systems alone in either country as the sole gauge of the range of political debate. Both systems operate in the context of the other factors we have identified.

POLITICAL FINANCING

With the (partial) exception of presidential campaigns, political financing in the United States is private, once derived largely from individual contributions but now flowing increasingly from corporations and interest groups and their political action committees (PACs). The Swedish system is based on public financing made available to parties in proportion to their share of seats in Parliament. These different financing arrangements introduce different dynamics into public debate in the two polities.

Great concern has been expressed in the American case over the possibility that politicians have become more responsive to funding sources than to voters (Ferguson 1995). Observers have noted several disturbing trends as a result of this finance system. First, the PAC system pushes the locus of representation away from a citizen constituency base and toward an increasingly national (but fragmented) issue agenda driven by concentrated economic and political organizations. Second, in the early years following the campaign finance reforms of the 1970s, the Republicans fared much better than the Democrats in attracting campaign money. The result was that to gain a competitive edge in the political money market, the Democrats abandoned their traditional rhetoric of jobs, welfare, and civil rights, while downplaying a host of moral issues in order to compete with the Republicans for adequate financing. The result, according to Ferguson and Rogers (1986), is that both political parties in the United States have been pushed rhetorically to the right of many voters, leaving those voters cynical and withdrawn from politics and leaving the Democratic Party searching for the reason for its own political existence.[3] In Chapter 6 we explore other accounts of how this finance system has affected the rhetorical patterns of recent campaigns. This paragraph is just one illustration of how institutions and ideas interact.

Prior to the mid-1960s Sweden also had a system of private political financing in the form of, mainly, membership fees and contributions from unions and business. Beginning in 1965, however, this system was gradually replaced with public financing on both the national and local levels. Every party represented in the legislative bodies now gets public funding in proportion to its seats. Not surprisingly, these parties have by and large been very appreciative of the system and made sure that the sums have increased substantially during the past quarter of a century (Gidlund 1983, 1991). Because all established parties benefit financially from the current system, there is little interest in discussing its pros and cons, let alone pressure to change it. Yet those groups and parties that do not get a piece of the public pie criticize the system for inhibiting new and fresh initiatives on the marketplace of ideas. Despite the merit of these claims, the Greens managed to break through the barrier in the 1988 elections, and they now benefit from the system as well. So did the New Democracy Party, which advocated the abolishment of public financing in its 1991 election platform. After the party got twenty-five seats in Parliament, however, its leaders seemed to come to the conclusion that using taxpayers' money for political purposes was not such a bad idea after all. The Swedish system provides an interesting contrast with the U.S. case, ensuring a range of different ideas in a communication system that could easily become (and has been) dominated by the SAP.

INTEREST GROUPS

Parties and elections are arguably the most visible and important forums for the exchange of political ideas. However, the daily undercurrent of public dialogue is important for fine-tuning the electoral agenda and developing ideas about future priorities. Sweden and the United States have substantially different interest group systems, with important consequences for the expression of political viewpoints and the representation of interests.

The dialogue that goes on between elections in the United States is carried forward largely through interest groups that push the specific agendas of their members. This system has been remarkably effective in bringing grassroots ideas to the attention of national representatives. Milk producers, tobacco growers, Mothers Against Drunk Drivers (MADD), small business associations, gun lovers, and environmental groups have all had great success in placing their issues on the national agenda. In some cases, these issues are either too narrow or too technical to receive much attention in electoral debate. In other cases, interest groups provide the momentum and pressure necessary to extract electoral promises and convert them later into political action. Sometimes the impact of interest groups on the rhetorical definition of issues is indirect, as when behind-the-scenes lobbying affects the content of legislation or regulation and thus limits the ways in which politicians can represent their activities to the public. To a remarkable degree, however, interest groups in the United States go directly to the public with rhetorical appeals, as was the case, for example, when tobacco companies funded advertising campaigns defining smoking as a "free choice" issue and labeling the attempts of various states to prohibit smoking in public places as a violation of smokers' "rights."

Despite the obvious importance of the interest group system in the American marketplace of ideas, there are some notable gaps and disadvantages in this particular form of dialogue between leaders and followers. First of all, groups without the resources to organize and make their points heard tend to have their ideas and interests excluded from the dialogue. Even when disadvantaged groups are able to organize (e.g., the National Welfare Rights League), they seldom have the resources to compete with more powerful groups. Thus, endangered animal species "spoken for" by environmental groups are more likely to have their interests represented in legislative forums and the media than, for example, are the more than 20 percent of American children living in poverty. More important, environmental groups have succeeded in constructing more emotionally arousing and attention-getting rhetorical images pertaining to the plight of animals than any that have been produced to draw attention to the problems of less fortunate, if not endangered, human beings. Second, the narrow focus of this type of dialogue may make it difficult to talk about, much less gain consensus on, big national priorities and broad visions for the future. Subject to interest group pressures, even modest national priority areas such as energy policy, education reform, and national health insurance easily become sidetracked or seriously compromised owing to the strategic advantages sought by conflicting interests. The result is often a dialogue in which some voices are raised more loudly than others in disproportion to the popularity of their ideas, and in which broad national priorities are often ignored because narrow issues advanced by well-organized groups occupy the dialogue space in political institutions and the media.

The Swedish interest group system deviates in interesting ways from the American case. Interest groups – and particularly labor market organizations – form an integral part of the Swedish model. It seems as if every large social group has its own organization, complete with statutes, board, magazine, and yes, even members. As in the United States, interest groups are increasingly active in promoting their issues through public relations efforts and the use of mass media. Direct contacts between powerful group leaders and equally powerful decision makers are also quite common (Petersson et al. 1990: Ch. 5). Very important in Sweden, but not in the United States, is the wide use of governmental commissions and the *remiss* system mentioned earlier. Almost every important piece of legislation is prepared through reports by specially appointed governmental commissions, usually consisting of parties, experts, and interest organizations. After a report has been worked out, everybody concerned is invited to react to the proposal and to send a remiss statement to the ministry in question. These reactions are then analyzed and reported in the final government bill. The whole procedure provides pressure groups with a unique opportunity to be heard and sometimes even to influence the content of a specific proposal (Johansson 1992; Premfors 1983).

During the past two decades, however, interest groups in Sweden have come under growing criticism for being out of touch with ordinary members and advocating positions that are not shared by a majority of the rank and file.[4] Union leaders who rhetorically champion the opinions of their members have quite often been accused of doing so without paying attention to what their members really think – which seems to occur in the United States as well. However, with the notable exception of labor, the interest group system in the United States involves much less bureaucratic distance between group representatives and members. The very survival of many issue groups depends on the direct financial support of members who review group positions vis-à-vis their personal political priorities. As a result, the U.S. interest group system is comparatively resistant to Swedish corporatist tendencies whereby high-level bargaining at the commission level and above can undermine the publicly stated differences between groups and governments.

However, corporatist tendencies in Sweden, though more pronounced than in the United States, may be undergoing change. A major study of power in Sweden (Petersson et al. 1990) hints at a possible weakening of the commission system accompanied by an opening up of the interest group system in general. The number of commissions decreased from 422 in 1980 to only 197 in 1987. Similar reductions have been made in allocated money and personnel.[5] All of this suggests that the policy consensus behind the rhetoric that once characterized the Swedish model may indeed be changing, leaving the Swedish system more open to U.S.-style breakdowns in agenda setting, policy making, and national planning (Micheletti 1991, 1995).

THE MEDIA

Communication media are important in regulating the flow of ideas and understanding between people and their leaders. In the words of Ben Bagdikian (1985: 97), former dean of the Graduate School of Journalism at the University of California, Berkeley:

The proper measure of a country's mass media is whether, by thorough examination and reporting, they increase understanding of important realities, and whether, through presentation of the widest possible spectrum of thought and analysis, they create an adequate reservoir of insights into the social process.

It is often argued that media ownership is one of the keys to the quality of public communications, either through a competitive capitalistic ownership structure or as a publicly funded operation separate from direct governmental or other monopolistic political control. Sweden and the United States provide interesting contrasts on this dimension. The overwhelming majority of print and broadcast outlets in the United States are privately owned. However, as Bagdikian points out, the news and information industry is becoming increasingly monopolized, with fifty large corporations controlling the majority of media output in 1980 and less than half that number dominating the mass media a decade later. The result in Bagdikian's view is the narrowing of political content, or as Herman (1985) puts it, the "marginalization" of minority and critical viewpoints in mainstream debate.[6] Sweden has a more mixed ownership pattern with print media largely in private hands (and often loosely affiliated with one political party or another), radio and television publicly owned under the operation of major interest groups (independent of government administration), and funded by license fees (the level of which is decided upon by Parliament). However, the Swedish media market, as previously stated, is now changing rapidly after the introduction of commercial radio and the explosive growth of cable television (Hadenius & Anderberg 1994; Petersson & Carlberg 1990: 65–76). The ironic result appears to be the introduction of more dramatized and personalized news coverage, inviting the trends toward strategic communication discussed earlier.

Which media system is more open and pluralistic? Which one provides for a greater range of ideas and issues to be reported and debated? There are no easy or clear-cut answers to these questions. In both systems views representing dissent or minorities have a hard time being heard. Both systems also seem, albeit for different reasons, to reinforce existing power structures and established ideas. Vietnam and Watergate may have gone down in history as fine examples of American investigative reporting, but in retrospect they stand out as exceptions rather than the rule. During the Reagan years, for instance, the U.S. press by and large played a subservient role, rarely asking the tough questions and missing such scandals as the Housing and Urban Development (HUD) debacle and the savings and loan disaster (Hertsgaard 1989). A Swedish newspaper cracked the Ebbe Carlsson affair, leading to a major political scandal in an election year (1988) and to the resignation of several top administration officials. But that, too, seems to have been an isolated event and is hardly typical of news reporting in general. In Sweden, elite groups are nowadays much more skillful in making use of the media, whereas women, ordinary workers, and minority groups are vastly underrepresented in the media coverage (Petersson & Carlberg 1990). In both countries, the uses of media have become central to election strategy and policy processes, with important effects on public communications (Arterton 1985; Diamond & Bates 1992).

HOW THE MARKETPLACE WORKS

The aims of our analysis are to show that ideas and rhetoric matter in shaping public opinion and mobilizing support or opposition around specific policies, and to illustrate how rhetoric is constrained by the institutional processes that characterize particular political systems. Precisely how the different regulatory mechanisms interact and how they affect rhetoric and public policy may differ from country to country and from issue to issue. What this perspective offers is a broad view of how institutional arrangements and the rhetorical calculations of actors in those institutions can affect power arrangements and the legitimacy of government decisions.

In addition to building a theoretical bridge between institutional analysis and political communication, this perspective may open the way to solving various puzzles of democratic theory, including the earlier question of how democracies that may be doing a reasonable job of interest representation have suffered such declines of public confidence and support. As noted in Chapter 1, the disjuncture may be caused by the symbolic representation of the decisions of government during the interest, election, and policy decision processes. For reasons having to do with strategic rhetorical calculations of actors within institutions, these symbolic processes may not produce satisfying or stable understanding of immediate government actions even though the outcomes of government are defensible by more distant empirical measures. At the same time, when policies or interest group gains are contradictory, another sort of political trouble may be created by the inability of institutions to support rhetoric that is more socially and intellectually cohesive. This implies that institutions may change in response to public pressures and that the policy results of those institutions may even reflect public preferences. However, the rhetoric that flows from those same changes may not represent either the institutions or the policies in ways that generate popular understanding, support, or stability of opinion. To put this bluntly, even if institutions are broadly responsive to public input, the rhetoric generated by disjointed institutional arrangements may not convey that responsiveness back to publics in generally acceptable ways.

What we have then is an idea market mediated by institutions that change in response to historical conditions and social preferences, but those changes may not be functional responses to those conditions or perfect responses to citizen input (which may not be formed or expressed all that clearly either, for that matter). Rather, we can imagine (and our cases document) a two-way causal flow in this marketplace. That is, social conditions and public preferences may lead to institutional changes, as when in the United States party corruption scandals (e.g., Watergate) and divisive policies (e.g., civil rights and the Vietnam War) led to pressure for various party and election reforms from direct primaries to campaign finance reform. Yet such reforms may have unintended effects on how party leaders and candidates communicate with publics. For example, less party discipline and more entrepreneurial candidates may generate short-term tactical rhetoric that often deviates from the grand governing ideas, whereas attempts to affirm the governing ideas may prove to be transparent when party solidarity is hard to deliver.

The interplay among these various mechanisms that constrain what political actors say to publics can be complex. Causality is not a simple matter of changing public preferences resulting in changing political ideas. Demands for change may result in institutional changes that seem responsive to those demands, but new institutional constraints may invite language choices that actually undermine the responsiveness of the government to citizen input. Thus, as we will see in Chapter 6, for example, campaign finance reform in the United States appeared in the mid-1970s to be a useful response to voter distress about party corruption. As the reform system evolved into PAC financing, candidates became increasingly independent financially, with the result that campaign rhetoric became increasingly personalized and independent of party or programmatic connection (Bennett 1996b). It is hard to determine whether the decline of party identification among voters or the decline of partisan messages from candidates was the stronger causal relationship here; the more compelling view is of an interactive relationship.

In another example of how interactions among institutions can produce effects among images transmitted to citizens, Patterson (1993) documents the increase in both coverage of elections as *horse races* and press attention to campaign strategy and personal defects of candidates following party nomination reforms in the United States after 1968. He attributes these changes to the failure of the media to rise to their new institutional responsibilities to become builders of voter coalitions in the wake of declining party control over nominations. Perhaps this is true, but we also suspect that this shift in party procedures and coverage patterns of media simultaneously created a new incentive system for increasingly independent candidates to produce more personalized, short-term, emotional rhetoric of the sort that Jamieson (1992) identifies as characteristic of the "dirty politics" of campaigning in the electronic media age. In any case, it seems too simple to say that television or press patterns have caused new campaign symbolism to emerge; rather, the adjustments among changing institutions have stimulated the production and distribution of particular types of images and devalued other rhetorical forms such as issue appeals and the publicity of party platforms. Patterson argues correctly that platforms still exist and that candidates continue to try to publicize their position papers. However, our perspective draws attention to the changing institutional contexts for these more traditional brands of campaign content. The rhetoric aimed by candidates at the media leaves voters suspicious of candidate issue pledges if only because of the perceived inability of parties to implement them if elected to govern.

Our perspective does not assume the primacy of institutions over communication or the independence of communications from institutions. Rather, we prefer a two-way causal linkage more familiar to social constructionists. Thus, we reformulate Patterson's argument to go beyond the "irresponsible press" explanation and point to a more general "devaluation" of campaign issues and platform rhetoric that results from changing finance practices, weakened parties, and related changes in media coverage. In this more systemic view, language and communication reflect the impact of institutional changes on the organization of government power, with the result that publics have implicitly devalued much of the issue rhetoric and party promises in campaigns as empty rhetoric and equally empty promises. As noted by one observer of election poll responses to a candidate issue position, that position is seldom regarded as being a serious issue by voters unless they "see the parties differing in their approach to it or their capacity to solve it."[7]

Looking at how institutions shape and are shaped by ideas allows us to see the irony of a marketplace that is not moved by some hidden hand of rationality but, like the economic marketplace from which we derive our framework, can produce various unintended consequences, inefficiencies, and breakdowns despite efforts at rational institutional reform and regulation. In the foregoing examples, it is ironic to note that several decades of party, election, and campaign finance reform have produced a rhetoric based on the marketing calculations of individual candidates that results in Jamieson's "dirty politics" – the abandonment of principle, the practice of deception, the creation of images that play on short-term emotions (fear, doubt, negativity), and the constant adjustment based on marketing research rather than efforts to rally support around more enduring rhetorical agendas. To compound these communication problems, the media representation of political candidates may further exaggerate these rhetorical tendencies by focusing increasingly on horse-race dramatics, individual attacks, personal images, campaign strategies over issues, and other types of communication content despite, as Patterson notes, the growing frustration of candidates, journalists, and voters alike with the lack of serious coverage of issues and agendas.

If we add up the various political institutions that affect how we communicate, we encounter a final dilemma confronting modern democracies: the possible eclipse of traditional political cultures through the continual initiatives of marketing research and strategic communication. Messages that target individuals at deep emotional levels may tear down the collective associations that draw citizens into public life. When finance arrangements or media formats keep new ideas from being circulated or prevent them from receiving the careful deliberation they must have in order to gain acceptance, the very vitality of culture as an evolving system of meaning that promotes stability and collective action becomes threatened.

A POSTSCRIPT ON CULTURE
AND COMMUNICATION

There are two arguments for keeping our analytical framework separate from the grand schemes of meaning that we call cultures. First is the traditional view of cultures as being inherently stable and protected from human tampering as a result of their being deeply embedded in the subconscious mind through early socialization and reinforced by rituals that give such everyday activities as elections a deeper mythological significance. In this view, the four regulatory mechanisms in our framework operate within culture-as-context – that is, as a stable interpretive system and the grand regulator of ideas in society. From this perspective, the enduring beliefs and values that define cul-

ture create expectations about who gets to say what, which ideas are more likely to be emphasized (e.g., property rights vs. welfare rights), and perhaps most
important, which ideas have little or no social standing at all (see Almond &
Verba 1963; Anton 1969, 1980; Lipset 1979; Tocqueville 1969; Wildavsky
1987). This most encompassing context of ideas reminds us that no matter
how open the party competition, how clean the financing, how strong the
group pressure, or how crusading the media, there are some ideas that simply
have little currency among the familiar rhetorical scripts that constitute a culture. All of which explains how culture differs from the other regulatory
mechanisms and why it should not be included at the same level of analysis:
Culture does not vary in the sometimes rapid (e.g., political reform), easily ob-
servable (e.g., party alignment), and often deliberate (e.g., interest expression)
ways that characterize the workings of regulatory mechanisms. Whereas the
interactions of regulatory mechanisms create a particular configuration of
policy or election rhetoric (sometimes contributing to incremental changes in
a political culture), culture constitutes the boundaries, whether loose or rigid,
within which acceptable and unacceptable policy thinking occurs in society
(see Merelman 1991). In addition, cultures are so wrapped in identity and difference that they often become residual elements in comparative analyses
rather than providing easily manageable terms for such analyses.

These hermetic views of culture have merit. However, there is another argument for keeping the everyday production of communication analytically
distinct from larger cultural processes – an argument that invites us to think
about culture as something that may be profoundly affected by politics,
power, and patterns of political discourse. Idea markets may move uneasily
against the cultural traditions that establish popular expectations about politics, government, and public life. Indeed, the market mechanisms that we
have identified may produce rhetoric that is unsettling to the stabilizing, consensual foundations of cultural values. Strategic communication can assault
the meanings of core values and beliefs on which polities depend for citizen
identity, legitimacy, and ultimately the evaluation and assimilation of new
ideas. The gradual erosion of governing visions and the resort to short-term
strategic communication may bypass traditional cultural practices that provide for some measure of broadly shared control over the democratic rituals
of policy making and election.

In his provocative work titled *Communication as Culture,* Carey (1989)
points out the limitations of the idea of communication as the mere trans-

mission of messages (i.e., the signal–receiver, stimulus–response attitude paradigms that dominate social science approaches). He recommends augmenting this view with a conception of communication-as-ritual that locates messages within broader contexts of community, identity, and social practice. He urges our reconsideration of Dewey's pioneering ritual approach to communication:

There is more than a verbal tie between the words common, community and communication. Men live in a community in virtue of the things they have in common; and communication is the way in which they come to possess things in common. What they must have in common ... are aims, beliefs, aspirations, knowledge – a common understanding – likemindedness as sociologists say. Such things cannot be passed physically from one to another like bricks; they cannot be shared as persons would share a pie by dividing it into physical pieces.... Consensus demands communication. (Dewey 1916: 5–6)

At first reading, Dewey may sound like the earlier hermetic perspective that assumes culture to be the self-regulating context for human affairs. However, Dewey leaves open the important question of how we communicate as being not solely determined by, but perhaps more important, as being the determinant of culture and its discontents. When rituals such as elections maintain an element of spontaneity and candidates can be observed to respond openly to challenges and criticisms of their positions, then the opportunity exists for new ideas to become tested and evaluated, perhaps even taking root in the cultural tradition if they become the basis for subsequent successful government activity. On the other hand, if open discourse is preempted by candidates who recite only the formulas produced by marketing experts and who avoid risky exchanges of ideas with opponents and audiences, then the ritual of elections becomes brittle and manipulated – what is commonly referred to as an "empty ritual." As the term *empty* becomes more synonymous with the terms *ritual* and *rhetoric*, it pays to consider the possible impact of everyday political discourse upon the culture that gives meaning to the common enterprise and in turn confers identifications on citizens. Thus, as we explore the transformations of public discourse in the case studies that follow, we will be mindful of the consequences not just for politicians, parties, and policies but for the integrity of cultures as well.

PART II

THE GREAT TWENTIETH-CENTURY GOVERNING IDEAS

3

The Rise and Fall of New Deal Liberalism in the United States

> The Democrats are in danger of again playing the role they did in the era of
> Grover Cleveland, that is of being the Everybody Else Party, a loose ragtag
> union, born of historical accidents and composed of ... disparate elements....
> To anyone living among the tired, two-jobbed, worried and scrambling
> middle classes, it should be obvious there are uncounted millions whom the
> Republicans do not and never will represent. But neither do the Democrats
> and the ones who led their party into this election should all be locked up
> under a witless protection program.
> – Nicholas von Hoffman, on the 1994 election

Within the bounds of culture and the fates of history, societies are often characterized most sharply by the political ideas that evolve to guide public debates. Governing ideas and the market mechanisms that act upon them (parties, finance arrangements, interest processes, and mass communications media) structure national debates on policy questions like tax reform, and they affect the clarity of choices, the credibility of promises, and the degree of party loyalty in elections. More generally, governing ideas set the terms for conflict and change in society.

In this chapter and the next, we explore the great domestic political debates of the twentieth century in Sweden and the United States, showing how two grand sets of governing ideas arose in response to the economic crisis of the 1930s and continued to set the tone of national politics until the 1990s. The important differences we identify are not so much the obvious contrasts between the Swedish and the American ways of thinking about society and its problems, but the deeper structure of political rhetoric itself. In the Swedish case, we find the development of an ideology that broke free of earlier conservative ideas, articulating a coherent set of social principles and goals, along with guidelines about how government should promote those goals. The key, and the irony, here is that this ideational break with Swedish conservatism was accomplished not through a forcefully articulated socialist ideology but with a more broadly appealing image of a government that would provide security, order, and respect for the members of society, much as a well-functioning home cares for all the members of a family. The contrasting American case reveals the formation of a weaker liberal vision that never fully rejected the principles of conservatism and therefore failed to produce an independent set of social principles or an easily defensible role for government to play in realizing a new social vision. This failure to identify a grand alternative to conservatism eventually led to the piecemeal legislative satisfaction of a growing clientele of interests within the Democratic Party, building to the historic moment in 1984 in which Ronald Reagan proclaimed that his rivals were the party of the special interests.

As a result of these different rhetorical formations, the nature of domestic policy debates has been very different in the two countries, and the success of the respective reformist parties in explaining and defending social welfare and economic policies has been correspondingly different as well. The Swedish case illustrates the rise of a dominant ideology in which a small set of positive social principles could be offered to explain and defend a large variety of programs and policies to a stable and knowing national constituency. The American case shows how the failure to develop an independent set of ideological principles left the Democrats frequently defending programs against principled attacks by the Republicans without being able to articulate an alternative broad social vision that linked different policies and constituencies together in a convincing, positive way. In this chapter we explore the rise and fall of this incomplete governing vision of the Democratic Party.

THE ETERNAL AMERICAN STRUGGLE WITH CLASSICAL LIBERALISM

As many observers have noted (e.g., Hartz 1955; Rodgers 1987), the dominant ideology in American politics has been classical liberalism, centered around something of a Holy Trinity of basic principles:

- The sanctity of business and private enterprise.
- The commitment to individual freedom in political expression and economic activity.
- And guaranteeing both of these principles by rejecting big government and bureaucracy.

Until the 1930s prominent national politicians generally competed with one another in their claims about who was most likely to conserve those hallowed principles of social life. Although the great issues like slavery, industrialization, money standards, and trade protectionism divided leaders and candidates for office, their policies and promises were generally framed within rhetorical contests over who was more conservative, by which was meant "loyal to the classical principles of liberal democracy."

It is no accident that beginning students of American political thought often have trouble understanding how conservatives can claim to adhere to the principles of true liberalism, just as it may be unclear how far modern-day liberals really depart from those same principles. The confusion is not misplaced: Both liberals and conservatives in present-day politics often return to the same foundations of liberal democratic theory when explaining themselves to voters, defending their programs, and attacking their opponents.

In this confusion lies the key to understanding the character of modern political debates in America and the limitations of the liberal rhetoric associated with the Democratic Party since the New Deal. The following analysis is based on candidate speeches, party platforms, State of the Union messages, and the rich secondary literature on political rhetoric from 1932 to the present. The purpose of this exploration is to document the rise and fall of contemporary liberal (meaning "left") rhetoric and to explain why a fully articulated ideological alternative to conservatism never developed in the United States the way it did in Sweden. In the process, we will also mark the final passing of New Deal liberalism in 1994, when the Democratic Leadership Council reprimanded the president it helped to elect as not being the true "New Democrat" he had promised to be, and instead harboring the kind of latent New Deal thinking that sabotaged the chances of national health care reform and lost the party its control of Congress. Like the grand symbol of the New Deal that it struggled so hard to replace, the idea of the New Democrat was also largely an empty category that cried out for definition.

THE ORIGINS OF NEW DEAL LIBERALISM

The New Deal fueled the great engine of government to solve social problems during the crisis of the 1930s and began the most sweeping period of social reform in American history. Supporters even called it a revolution (Frederick 1933). Establishing an activist role for government also marked a significant departure from one of the three basic conservative principles: the ideal of small, passive government. This change was both dramatic and enduring enough to create a new political label for the rest of the century: liberal. Yet these new liberals who would advocate governmental solutions to society's problems for the next fifty years have always struggled with a serious political handicap because they have never established a convincing, widely accepted rhetorical break with either of the other two foundations of the conservative ideology. The new liberalism became something of a hybrid, or mongrel, ideology: a less conservative version of classical liberalism.

The reluctance of the New Deal reformers to make an ideological break with conservatism and outline a new set of governing principles was evident from the very beginning. In 1932 Franklin Roosevelt ran for office, attacking President Herbert Hoover for being a big spender while promoting a Democratic platform that promised a return to tried and true policies of reducing taxes, cutting public expenditures, and balancing the budget. On the high ground of principles, the campaign of 1932 offered fairly conventional rhetorical fare, with each candidate trying to represent himself as being more conservative than the other.[1]

Yet, as popular comedian Will Rogers was fond of saying, it was a time of crisis, and the people would have supported almost anything that looked like action from Washington:

They know they got a man in there who is wise to Congress, wise to our so-called big men. The whole country is with him, just so he does something. If he burned down the Capitol we would cheer and say: "Well, we at least got a fire started anyhow." (Schlesinger 1958: 12)

What Roosevelt offered by way of distinctive rhetoric was a large dose of Jeffersonian pragmatism, promising to experiment and to try new solutions until something worked. It was this promise to experiment, and not the introduction of a new set of principles, that characterized the rhetoric of the 1932 election and the defining years of the New Deal itself (Hanson 1985: 276). Lines like this one filled Roosevelt speeches: "The country needs, and unless I mistake its temper, the country demands, persistent experimentation. It is common sense to take a method and try it. If it fails, admit it frankly and try another. But above all, try something" (Hofstadter 1973: 410).

The idea of an activist government was not revolutionary in itself. Years before, the Progressives and the Populists of the 1890s before them had promoted government as an engine of political and economic reform. But the Progressives were a movement for correcting deviations from classical liberal traditions and aimed as much at the Republican corruption of business principles of free enterprise and open competition as at the Democrats' embrace of corrupt urban political machines. By contrast, the activism of the New Deal was epitomized by Roosevelt's relentless pragmatism and problem-solving rhetoric. This almost antiphilosophical activism had plenty of room for human compassion, as derisive conservative attacks on "bleeding heart liberalism" have charged for decades. However, the new liberals refrained from promoting their ideas as ideological or moral dogma. As Thurman Arnold (1935, 1937) explained in his great works debunking the perceived mythologies of government, law, and economy, political moralism of any ideological stripe inevitably descended into a kind of religious mystification, hiding greed, corruption, and inefficiency even from many of the true believers themselves. At least that is how many of the founding New Dealers understood their distinctiveness from both conservatism on the right and socialism on the left.

For Arnold and many others in the Roosevelt brain trust, the error of the earlier Progressive activists was that they, too, were slaves to moral principle, meaning that they often settled for using government as a purifying ritual to impose moral codes (e.g., elaborate antitrust laws), while accomplishing relatively little in practical terms (e.g., actually breaking up corporate trusts). Richard Hofstadter identified the key rhetorical terms of Progressivism as "patriotism, citizen, democracy, law, character, conscience, soul, morals, service, duty, shame, disgrace, sin, and selfishness," while noting a sharp moral break in the vocabulary of the new liberalism outlined in the writings of Arnold: "needs, organization, humanitarian, results, technique, institution, realistic, discipline, morale, skill, expert, habits, practical, leadership" (Hofstadter 1955: 320).

Here, then, lies the enduring tension of modern American political rhetoric: a social problem-solving pragmatism that is suspicious of mystifying political doctrines versus a litany of conservative principle that is suspicious of unrestrained government activism. For nearly any liberal problem-solving effort from the New Deal on, conservative opponents have raised the challenging questions: But what philosophy drives these experiments? What principles govern the choice of methods or the evaluation of success? Beyond the liberal response that government must address self-evident human needs, there has been remarkable ideological silence on these questions. Ample evidence suggests that this silence was not born of some conspiracy to cover up a secretly shared set of subversive principles too radical to spring on an untutored public. Beneath the grand symbol of twentieth-century liberalism in American politics – the foundation of much everyday rhetoric in both the policy arena and the election campaign – there is an aversion to principle that encourages the largely unchanging rhetoric of the conservative opposition. When George Bush accepted the Republican nomination for president in 1992, he uttered words that might have been spoken by Ronald Reagan, Richard Nixon, Dwight Eisenhower, or Herbert Hoover before him: "And so we offer a philosophy that puts faith in the individual, not the bureaucracy. A philosophy that empowers people to do their best.... We start with a simple fact: Government is too big and spends too much."[2] In fact, before the happy, and largely accidental birth of the New Deal, these words might well have been delivered in one of Franklin Roosevelt's speeches charging none other than Herbert Hoover with wandering off the true path of American political tradition.

The Rhetoric of Pragmatism

In the beginning, the phrase "new deal" was coined by a speechwriter as a dubious amalgam of Theodore Roosevelt's "Square Deal" and Woodrow Wilson's "New Freedom," and was thrown in without much clarification at the end of the 1932 acceptance speech: "I pledge you – I pledge myself to a new deal for the American people."[3] The phrase was seized upon by a cartoonist who played on the imagery of Roosevelt's dramatic and unprecedented plane trip to Chicago to deliver his acceptance in person. In Roland Kirby's cartoon, "The New Deal" was written on the wings of the plane flying on its allegorical rescue mission through bad weather as it carried the candidate from Albany. (See Dorothy Rosenam's account in Loucheim 1983: 11.) Although seldom used by Roosevelt or later Democratic leaders until the party attempted a rhetorical rebirth in the 1950s and 1960s, the term was quickly popularized by the press looking for a capsule version of an alternately grandiose, detailed, and uneasily conservative speech. For much of the rest of the decade of the 1930s, the "New Deal" became an easy category in which to place rhetoric and policies that eluded easy ideological labels. As in the case of the Swedish *folkhem* discussed in Chapter 4, the grand idea itself was seldom invoked in everyday discourse but served as the constant, implicit interpretive context for the popular rhetorics of the day.

Recognizing that the phrase lacked much distinctive substance, speechwriter–adviser Samuel Rosenman counseled Roosevelt to call in a brain trust of academic advisers to come up with ideas to fill the new and rather empty rhetorical category. True to his belief in experimentation, Roosevelt assembled the now famous coterie that included Berle, Tugwell, Moley, Morgenthau, and others, who often disagreed on what to do, and even when they reached consensus, often had trouble explaining their proposals to the boss. In cases of conflicting advice, Roosevelt was notorious for simply combining different ideas in the same program and seeing if it would fly. As Tugwell described the process: "We could throw out pieces of theory. We could suggest relations; and perhaps the inventiveness of the suggestion would attract his notice. But the tapestry of the policy he was weaving was guided by an artist's conception which was not made known to us" (Wright 1982: 94).

When Tugwell had trouble explaining his agriculture program that would become the foundation for the Agricultural Adjustment Administration (AAA), Roosevelt's reaction was to say: "Well, Professor, put it in a telegram – two or three hundred words – and we'll work it into a speech. I'll take your word for it that it's the latest and most efficient model" (Wright 1982: 94). When those speeches were made, they contained a combination of dense facts and figures in the context of optimistic pronouncements and calls for support, all held together by the enduring faith in experimentation, action, and more action. In a typical Fireside Chat, the AAA was discussed first at a dizzying technical level explaining the peculiar problems of cotton, tobacco, wheat, and corn–hog farmers, and then the rhetoric jumped to the continuing imperative for action:

I do not hesitate to say in the simplest, clearest language of which I am capable, that although the prices of many products of the farm have gone up and although many farm families are better off than they were last year, I am not satisfied either with the amount or the extent of the rise, and that it is definitely a part of our policy to increase the rise and to extend it to those products which have as yet felt no benefit. If we cannot do this one way we will do it another. Do it, we will.[4]

Perhaps the most striking characteristic of the Fireside Chats taken as a group from 1933 to 1939 is their mixture of almost dizzying detail and continual hopefulness (spiced with attacks on the enemies of progress), creating a continuing sense of activity from government without offering much higher reason for that action than the sheer need to do something in a crisis. This call to action was, as Will Rogers noted, a welcome message in a nation filled with unemployed and anxious people. The chats were also aided by the intimacy of the radio medium, which suited the fatherly tone of the frequent minilectures on subjects like how the banking system worked and why it failed, or how farm commodity prices were established and why the government needed to regulate that marketplace. For example, the first Fireside Chat (March 12, 1933) was titled "An Intimate Talk with the People of the United States on Banking." The second (May 7, 1933) was called "What We Have Been Doing and What We Are Planning to Do." The fourth and final chat of 1933 (October 22) was an exhortation called "We Are on Our Way, and We Are Headed in the Right Direction." The first chat of 1934 was one clearly studied by Ronald Reagan's speechwriters in 1984 (June 28) called "Are You Better Off than You Were Last Year?" A minilecture on soil erosion (September 6, 1936) interspersed with heroic vignettes about farm families was called "We Are Going to Conserve Soil, Conserve Water, Conserve Life."

Even the disciples of the New Deal were often hard-pressed to discover its deeper principles or its countermessage to the reigning conservative ideology. Following a speech before a group of midwestern businessmen, Alvin Hansen was asked to reflect on eight years of New Deal policies from his vantage as an economic adviser: "In your opinion is the basic principle of the New Deal economically sound?" His reply: "I really do not know what the basic principle of the New Deal is. I know from my experience in the government that there are as many conflicting opinions among the people in Washington under this administration as we have in the country at large" (Brinkley 1989: 85).

On the important issue of trade protectionism, for example, Hoover never wavered from the clear statement in his 1932 acceptance address, to wit: "I am squarely for a protective tariff."[5] Meanwhile, Roosevelt clouded the tariff issue in his acceptance speech and continued to do so until the final address of the campaign when advisers argued that he needed to react to Hoover's continuing statements of principle on the issue. Yet when those advisers pointed out that he must choose between opposed schools of thought like Free Trade or Protectionism, Roosevelt replied "Fine! Fine! Weave the two together!" (Wright 1982: 94). And so, Roosevelt's final words on the matter merged three speechwriters' drafts along with his own introduction, leading one scholar to refer to Roosevelt as "an ideological fixer" (Wright 1982: 95).

New Deal Pragmatism Survives a Challenge from the Left

If this thesis about the failure of New Deal liberalism to differentiate itself from the prevailing conservative ideology is to hold up, it must account for the seemingly more radical policies and rhetoric, highlighted by the Social Security and Wagner Acts of 1935, that scholars have termed the second New Deal (Leuchtenberg 1963). It is true that the rhetoric of the mid-1930s heated up considerably, with appeals to labor and veiled attacks on greedy and selfish business interests. This was the era in which Roosevelt called for passage of a tax reform that would "soak the rich." The acceptance speech at the 1936 Democratic Convention condemned the "modern economic royalists," the "new economic royalty," and the "new economic dynasties" who threatened the freedom of individuals that had been hard-won and hard-preserved since the Revolution of 1776.[6]

Although fiery, this rhetoric was careful never to take aim at capitalists as a class, only at the wayward few who gave the marketplace a bad name. Nor were the victims of these greedy elements identified primarily as a working class or a labor movement but (similar to a later development in the Swedish case) as "wage earners," families, and consumers who stood for the higher principles of individual freedom and free enterprise – the same principles that the Republicans claimed were being undermined by New Deal policies.

Upon close inspection, the historical evolution of both the second New Deal policies and the rhetoric used to sell them to the public suggests that once again pragmatism and not the evolution of an ideologically distinctive opposition to conservatism guided Roosevelt's actions. The key factor explaining both the rhetoric and the policies of the second New Deal was growing political opposition to the whole reform program from both the left and the right. The Supreme Court overruled key provisions of the National Industrial Recovery Act, which was heralded as the centerpiece of the first New Deal and defined rhetorically as a practical effort to bring business and labor together to forge wage and price policies.[7] At the same time that it was being undermined from the right, the business–labor partnership created by the National Recovery Administration (NRA) was dismissed derisively as the "National Run Around" by many labor groups (Hofstadter 1973: 438).

Even though the Democrats did very well in the 1934 elections, the new crop in Congress was more ideological than Roosevelt, and the "thunder on the left" coming from Populists like Huey Long threatened to steal Roosevelt's rhetorical thunder as well as his legislative initiative. Thus, the sudden shift to a "soak the rich" rhetoric in the second New Deal can be understood as an early instance of strategic communication aimed at stealing the thunder from the left, not as an evolution toward a more coherent set of governing principles. Consistent with this interpretation is the widely accepted analysis that the much heralded tax reform netted little revenue gain for the government treasury. Moreover, from the outbreak of World War II onward, the American labor movement was steadily relegated to a fairly well-behaved interest section within the Democratic Party and was represented by pragmatic unions that articulated little more radical vision than that workers should have their share of the American Dream.

The Politics and Rhetoric of Political Expediency

In these political interpretations of the brief New Deal rhetorical movement to the left, we begin to see a pattern in both the rhetoric and the policies of the middle to late New Deal years (roughly 1935 to 1939). It is a pattern that explains a great deal about the lack of an evolved American leftist alternative to conservatism and at the same time explains the enduring vulnerability of liberal rhetoric to conservative challenges. Many of the programs that are regarded today as the core of the liberal reform legacy in government were issues in which Roosevelt was not particularly interested at the time. However, he recognized that a more radical rhetoric was useful for maintaining popular support and that embracing the new policy agenda gave him the appearance of leading Congress. Consider in this light Hofstadter's account of the Wagner Act that unleashed – for a short and politically expedient period – an activist labor movement that was for the first time in history sanctioned by the government:

> The Wagner Act had never been an administration measure. It had been buffeted about the legislative chambers for more than a year without winning Roosevelt's interest.... Yet under the stimulus of recovery and the protection of the NLRB [National Labor Relations Board], unions grew and flourished and provided the pressure in politics that gave the second New Deal its dynamic force. "A good democratic antidote for the power of big business," said Roosevelt. (Hofstadter 1973: 440)

Likewise, the much heralded "soak the rich" tax reforms of the Revenue Act of 1935 were scarcely high on Roosevelt's political priority list. To the contrary, his main economic program continued to be guided by traditional conservative principles of low taxes, low government spending, balanced budgets, and free enterprise. Data from Mark Leff's study of the actual redistribution of wealth following the tax reforms of the second New Deal led to his somewhat surprised conclusion that:

By no stretch of the imagination was the New Deal tax system a vehicle for the broad income redistribution to lift up those at the bottom of the economic pyramid. For various reasons ... the share of tax collections drawn from potential sources of redistributive taxation ... was considerably *lower* in the New Deal than in World War I, the 1920s, or the decades succeeding the New Deal....

Franklin Roosevelt's slashing oratory in the colorful 1935 Revenue Act fight can encourage the supposition that New Deal taxes must have eased income inequality in favor of the "forgotten man." Such conclusions are extravagant at best; high rates on upper income brackets were counterbalanced by ... taxes that obtained more impressive collections from the poor. To this extent, the government acted as a bourgeois Robin Hood, taking not only from the rich, but also at times from the poor to rescue the merely comfortable from the tax man. (Leff 1984: 2)

What inspired the slashing "soak the rich" oratory? As Hofstadter (1973: 440) put it, "Since Roosevelt was baited and frustrated by the right and adopted by the left, his ego was enlisted along with his sympathies in behalf of the popular point of view." More than this, however, Roosevelt increasingly faced popular competition from within his own party, and eventually decided to capitalize politically on the willingness of voters to adopt candidates who talked the leftist talk, even if their subsequent policies did not always measure up to the rhetoric. In Leff's analysis:

[Roosevelt's initial efforts to suppress the political discontent from both sides] and salvage a middle way floundered as it became clear that recovery had revived intense business opposition. Roosevelt chose to stem the disintegration of his support by ceremoniously driving the "overprivileged" out of his coalition. Rhetoric was the most direct way of dramatizing this rift and of binding together what was essentially a negative coalition. The quintessence of this strategy was its fearsome shadow, not its more limited substance. Thus the celebrated Revenue Act of 1935, though financially frivolous, was politically crucial to Roosevelt's broader strategy. (Leff 1984: 7)

Thus did Roosevelt's rhetoric shift from a somewhat apologetic explanation about welfare "chiselers" in the April 1935 Fireside Chat to an unapologetic Labor Day address the next year in which he boldly announced:

Our aim must be to achieve and maintain a national economy whose factors are so finely balanced that the worker is always sure of a job that will guarantee a living wage. By a living wage, I mean a wage which will assure the worker and the worker's dependents a living in accordance with American standards of decency, happiness and self-respect. The wage earners of America do not ask for more. They will not be satisfied with less.[8]

For reasons to be outlined in the analysis that follows, these strong words never developed into an ideology that opposed the core economic or individualistic principles of conservatism, as those principles had been fashioned from classical liberalism. Even Roosevelt's later embrace of Keynesian economics, along with the abandonment of promises about balancing budgets, were not championed as matters of economic principle but political necessity. In his State of the Union Message of 1938, for example, he promised a budget that would decrease the deficit but not eliminate it, citing an obligation to people who continued to need help from government. Like a host of Democrats and Republicans since, he promised to reduce the deficit through a combination of economic growth and better methods of tax collection.[9]

In these later years as in the beginning, the rhetorical drumbeat of the New Deal was the naming of specific programs and policies and listing benefits to particular groups. Although those programs no doubt appealed to their immediate beneficiaries, they also invited attacks from vocal opponents (e.g., Dewey 1940) who opposed nearly every one on the principle that they undermined free enterprise, individual self-reliance, and the ideal of small government with limited powers. Following the bruising battle with Congress over adding new members to the Supreme Court, and the eventual relaxation of the Court's opposition of many of the regulatory policies he supported, Roosevelt appeared to recognize that short of articulating a grand but ideologically divisive governing vision, the political, and more important, the rhetorical capital of the New Deal had been spent. As Hofstadter (1973: 445–446) describes it, the growing opposition within his own party:

... augured the political bankruptcy of the New Deal. The reform wave had spent itself, and the Democratic Party, divided by the Supreme Court fight and the purge and hamstrung by its large conservative bloc, was exhausted as an agency of reform. Always the realist, Roosevelt rang the death knell of the New Deal in his annual message to Congress on January 4, 1939. "We have now passed the period of internal conflict in the launching of our program of social reform," he declared. "Our full energy may now be released to invigorate the process of recovery in order to preserve our reforms." Almost three years before Pearl Harbor his experimentation had run its course.

THE BIRTH OF INTEREST GROUP LIBERALISM

There was, however, an important rhetorical legacy of the New Deal era, one that would affect the character of American public debate for the next half century and at the same time explain much about the often convoluted and ideologically compromised policies that later emerged in areas like civil rights, affirmative action, labor and wage regulation, and the broad domain of social welfare. This conceptual invention of the New Deal Democrats was the idea of government as social problem solver. This idea was outlined in numerous statements throughout the New Deal era but perhaps stated most clearly in Roosevelt's 1936 message to Congress:

> You the Members of the legislative branch, and I, the Executive, contended for and established a new relationship between government and people.
>
> What were the terms of that new relationship? ... Government became the representative and the trustee of the public interest.[10]

Looking back several years later on the era he had dominated rhetorically, Roosevelt fashioned this governing idea into something of a political tradition of his own invention:

> Generally speaking, in a representative form of government there are usually two general schools of political belief – liberal and conservative.... The liberal party is a party which believes that, as new conditions and problems arise beyond the power of men and women to meet as individuals it becomes the duty of government itself to find new remedies with which to meet them....
>
> The conservative party in government honestly and conscientiously believes the contrary. It believes that there is no necessity for the government to step in, even when new conditions and new problems arise. It also believes that, in the long run, individual initiative and private philanthropy can take care of all situations....
>
> The clear and undisputed fact is that in these later years, at least since 1932, the Democratic Party has been the liberal party, and the Republican Party has been the conservative party. (Green 1987: 119)

Why Liberals Are the Perennial Poster People of Conservatism

Although the idea of government as problem solver has become the defining characteristic of the new (i.e., post–New Deal) liberalism in American politics, the rhetorical structure supporting it is not as easily separable from conservatism as Roosevelt suggested. Ever since this uneasy brand of liberalism was invented, conservatives have charged that its defining principle – government as problem solver – is inconsistent with the other two foundations of the American governing tradition. Put most simply, government intervention almost invariably undermines both individual self-reliance and business enterprise. For example, Herbert Hoover, long a rhetorical standard-bearer of the Republican Party, called for the abandonment of this disagreeable un-conservative notion so that the nation might return to the coherent and conservative foundations of "true liberalism." Russell Hanson summarized Hoover's argument as an archetype of modern conservative rhetoric: "True liberalism did not strive to spread bureaucracy, but set bounds on it.... Liberalism was a force proceeding from the deep realization that economic freedom could not be sacrificed if political freedom was to be preserved." Or as Hoover himself concluded:

It is a false liberalism that interprets itself into dictation by government. Every step in that direction crushes the very roots of liberalism. It is the road not to liberty but to less liberty. (Hanson 1985: 264)

The resulting historical pattern is that conservative rhetoric has maintained a structurally more powerful foundation consisting of a small number of logically consistent and generalizable principles. This enduring and elegant ideological structure has been used as the basis for perennial attacks on the waywardness and inconsistency of liberals who foolishly altered one of the founding principles of the American creed, without recognizing that the other two unchallenged principles of classical liberalism required the principle of small government in order to survive. Worse still, say the conservatives, the new liberals altered the principle of limited government without establishing new principles around it to explain what general social goals big government would serve, or what natural restraint would keep its bureaucracy and budgets in check.

Two notable patterns of public debate and persuasion flow from this structural imbalance in modern liberal and conservative rhetorics. First, there is what might be called the *self-limiting* tendency among liberals to balance promises and policies against assurances that individual initiative and economic free enterprise will not be compromised. Second, we note a pattern that might be termed "pragmatism meets the pork barrel," in which liberals represent their programs as solutions for problems experienced by various social groups, without much historical success (or effort) to link the growing list of groups and government programs together within a common ideological vision. Both patterns have had important consequences for the definition of political choices, the success and failure of policies, the balance of power between the parties, and the difficulty of generating new governing ideas in response to changing social and economic conditions. Data illustrating these rhetorical patterns are reviewed in the next two sections.

Self-Limiting Liberal Rhetoric

Much as Roosevelt promised social change that would not disrupt the core values of individualism, enterprise, and the ideal of a manageable government, so too have leading Democrats ever since imposed these value limits on their programs. Even as possible new ideological principles were introduced over the years, they were invariably limited by rhetorical linkage to the classical liberal tradition, assuring they would not develop structurally into full ideological visions. Thus, for example, Adlai Stevenson in 1952 promised "justice" and "human dignity" while celebrating the Democratic Party's traditional defense of free enterprise: "... the greatest danger to free enterprise in this country died with the great depression under Democratic blows."[11] John Kennedy introduced potentially radical concepts like "human rights" and "civil and economic rights" in 1960 and then tempered them by calling on the people to create a society in these terms, not to expect government to do it for them:

> Woodrow Wilson's New Freedom promised our nation a new political and economic framework. Franklin Roosevelt's New Deal promised security and succor to those in need. But the New Frontier of which I speak is not a set of promises – it is a set of challenges. It sums up not what I intend to offer the American people, but what I intend to ask of them. It appeals to their pride, not their pocketbook – it holds out the promise of more sacrifice instead of more security.[12]

When Lyndon Johnson called for "Equal justice under law for all Americans" and "war against poverty" he invited the nation to "extend the hand of compassion and extend the hand of affection and love," without fear of losing freedoms in the process:

> The man who is hungry, who cannot find work or educate his children, who is bowed by want – that man is not fully free. For more than 30 years, from Social Security to the war against poverty, we have diligently worked to enlarge the freedom of man, and as a result, Americans tonight are freer to live as they want to live, to pursue their ambitions, to meet their desires, and to raise their families than at any time in all of our glorious history.[13]

Even the campaign that may stand as the most radical in the last half century in terms of policy proposals, the 1972 candidacy of George McGovern, was careful to avoid pushing new ideological principles. McGovern adopted, instead, a rhetoric of jobs, tax fairness for working people, and an end to government corruption and giveaways to the rich, all limited ideologically by his call for America to come "home to the founding ideals that nourished us in the beginning."[14]

Meanwhile, win or lose, Republicans have attacked Democratic programs and appealed to voters with a rhetorical consistency that might have been penned by the same speechwriter: such is the advantage of having a core ideological structure that changed little due to the absence of an evolving counterideology from liberal opponents. In 1968 Richard Nixon condemned the Great Society of the Democrats with a simple review of conservative principles:

> We are a great nation. And we must never forget how we became great. America is a great nation today, not because of what government did for people, but because of what people did for themselves over 190 years in this country....
>
> Instead of Government jobs and Government housing and Government welfare, let Government use its tax and credit policies to enlist in this battle the greatest engine of progress ever developed in the history of man – American private enterprise.
>
> Let us enlist in this great cause the millions of Americans in volunteer organizations who will bring a dedication to this task what no amount of money can ever buy....
>
> Black Americans – no more than white Americans – do not want more Government programs which perpetuate dependency.[15]

In 1980 Ronald Reagan did nothing less than retell the American story itself, beginning in 1620 with the Mayflower Compact, and in the process turned the pantheon of leaders from Tom Paine to Abraham Lincoln to Franklin Roosevelt into exponents of the same American ideological tradition conserved only by Republicans in the modern era. Reagan drew his acceptance to a close by quoting none other than Roosevelt's own promise from 1932:

> For three long years I have been going up and down this country preaching that government – Federal, state and local – costs too much. I shall not stop that preaching. As an immediate program of action, we must abolish useless offices. We must eliminate unnecessary functions of government.
>
> We must consolidate subdivisions of government and, like the private citizen, give up luxuries which we can no longer afford.
>
> I propose to you my friends, and through you, that government of all kinds, big and little, be made solvent and that the example be set by the President of the United States and his Cabinet.[16]

And so, the whole spectrum of Republican response can be understood to spring from those three ideological principles outlined earlier, from Alf Landon's 1936 admonition that "American initiative is not a commodity to be delivered in pound packages through a government bureau,"[17] to George Bush's "thousand points of light" reference to voluntary solutions, delivered along with his 1988 promise to "see to it that government intrudes as little as possible in the lives of the people."[18] In light of this nearly unbroken tradition, one can only marvel at the breathless announcement by a Republican consultant about the 1992 Bush acceptance speech: "It is the speech we've been waiting for and the message we've been waiting for ... Government shouldn't be the master of individuals."[19] Nor should it have come as much surprise when Bush launched his 1992 ad campaign around the theme "America must change. But change must be guided by principle."[20]

What is more important, however, is that liberals have continued to limit their rhetoric in the modern era to avoid rejecting those same conservative principles. As Franklin Roosevelt was the first liberal in this tradition to promise to shrink government, so too Bill Clinton in 1992 carried on the self-limiting rhetoric of the Democrats in this speech from a western campaign trip: "I'm going to carry the West in this election partly to prove that not all Democrats are oriented to Washington, D.C., and the Federal government solving all problems."[21] Although Clinton, the New Democrat, won the election, his proposals on health care eventually belied his words, convincing many voters that the idea of activist government fits awkwardly at best with the ideas of self-help and free enterprise that have always claimed primacy in the American tradition. The dilemma was that for Clinton (and, for that matter, any Democrat since Roosevelt) to abandon the premise of activist government, he would revert to little more than Republicanism with a slightly more ragtag following.

CONSERVATISM AS THE AMERICAN RHETORICAL DEFAULT OPTION

The important result of this rhetorical pattern is the continuing, implicit reinforcement of a single, dominant ideology in American public life. The failure of the liberals to create an independent set of governing ideas has opened virtually all their political programs to compromise, while severely limiting the development of the broad social welfare and labor market policies found in most European polities. It is by now commonplace to hear liberal Democrats defend their programs on what turn out to be essentially conservative terms: for example, that welfare is really "workfare" and will not undermine self-reliance; that legislation against job discrimination will help minorities without infringing on the freedoms of white male workers or costing business in profit-reducing paperwork; or that health care reforms will not limit freedom of medical choice, restrict the free enterprise of doctors and health care companies, or create huge government bureaucracies to further complicate health care delivery.

The dynamics of many policy debates have thus been essentially defensive on the liberal side, inviting conservative opponents to cut policy proposals back on precisely the terms opened up by liberal rhetoric. Thus did Harry Truman suffer defeat of his twenty-one-point domestic program described by one historian as the most "boldly comprehensive domestic program" proposed by any modern president, including Roosevelt.[22] Adding injury to insult, conservative opponents replaced the Wagner Act with conservative Taft–Hartley labor legislation that put the labor movement on the permanent political defensive. And thus did Republican presidents from Richard Nixon through George Bush (and more recently, Congress under the rhetorical leadership of Newt Gingrich) restructure the federal–state power relationship, cutting back many of the social programs that had been passed since the New Deal.

Perhaps most important from a policy standpoint, the failure to develop a fully independent ideology on the left presents serious problems for both policy implementation and for legal interpretation when policies are challenged in the courts. The tortured history of Supreme Court rulings on civil rights statutes aimed at resolving problems of discrimination in the workplace offers a good illustration here. When there is essentially only one ideologically clear basis for political and legal reasoning in a society, it should come as no surprise that there is no clear precedent for having both equality and the protection of individual rights at the same time. Yet the traditional interdependence of liberal and conservative rhetoric leads both politicians and jurists alike to continue presuming – or at least saying – that these and other conflicting ideals can coexist. Rhetorically speaking, there has been no clear basis for separating them.

The Fatal Liberal Attraction: Pragmatism Meets the Pork Barrel

There have been, of course, plenty of liberal political victories throughout this period. Indeed, many have argued that the last half century has been dominated more by the New Deal and the Great Society and the coalitions that governed in their names than by the social moralism of the conservatives. Moreover, the electoral and legislative victories of the liberals were not just the results of dressing up candidates and policies in conservative rhetorical terms. Both the electoral success and the political limits experienced by modern liberals can be explained in large part by a second established rhetorical practice of the Democrats since Roosevelt: advertising the policy victories of their administrations and listing the specific social groups those policies benefit. Party rhetoricians then explain that service to so many groups makes the Democrats the party of the people, as opposed to the Republicans who serve the special interests:

The people know the Democratic Party is the people's party and the Republican Party is the party of the special interests and it always has been and always will be. (Harry Truman, 1948)[23]

The Democratic Party is the people's party, not the labor party, not the farmer's party, not the employer's party ... it is the party of no one because it is the party of everyone. (Adlai Stevenson, 1952)[24]

We offer ourselves on our records and by our platform as a party for all Americans, an all-American party for all Americans! (Lyndon Johnson, 1964)[25]

Over the years, this pattern of listing groups, problems, and solutions as the core of liberal Democratic rhetoric grew more pronounced. For example, a study conducted for this project by John Klockner of the party platforms since the mid-1800s shows that by three measures (the number of paragraphs, the number of lines, and the number of topic headings or titles) the level of topical detail in both party platforms remained both small and remarkably equal until after World War II. From 1948 on, however, the length of both parties' platforms grew as measured by the number of paragraphs and lines, reflecting increasingly heated contest for power at the national level and the devotion of increasing attention to world affairs and national security issues. However, the number of topic headings or titles for the Democrats grew much faster than that of the Republicans over the elections from

1948 to 1972, reflecting the Democratic rhetorical strategy of selling specific proposals to specific constituencies, along with the resulting greater degree of coalitional conflict within that party. These trends are illustrated in Figure 3-1.

This pattern of advertising group benefits has opened the Democrats to continual attacks from Republicans, who charge the liberals with having no principles for steering their domestic policy course. Particularly in the area of welfare policies, the Democrats have been attacked in every election since 1932 as having no ideological basis for their persistent benefits-mongering. Meanwhile, the core Republican philosophy of laissez-faire was seldom even addressed in the history of modern Democratic acceptance speeches.[26] In domestic affairs, Republicans have had the luxury of advertising what they have not done, or what they have prevented the Democrats from doing, as victories of higher principle. On the foreign policy front, Democratic candidates have played a continual rhetorical game of catch-up to prove themselves as tough and as experienced as Republicans.[27]

The tacit and often explicit embrace of conservative principles, while offering no fully independent ideological alternative of their own, left the Democrats open to charges that they virtually sold their policies in exchange for political support. This left the Democrats vulnerable to Ronald Reagan's devastating, if ironic, attack upon them in 1984 as the party of the "special interests," along with his grand category reversal that defined the Republicans as the party of "the people":

> The choices this year are not just between two different personalities, or between two political parties. They are between two different visions of the future, two fundamentally different ways of governing....
>
> Their government sees people only as members of groups. Ours serves all the people of America as individuals.[28]

From the New Deal to the "L" Word: The End of an Idea

With this, Reagan had finished the rhetorical task of cleansing the Democrats of their single, wayward governing principle: the ideologically homeless idea of governmental activism. In the process, he reconstructed Franklin Roosevelt as a true conservative. At the same time, he explained why he, himself began his political career as a Roosevelt Democrat and later abandoned the party because of its random drift without guiding principle. Reagan had, in

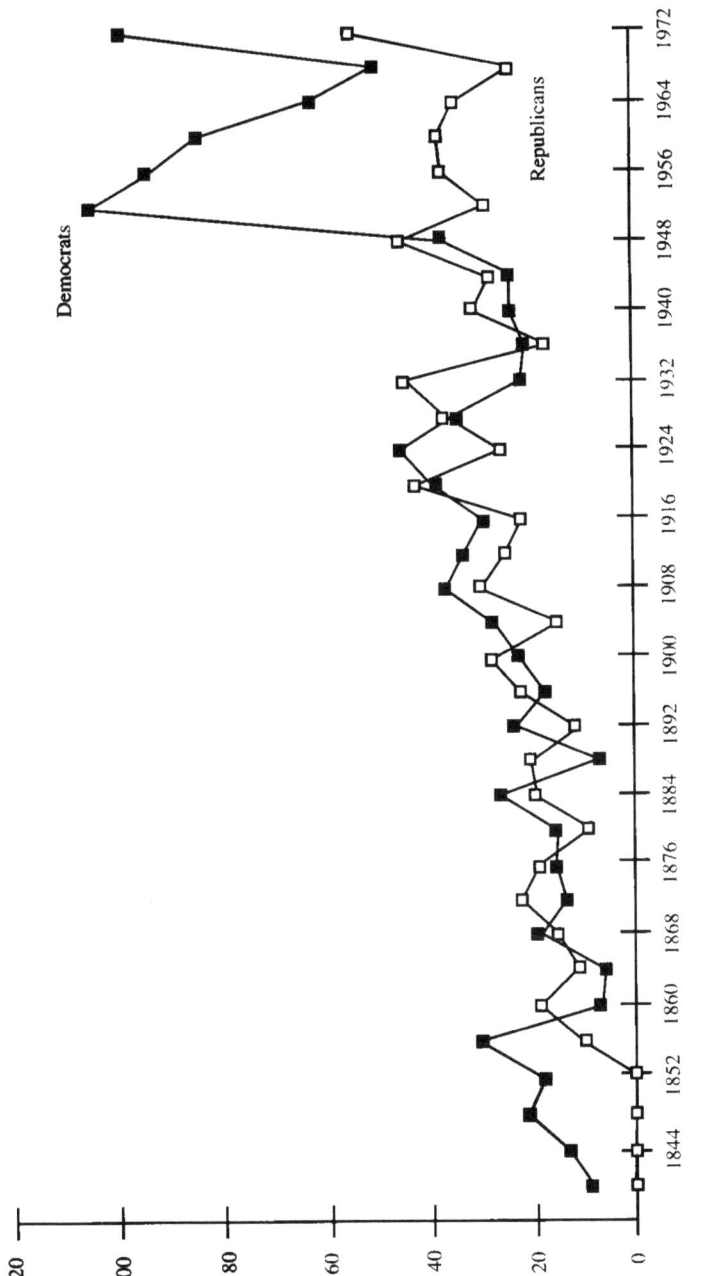

Figure 3-1· Number of Subject Headings (Titles) in Party Platforms, 1840–1972

effect, completed the rhetorical mission called for by other conservatives since Herbert Hoover, restoring the logic of the Holy Trinity of classical liberalism and sending modern-day liberals fleeing from their own self-defined label. Coming full circle from the New Deal, which introduced the new definition of liberal, Reagan was able to propose in 1984 the "New Beginning," which restored liberalism to its "true" conservative context back within the Holy Trinity. This placed the very concept of "liberalism" in jeopardy, giving it the infamous stigma of the "L-word" in the 1988 contest.

Neither the Democrats nor the liberals were physically banished from the kingdom of Washington by the so-called Reagan Revolution, but they began a somewhat desperate effort to reconstruct themselves rhetorically, if not ideologically, after the presidential defeats of 1980, 1984, and 1988. Much of this effort became focused on the use of marketing and polling strategies to find political ideas that sold well in the existing electoral marketplace. The first success story was Bill Clinton, the first New Democrat to win the national prize. Yet Clinton's promise of everything to everyone eventually sounded hollow to many voters who began to suspect a closet New Dealer in a New Democrat's clothing. Not surprisingly, even the Clinton success eventually proved futile – at least as measured by the repudiation of the 1994 election – since the marketplace itself had been structured by deeper political forces that continued to condition the rhetoric of the two parties. In other words, as long as the Democrats were defined by the same basic interest groups, financial arrangements, internal party politics, and media strategies that had governed their fate to date, their efforts to reinvent themselves rhetorically could not get them far beyond the same ideas they were trying so desperately to escape.

Looking at the market forces that shaped and limited the historic efforts of the Democrats to define themselves ideologically offers a different perspective on a number of questions: Why is liberal rhetoric self-limiting? Why does the contemporary Democratic Party seem unable to redefine its governing ideas beyond either pragmatic liberalism or self-limiting conservatism? Why does the political system seem to be stuck in these rhetorical patterns despite widespread citizen dissatisfaction?

The all too easy answer is that American political culture is enduringly liberal in the classical sense. This response is ultimately unacceptable because it is both circular and historically deterministic, offering no room for explaining change. If the culture has become stuck within a particular ideological frame, it is because the institutional arrangements for buying, selling, and maintaining relations of power in the political marketplace have continued to promote essentially conservative ideas over other possibilities. Cultures do not persist by the sheer force of their ideas alone, particularly at times like the present in the United States when large numbers of people are calling for new ideas, yet find little reason to hope that national elites will depart very far from the old ones. A market explanation suggests that the Democratic Party and, more generally, liberal political actors have had, and continue to have, both ideological and rhetorical choices. At key historical junctures, however, market conditions have led party leaders to make choices aimed at maximizing short-term electoral success, even at the possible sacrifice of long-term ideological development and governmental dominance. This communication spiral toward strategic short-term rhetoric has been intensified over the past decade with the decreasing rhetorical viability of the lone Democratic idea of activist government.

IDEAS, MARKET CHOICES, AND THE
DEMOCRATIC PARTY DILEMMA

For many political analysts, the American party system alone may be enough to explain the ideological patterns we have described. A two-party, winner-take-all election system promotes a drift to the ideological middle (Page 1978). This drift is compounded by the plight of the Democrats, who have historically needed their conservative southern flank to remain in control of Congress. Yet this simple explanation overlooks two factors. First, we are not talking about a two-party drift to the middle but a historical and structural tie of both parties to ideas of the right. Second, if other choices had been made by party leaders at key historical junctures, the result might have been the evolution of a fully opposing ideological alternative to conservatism, prompting a restructuring of the parties and of political power more generally. We can only imagine the political aftershocks of an ideological formation strong enough to drive conservatives out of the Democratic party while energizing masses of poor, low income, and minority voters who have historically participated at low rates and felt poorly represented by either party.

The tendency among analysts is to assume that a clear ideological break with conservative values is impossible because of the unquestioned dominance of classical liberalism in American politics. Our analysis questions the foundations of that dominance: We contend that there were market choices to be made at numerous historical junctures, and that the ones opted for by the Democrats were responsible for restricting ideological development and keeping an unwieldy and ultimately self-limiting domestic policy coalition together. The interplay of party systems, money in politics, media strategies, and interest processes all explain why an alternative to conservatism never fully developed into a systematic and mutually independent ideology with its own governing principles.

Party Finance as an Enduring Limit on New Democratic Ideas

The first great market choice occurred at the time of the second New Deal when the rhetoric from the left heated up, but the Democratic Party money brokers began working out important financial arrangements with business interests. At the time, it was clear that the old effort to put together a business–labor coalition under the NIRA failed not just because of friction between business and labor but because of friction within the business community itself. Key issues on wages and tariff policy were disputed on the one side by domestic manufacturers that saw tariffs as useful and low wages as essential, and on the other side by the growing ranks of international banks and businesses that opposed tariffs but did not actively oppose liberal wage policies because they were not representing labor-intensive industries. The Roosevelt Democrats broke this gridlock by easing domestic manufacturing interests out of the picture while inviting both labor and international business interests to play key roles in the party.

In Ferguson's (1989) analysis, aligning Democratic Party financial support with the internationalists stabilized party financing, and, because labor activism did not threaten international business interests at the time, permitted the party to adopt a more heated populist rhetoric that proved useful for keeping the Democrats in office with high levels of voter support. At the same time, however, the business coalition behind the rhetoric prevented the party from developing the kind of economic and social theories that would have become the basis for a counter ideology.

Ferguson concludes that the rhetoric advertising the Democrats as the party of the people and condemning the Republicans as the party of big business created enduring popular expectations that broader social reforms would go forward under the Democratic banner. Yet time and again, key reforms were either not proposed at all or, like the Truman domestic package or the Clinton health reform, were defeated by coalitions of Republicans and conservative Southern Democrats. It is hard to imagine a clear governing ideology emerging from an organization that continually had to negotiate its promises with three such disparate groups as its national electorate, its key conservative Southern voting bloc in Congress, and its big business backers at the same time. The failure to understand this self-limiting coalition held together by money has, in Ferguson's (1989: 24) words, left many ordinary Americans:

... alternately confused, perplexed, alarmed, or disgusted, as they tried to puzzle out why the party did so little to help unionize the South, protect the victims of McCarthyism, promote civil rights for blacks, women, or Hispanics, or, in the late 1970s, combat America's great "right turn" against the New Deal itself. To such people, it always remained a mystery why the Democrats so often betrayed the ideals of the New Deal. Little did they realize that, in fact, the party was only living up to them.

Not surprisingly, the party's self-limiting rhetoric became a source of continuing problems. Open to attack whenever they contradicted their stated sympathies for free enterprise and individualism, liberals became active, if rhetorically reluctant, participants in establishing limits on labor and social welfare policies. Whereas Sweden made peace between business and labor by adopting low taxes on corporate profits coupled with a "social Keynesianism" aimed at a full employment economy primed by social welfare spending, the United States developed a "commercial Keynesianism" aimed at curbing inflation and stimulating business growth (Weir & Skocpol 1985). The result was increasing friction in the Democratic Party between business and labor, and later on, between both groups and other constituencies such as women, minorities, and the poor. Thus, interest group politics cloud the rhetorical picture and push party communication into the perilous direction of short-term opinion strategies.

Divided Interest Groups and the Failure to Find a Common Rhetoric

The continuing rub was the Democratic rhetoric of government as social problem solver, which not surprisingly fueled popular expectations and stimulated persistent claims by new groups to have their problems solved. Thus, new groups sought entry into the Democratic coalition, and the party had little ideological reason either to exclude them or to integrate them within a common vision of society. The result was that almost any new social policy initiatives created problems: with financial backers who opposed the economic consequences of social Keynesianism; with conservative Southerners who threatened to bolt the voting coalition if liberal policies were extended; or with the new voter groups themselves, who often found the "party of the people" less open to them than its rhetoric implied.

Not surprisingly, these conflicts of interests only grew more intense over the course of the Democratic Party's long struggle to maintain a coherent political organization in the absence of ideology. The irony is that history continued to present the Democrats with rich opportunities for ideological self-definition, yet the internal pressures to maintain financial solvency and balance competing demands within the coalition only set the party's interest group time bomb to ticking faster. For example, an important opportunity for ideological self-definition was lost during the great labor strikes following World War II. This labor unrest, highlighted by the strike against General Motors, provided the ruling Democrats with the opportunity to continue their wartime industrial management policies and respond affirmatively to labor's call for a European-style corporatist state apparatus. Despite Truman administration prolabor rhetoric, government policy tacitly endorsed business claims that labor had turned socialistic and represented a threat to the public interest.

The Democrats entered this era politically strong, with the victory in the war and the economy out of depression, yet vacillation about how to respond, along with escalating labor unrest, gave both business and the Republicans a political boost. The opportunity to institutionalize a postwar Democratic-labor-industrial regime was thus lost when the Republicans scored major electoral victories in 1946 and passed the Taft–Hartley Act over Truman's veto in 1947. All of which sealed the fate of labor, along with the possibility for a viable political base to sustain any prolabor, or more generally, social-Keynesian governing ideology (Lichtenstein 1989). Rather than speaking with an ideological voice, labor was permanently reduced to being just another interest group in an already unstable Democratic coalition of interest groups.

The next great lost ideological opportunity came with the limits imposed on the War on Poverty, the cornerstone of the Johnson administration's Great Society effort to rekindle New Deal activism. Like the Democrats following World War II, the Johnson-led party was strong enough to propose an ideological shift in social and economic thinking: They had just scored (what seemed at the time) a fatal blow against the Goldwater Republicans in 1964, and the unfinished agenda of John Kennedy provided a powerful rhetorical means of advancing new social visions. Characteristically, however, no new social or economic theories were advanced. The Great Society programs in general and the War on Poverty in particular were, in Katznelson's (1989) view, adjustments at the margins of an existing political and economic order. Thus, although the rhetoric again appeared liberal or even radical to some, the political conflicts and ideological limits in the underlying Democratic coalition meant that the policies themselves would be compromised and their presentation to the public would be ideologically confounded. In Katznelson's (1989: 198–199) analysis, with the exception of Medicare, the Great Society program:

... did not promise any significant changes in the life conditions of the majority of Americans, or even the majority of supporters of the Democratic party. Substantively, it stopped well short of attempts to reorganize and modify the marketplace. It entirely left alone the organization of work, the patterns of investment, and the role of the business class....

The most compelling characteristic of the Great Society was that it was a program of mainstream economists and technicians who conceded from the start the framework of ideas and practices of the larger political economy. It sought to correct inequities and problems on the margin of a thriving system of production and consumption.

In the process, we might add, the Great Society also converted poor people, as was labor converted in a previous era, into another interest group with programs to maintain but no basis in ideological principle for defending those programs or for joining ranks with other groups to fight together politically when those programs were threatened. Thus, the interest group structure of the Democrats became unwieldy at best and a political liability at worst, always threatening to unleash antagonisms rather than develop principled agreements within the party organization. The sweeping civil rights legislation of the 1960s offers further illustration of this point.

On their own terms, the civil rights acts of 1964 and 1965 can hardly be faulted for promoting the ideal of equality under the law for all Americans. Yet the very boldness of that legislation illustrates the internal dilemma faced by a political organization not united by a strong ideological vision, much less joined by a sense of shared social interest. True to Lyndon Johnson's fears, the Southern Democrats bolted the party at the presidential level, reconstituting a winning Republican voting coalition at just the moment when it ap-

peared that the conservative party had exhausted its ideological capital. In
the process, minorities followed in the tradition of labor and poor people before them, joining the Democrats as separate interest constituencies that
would eventually become political liabilities under Ronald Reagan's efforts to
label the Democrats as the party of special interests.

Perhaps the greatest ongoing tactical error in the evolution of the Democratic Party has been this tendency to bring new constituencies into the party
as special interests with the promise to deliver benefits that are not broadly
shared by all members of the party. By contrast, the cornerstone of the European welfare states, exemplified most clearly in Sweden, is that all citizens
share broadly in the same benefits, providing for policy stability and a greater
sense of common interest, in some cases stretching across the ideological di-
vides that separate parties. In America, only Social Security and Medicare
have escaped the divisive stigma of "welfare" that haunts so many of the
Democratic social reforms that have become the subjects of political turf battles between groups and the objects of conservative rhetorical attacks as
being unprincipled giveaway programs.

Modern Party and Campaign Finance Reforms:
Idea Caps on Both Parties

Confident of capturing the formerly Democratic South at the presidential
level after 1968, Republican strategists saw the way to assemble a new coalition around their enduring ideological precepts. The potentially fatal blow
was delivered to the Democrats when the conservative party adopted free
trade policies. The always fragile Democratic interest coalition was strained
to the maximum by pressures to make further conservative concessions in
order to keep what business backing it could – pressures that mixed poorly
with the grass-roots coalition that took over the party and reformed its nom-
inating process between 1968 and 1972. From this point on, Democratic concessions to labor, minorities, or the poor came directly at the expense of the
party's financial support base.

Once again, however, the Democrats were offered a golden opportunity
for ideological redefinition in the form of the Watergate scandal that rocked
the Republicans in the mid-1970s. With Congress opened up by the election
of a class of reform-minded Democrats in 1974 and the arrival of a Democratic president on the scene in 1976, the party had still another chance to ar-

ticulate a set of governing principles and finally to unload the liability of self-limiting liberalism. Yet the reforms of Congress undermined the power of the party leadership, and the campaign finance reforms passed in the same era only invited more – and more fragmented – interest groups into the party's tattered coalition.

In narrow pragmatic terms of winning elections, those reforms clearly made sense. By the mid-1980s, the congressional Democrats were stronger both financially and electorally than were the Republicans. However, the political debts incurred by the party in exchange for its financial solvency further undermined the possibilities for any definition of governing principles to explain what the Democrats stood for or how they differed from the Republicans.

Ferguson and Rogers (1986) suggest that the Democrats have made a fateful right turn ideologically over the past twenty years, offering the voters less and less meaningful ideological differences from their conservative rivals. This analysis may attribute too much ideological coherence to the Democrats in this period, however. From our view, the party has always been tied ideologically to the right through failures to define standalone alternatives to classical liberalism, although party rhetoric made periodic overtures to a self-styled left whenever it was politically expedient or possible to do so. In the recent period, however, preoccupation with balancing an increasingly unwieldy financial coalition with its crazy quilt of policy demands left the party with relatively little that it could offer to the voters as a coherent domestic program.

In the absence of either a program or a governing vision to sell, the party turned to increasingly short-term efforts to offer key voter groups small tangible rewards for their support. In particular, this delivery of legislative services (from finding lost Social Security checks to adding amendments to include new group benefits in existing laws) worked well enough at the congressional level to keep a motley coalition in power until 1994. It is ironic that the coalition members recognized their respective self-interests clearly enough to produce the highest levels of party solidarity in legislative voting on selected issues since the early years of the century. However, as noted, the rhetorical transparency of the Democratic program was apparent at the national level where the party became vulnerable to Republican attacks as being the party of the special interests. And in a sense the Republicans may have been right. The Democrats had won the PAC game in Congress and had delivered an impressive array of legislative benefits to a broad spectrum of business, banking, agriculture, and widely scattered voter blocs.

Media-Driven Rhetoric as the Alternative to New Ideas

All this legislative largesse not only defied ideological explanation but proved nearly impossible to market nationally as a coherent political, much less intellectual, program. Not surprisingly, the Republican media strategy from the early 1980s on effectively turned the term *liberal* into a political epithet, the dreaded "L" word. For their part, the Democrats abandoned the effort to defend their own self-created liberal label, much less to try to fill it up with some structurally coherent idea content (Bennett 1996b). An irony of this effective labeling of Democrats as the nonconservative "other" in American politics was that the Republicans locked themselves into a peculiar symbiotic, if symbolic, relationship with their rivals for power. Given the interplay of the institutional, or market regulatory mechanisms discussed earlier, neither side has proved able or willing to think itself out of its symbolic trap. For all of its ideological coherence, the Republican rhetoric has not attracted much greater appeal than it had in the 1950s. To the contrary, the Reagan Revolution was produced by merely 28 percent of those eligible to vote in 1980. This stands as a revolution only when compared against the GOP 21 percent landslide of 1994. In this light, Republican rhetorical strength can be measured only by corresponding Democratic weakness.

Without major reforms of the party and representation system, the new ideas that enter this system are likely to have only limited popular appeal. For the Republicans, the main pressure for redefinition has continued to come from the moralistic right wing of the party, a direction that has proved its own self-limiting appeal in the voter marketplace, particularly among women. Thus, although traditional GOP conservatism would always be vulnerable in times of economic strain, as Republicans from Herbert Hoover to George Bush continued to discover, the party had little general incentive to alter its idea base as long as the Democrats continued to endorse much the same governing vision. As for the Democrats, as long as internal pressures for redefinition continued to come from neo-Centrists like David Gergen or "moderates" like the Democratic Leadership Council, party rhetoric would continue to spin a middle-class appeal with the self-limit of being a pale imitation of Republicanism.

In light of these structural limits imposed by the dominant institutional arrangements of electoral politics and policy processes, it is not surprising that by the late 1980s both parties had adopted unabashed communication strategies based on voter market research and media-driven rhetoric aimed at winning the next election rather than forging long-term governing coalitions. By this time, the Democrats had also abandoned all but the pretense of being the party of the people. Michael Dukakis's and Bill Clinton's unapologetic appeals to the "forgotten" middle class suggested once again that in place of articulating governing ideas, the party was struggling to capture short-term voting leverage. "The people" in the New Democratic politics were those in the economic and political middle for whom political independence had become something of a defense mechanism against empty promises and tired rhetoric. Yet many of those very same voters were clearly sympathetic to the rhetoric and the ideology of conservatism offered by the Republicans, particularly – as the landslide of 1994 revealed – when Democratic promises to be all things to all people collapsed under the weight of poor governing performance.

The system for mobilizing national political power had, in short, become stuck within the very institutional reforms and changes created largely by the parties themselves. In place of proposing broad new programs for social or economic renewal (and thereby disrupting the delicate party finance balance provided by interest groups), both parties seemed relatively content at the close of the century to promote increasingly similar brands of conservatism, differing mainly at the rhetorical margins on moral and religious issues. To fill the rhetorical void, Democrats and Republicans alike were forced to rely increasingly on negative media campaigns that bashed each other – and government too, for good measure – and to play the voter market for essentially the same swing voters. Meanwhile, large numbers of voters stayed away from the electoral process and from government itself, feeling that neither party spoke to them or for them. All of this suggests that in the absence of broadly appealing, or at least broadly competitive, governing ideas the idea of democracy itself might be the ultimate loser.

GOVERNING IDEAS AS IMAGES OF
THE GOOD SOCIETY

As long as the Democrats continued to pursue their channels of special interest funding and middle-class vote mongering, while advertising themselves ineffectually as the party of the people, the spiral of governmental drift could only deepen. If they are to break out of this spiral of interest group politics and ideological fragmentation, the Democrats would do well to learn from their own history and not run from the chance to redefine themselves rhetorically when their next political opportunity arrives. This rhetorical re-birth of the party does not mean that there is some obvious direction the new rhetoric must take. In fact, none of the foregoing analysis presumes what the most effective Democratic alternative to conservatism might have been. It is too easy to assume that the Democrats could or should have moved in more socialist directions at any of the historical opportunities they missed. It is worth recalling in this context how the Swedish labor party made its great-est political gains when it threw out its Marxist rhetoric in the 1930s and began a slow, trial-and-error process of filling in an ideological definition for the more broadly appealing idea of the *folkhem,* or the "people's home."

Perhaps Democratic intellectuals in the United States are trying too hard to imagine ideology in stereotypical, left–right terms when there are plenty of familiar, everyday, and appealing political ideas that might serve as points of departure for new ideological definition. For example, much as the Swedish Social Democrats stole the thunder from the right by appropriating the *folkhem,* the Democrats in the United States might put their own ideo-logical spin on the Republican idea of family values. One can imagine a fam-ily values program that is not just a collection of moral precepts but a set of defining social goals linking family life to society and economy and aimed at creating broader support for policies involving day care, education, parental leave, health insurance, and other matters that are currently adrift in a sea of special interest politics.

As great thinkers about ideology from Gramsci to Mannheim have recog-nized, ideologies cannot simply be invented whole and sold to people. They emerge from familiar concepts, evolve gradually, and take root in life experi-ence. If American society is currently suffering a crisis of divisiveness and fragmentation, perhaps the place to begin building governing ideas is with familiar concepts that speak to personal hopes for social harmony and stabil-ity. Just as the rhetoric of family and community has become a tool for revi-talizing enduring conservative beliefs, so too these or other everyday life cat-egories might be filled with visions of a society in which all citizens shared common benefits from government. Perhaps the home, school, workplace, and sports arena could surround the family and create a rhetoric of commu-nity as an organizing symbol for a new American governing vision. From there it would be a short rhetorical jump to a definition of industry that was community-centered and that offered business the motivation of tax or fed-eral contract benefits for employment and production programs tied into their surrounding communities.

The moral of this story is that ideas matter, perhaps not so much to win short-term electoral support but for the more important task of governing a nation and maintaining the health of a democracy. To break out of its current negative spiral, the political marketplace itself must be adjusted in terms of campaign finance arrangements, interest group affiliations with parties, and perhaps by using the media to hold dialogues with citizens rather than merely to sell candidates to voters on increasingly meaningless grounds. These market reforms must be guided by something beyond the short-term goal of just winning the next election. Winning elections is a necessary but not sufficient condition of governing, as the political drift of recent years illustrates all too clearly. Nor is simply passing well-intentioned legislation – when the governing party has the power to do so – enough to constitute good government, as the troubled history of Great Society programs, welfare policies, and civil rights laws indicates. Perhaps the highest goal of governing is to work out a vision of society that not only leads people to identify with a political party but that leads them to identify with one another as members of society as well.

4

The Rise and Fall of the
Folkhem in Swedish Politics

Per Albin [Hansson] was an extraordinarily adept manipulator of political symbols. He knew the dangers of attacking such sacred bourgeois values as peace, unity, the home, the flag, and the nation; instead he appropriated them for Social Democracy. The conception of the "people's home" not only took a central opposition symbol to convey the Social Democratic values of security, equality, and solidarity, but it equipped Swedish society with a great symbol of the democratic community in opposition to Nazism. Humankind does not live by policy statements and rational choice alone, a fact Per Albin appreciated and utilized by elaborating an extraordinarily evocative and effective political image.

– Tim Tilton

The dominant political idea of the twentieth century in Sweden has been the *folkhem,* the vision of government as a home that protects the nation's people much as a family's home protects each of its members. Like the New Deal, this vision introduced the idea of an active and protective government to a nation that had previously embraced a much diminished role for the state in the welfare of society. However, unlike the New Deal, the *folkhem* provided a rhetorical foundation for what became the most evolved welfare state among the world's democracies. The evolution of such a sweeping policy agenda did not happen without political struggles and social conflicts, yet these periods of turmoil are often overlooked by observers who see Swedish Social Democracy as more consensual than conflictual. We argue that it is precisely the overriding rhetorical direction provided by the *folkhem* idea that enabled leaders to turn potentially serious conflicts into remarkable levels of consensus for roughly half a century. In this sense, the alternative views of conflict and consensus in Swedish politics represent a false dichotomy that can be reconciled only by understanding the pragmatic uses of this grand political symbol. Similarly, the recent discontent of voters can be understood less as a return to some sort of class conflict or as an abandonment of consensual politics than as a growing failure of the *folkhem* vision to offer new solutions to today's changing political conditions.

CONFLICT, CONSENSUS, AND THE IMPORTANCE OF RHETORIC

Two competing interpretations dominate the literature on Sweden's political development during the twentieth century. The *conflict thesis* holds that Swedish politics must be viewed as a struggle between two adversarial sides, socialists and nonsocialists, labor and capital, and it tends to focus on some of the most contested issues in recent political history, such as the struggles over universal suffrage, parliamentary rule, state intervention in the economy, and so on (Hedborg & Meidner 1984; Korpi 1983; Lewin 1988). The *consensus thesis,* on the other hand, has a different focus and brings forth the country's homogeneous political culture and the fact that issues are usually settled through peaceful negotiation and compromise (Kelman 1981; Rustow 1955; Uddhammar 1993). Whereas the former thesis tends to emphasize class confrontation, depicting the formation of a unique Swedish model, the latter portrays the country as one example among many of a basically "consensual democracy" (cf. Elder, Thomas, & Arter 1988). The two schools converge, however, in their assessment of the dominant role played by the Swedish Social Democratic Labor Party (SAP)[1] in transforming the country from poverty to affluence. References to the "Social Democratic hegemony" and to the party as the "hegemonic force in postwar Swedish politics" abound (Ginsburg 1992: 31; Milner 1989: 9; cf. Pontusson 1987: 527).[2]

It is true, as we argue throughout this book, that the influence of Social Democracy's governing ideas – general welfare policy, solidarity, and equality – has been pervasive in Sweden. The best evidence of that is perhaps the extent to which these ideas have been accepted or emulated over the years by the party's political opponents (cf. Tilton 1991: 6–8). However, both schools tend to overstate the role and power of the Social Democrats in modern Swedish society, describing the country as being practically devoid of counterbalancing forces. The labor movement has certainly been the most important agent of change in Sweden, at least since the mid-1930s; in that sense the accounts we have alluded to are quite accurate.[3] What rarely gets mentioned is that over the years the SAP has occasionally had to deal with stiff opposition and has often been forced to make policy compromises in order to get its proposals through the *Riksdag*. In only two national elections – 1940 and 1968 – did the party achieve an outright majority of the seats in Parliament (Petersson 1993: 194; Tilton 1991: 2). Thus, the party leadership has felt it necessary to govern by building coalitions and by adapting its ideology to changing historical circumstances. It soon realized, for instance, that most of its goals could be attained by working within the confines of the market economy, thereby setting the stage for the general move toward the center that has been such a striking feature of post–World War II politics in Sweden.[4]

In this chapter we argue that the consensus theorists have it right, by and large, when they emphasize the importance of compromise over confrontation as the basic trait of Sweden's modern political development.[5] However, we try to demonstrate the validity of the consensus argument not by examining the debate on the grand political issues or by studying actual parliamentary decision making (Lewin 1988; Uddhammar 1993), but, rather, by focusing on *how political language has changed* in the period following World War II. To illustrate the changing role of language as well as the interplay between language and social institutions, we analyze the rise and decline of the key metaphor in twentieth-century Swedish politics: the idea of a *folkhem*, or "people's home." Our main argument is that the influence of Social Democracy in Sweden should be viewed not only as a result of specific policies or superior organization (Therborn 1992); it also has a lot to do with the appeal of its rhetoric.[6] One cannot fully appreciate the party's role and influence over the years without taking account of the changing ways in which its principal players have communicated with the outside world.[7]

Neither the conflict argument nor the consensus thesis pays much attention to language in analyzing the ebb and flow of Swedish politics. Furthermore, they do not tell us where the dominating political ideas came from or why they eventually dissipated and fell apart. Reading the leading theorists, one is at a loss to understand how a nonsocialist government could come into power in 1991 and how the first conservative prime minister since 1930 could proclaim, in his opening speech to the new Parliament, the "end of the collectivist era" in Sweden.[8] Here is where an analysis focusing on the changing role of language might prove to be useful. Such an analysis would find, among other things, that prior to the ascendancy of Social Democracy there did exist competing governing ideas, some of which the 1991 Conservative-led coalition continued to build on. Well before the *folkhem* and the "welfare state" became household words, Swedish politicians tried to govern with quite a different set of principles in mind. We begin this chapter by looking at what these principles were. We then move on to see how the principles were discredited and replaced as market forces introduced another set of ideas into the political playing field.

LIBERALISM IN SWEDEN:
THE DEMISE OF A GOVERNING IDEA

The most influential ideology in middle to late nineteenth-century Sweden was liberalism. At the heart of the liberal philosophy lay the principles of the French Revolution: liberty, equality, and fraternity. Proponents of the liberal view sought far-reaching changes in the existing political and economic order. They were unhappy with the monarchy and with the ruling elites, preferring a republic to the monarchy and demanding an end to privileges and regulations in the economy. The middle class should play the leading role in society, according to the liberals, not the old aristocratic and clerical groups. Although championing the individual's political and economic rights, however, the liberals did accept "natural" inequalities that were the result of education and private wealth. They called for a more "humane" society, one in which voluntary contributions from the better-off rather than government action would assist the less fortunate. In essence, nineteenth-century "bourgeois liberalism," as it has been called, believed in individualism, progress, humanism, and nationalism, the latter aspect being emphasized partly as a tactical move to ward off criticism from the main competing ideology of the time, conservatism (Nilsson 1975: 148–151).

Many of the ideas of this old liberalism survived in one form or another and guided the nonsocialist governments of the 1920s and early 1930s.[9] During that decade, the liberal or conservative cabinets, unstable as they were, actively sought to promote ideas of individualism, free enterprise, and private ownership of the means of production. The leading nonsocialist politicians of the day clung to an ideology of essential market harmony in economic life and individual responsibility in private life (Ekman 1928b; Lindman 1931). However, this ideology differed in one important respect from the American Holy Trinity, as discussed in Chapter 3: It did not as a matter of principle exclude government intervention in the economy. True, the nonsocialists clearly preferred a passive government to an active, or intrusive, one. The liberal ideas they espoused entailed a freedom *from* and not a freedom *to*. But they also left open the possibility that if the market system did not operate satisfactorily, government might have to step in and steer an ailing economy on course. The caveat was that government should not intervene in such a way as to impair the "mechanisms of wealth" (i.e., the basis of the market system itself) (Lewin 1970: 7–22). This more pragmatic view of the role of the state is an important difference between the ruling predepression ideologies in Sweden and the United States.

The Social Democrats, on the other hand, were early influenced by the Marxist version of socialism. The party had come into being in 1889. Seven years later the party leader, Hjalmar Branting, was elected to Parliament on a liberal ticket. By 1914, six national elections later, the SAP had become the largest party in the popularly elected Second Chamber, a position it has retained ever since. In 1917 the first Social Democratic ministers were appointed, with Branting serving for a while as minister of finance. Three years later the party formed a minority cabinet of its own, the first such government in the world (Hadenius, Molin, & Wieslander 1991: 348–353, 363–364). Around that time the country's well-known five-party system was already in place. The Social Democrats and the Communist Party constituted the left, whereas the Conservatives, Liberals, and Agrarians (later the Center Party) were considered to belong to the right. This party system was to stay in place, by and large, until the late 1980s, when various mechanisms in the political marketplace would contribute to an unraveling of the traditional parties' voter support.

The SAP's Marxist vestiges came out clearly in its 1920 party program. Many of the familiar ideas were there, such as socialism and socialization, class struggle, exploitation, the emphasis on the working class, and so on. The capitalist mode of production was sharply criticized, although it was not entirely clear what was going to replace it once the conditions seemed ripe for a development toward socialism (Tingsten 1973: 212–238, 702). Despite this common theoretical base, however, the SAP of the 1920s was a divided and relatively weak party, torn between radicals who wanted to devote all the attention to the working class and reformists who insisted that the party must also get support from the broader middle strata in society. These divisions produced an ambiguous and fuzzy rhetorical message that could not effectively compete with the still powerful liberal ideology (Schüllerqvist 1992: 61–74).

After the introduction of universal suffrage in 1919 (first enacted in 1921), many party activists had been confident that the party would soon reach majority status among the electorate. That did not happen. As it turned out, getting overwhelming support from the industrial workers was not enough to form a lasting government, and the debate over which strategy to choose – pitting the class strategy versus the *folk* (people's) party strategy – continued to rage within the movement during most of the 1920s (cf. Schüllerqvist 1992: 286). After the 1928 election, however, when the Social Democrats lost badly after running a campaign on a radical platform advocating, among other things, higher inheritance and property taxes for the rich, the reformist, or more "moderate," faction of the party took charge and changed the SAP outlook fundamentally in just a couple of years. The SAP that appealed to the voters in the 1932 election was in many ways a new and different party, much more homogeneous and centralized and with a unified rhetorical theme. The new leadership, headed by party leader Per Albin Hansson, was able to produce a much more coherent rhetoric that would not only become an alternative to the nonsocialist vision but that would eventually dominate Swedish politics and debate for many decades to come. How that rhetoric was shaped is the subject of our next section.

THE *FOLKHEM* IN SWEDEN:
THE RISE OF A GOVERNING IDEA

Most writers who have dealt with the history of the *folkhem* in Sweden start their analysis with Per Albin Hansson's famous 1928 *Riksdag* speech. But the idea of a common "people's home" is older than that and has a history that is much too interesting to ignore. It is without a doubt the great metaphor of twentieth-century Swedish politics, but it did not originate as a Social Democratic catchword. The first Swedish politician known to have used it was Alfred Petersson, a farmer and cabinet minister, who in 1909 upon leaving the conservatives for the liberal party, came up with the concept as a way of summarizing the aim of politics in a good society (Isaksson 1985: 248; 1990: 258–259).[10] At that time it was more of a vague sentiment than a well-developed ideology, and it had a decidedly conservative tinge.

A more ambitious explication of the concept was proposed by Rudolf Kjellén in a series of publications at the beginning of the century. Kjellén was a prominent political scientist and a conservative member of Parliament, and his writings had a strong nationalist orientation. Key concepts were the nation, the state, and the notion of the common good. His immediate concern was to heal the wounds caused by the breakup of the union with Norway in 1905, which had threatened to tear both societies apart. Kjellén issued a plea for national unity, something that could be attained, he thought, only by bringing the growing Social Democratic movement into the public dialogue. He viewed society as an organism in much the same way as earlier nineteenth-century European conservatives had done. The most important thing of all, according to Kjellén, was to keep society intact, avoid divisions, and inspire everyone to work together for the common good – for the Swedish *folkhem* (Elvander 1961: 257–325; Larsson 1994: 63–65).[11]

The purpose of the preceding paragraphs is to emphasize that the idea of a *folkhem* was not novel by the time it was picked up and transformed by the Social Democrats. It was already in the public domain, still rather obscure and ill-defined, but attractive enough to lure politicians from many different parties into using it. No one had as yet conquered the rhetorical arena and succeeded in identifying policies with the term. The person later alleged to have made that conquest was Per Albin Hansson, who was elected SAP leader in 1928. However, the words *conquer* and *conquest* imply that he grasped the term swiftly and deliberately, but that was hardly the case. Instead, it seems that Hansson approached the concept slowly over a number of years and only gradually came to understand the full rhetorical power it possessed.

Per Albin, as he was often called, started to allude to what would become the *folkhem* ideology in the late 1910s. He first used the word *home* in a 1918 speech in which he emphasized the connection between democracy and social reform (Lindgren 1950: 402–404; Lindström 1952: 57–58).[12] The very word *folkhem* was first used by him in 1925 and then again in a 1927 article in which he specifically appealed to women to join in building the "great people's home" (Hallberg & Jonsson 1993: 17–18, 26–29, 31–32; Hirdman 1989: 89–90). Prior to using that term, however, Hansson had spelled out the essential content of the idea in many articles and speeches in which he took issue with his opponents both inside and outside the party. The way he went about this is a textbook case of how to co-opt and disarm your opponent's best arguments in politics. Determined to outdo the conservatives on their own home turf, he first adopted their nationalist rhetoric and claimed that the Social Democrats were the most patriotic party in the country. And the most patriotic task, he suggested, was to arrange society in such a way as to make everybody feel that they had a comfortable "home" devoid of outsiders or favorites (Hallberg & Jonsson 1993: 19–23).

Next he started to include the very term *folkhem* in his narrative. This is how he outlined the contours of a good society in his 1928 speech:

The basis of the home is togetherness and common feeling. The good home does not consider anyone as privileged or unappreciated; it knows no special favourites and no stepchildren. There no one looks down upon anyone else, there no one tries to gain advantage at another's expense, and the stronger do not suppress and plunder the weaker. In the good home equality, consideration, co-operation, and helpfulness prevail. Applied to the great people's and citizens' home this would mean the breaking down of all the social and economic barriers that now divide citizens into the privileged and the unfortunate, into rulers and subjects, into rich and poor, the glutted and the destitute, the plunderers and the plundered.

The genius of this formulation lay in the fact that it appealed to sentiments and experiences shared by people across the entire political spectrum. Hansson did not start out with a theoretical exposition on Marxism, an ideology the party was about to leave anyway. His focus was much more familiar. Everyone knew what a home was and how a good family should ideally function, and what Hansson did was to play to those feelings and try to demonstrate that they in fact entailed essential Social Democratic values. In the speech he also made sure that everyone understood that his vision was one thing and reality quite another. He used the *folkhem* image as a critical device, contrasting it with the shortcomings of the existing social order:

Swedish society is still not the good citizens' home. Here to be sure there prevails formal equality, equality of political rights, but socially the class society still endures and economically the dictatorship of the few prevails. At times the inequalities are flagrant; while some live in palaces, many consider themselves lucky if they can continue to live in their garden huts even during the cold winter; while some live in opulence, many go from door to door in order to beg for bread.... If Swedish society is going to be a good citizens' home, class differences must be eliminated, social services developed, economic equalization achieved, workers provided a role in economic management, democracy carried through and applied both socially and economically.

As these quotations show, the *folkhem* speech had two main themes, one emphasizing cooperation and consensual democracy, the other egalitarianism and social reforms. The speech has often been associated with the consensual aspect only, possibly because the image of a home first and foremost appeals to traditional conservative ideals. But it was just as much a plea for extending democracy to the social and economic sphere, as in this telling passage:

I have already indicated that in a political democracy economic oligarchy must also fall. In the long run a politically mature people will not accept a situation where the most important means for the production of life's necessities, for the maintenance and improvement of their welfare, lie in the hands of a few capitalists who, in order to satisfy their desire for profits, set aside consideration for production and other general interests.

Having made rhetorical appeals to both his own hard core as well as to his adversaries, Per Albin finally urged the nonsocialists to adhere to their long-standing liberal values of liberty, equality, and fraternity and to join in a common effort "to make our country into the good citizen-home with a secured existence for those who work and live there, with everyone co-operating for the common good."[13]

THE FOUNDATIONS OF A CONSENSUAL RHETORIC

It is important to note what the *folkhem* speech was and was not, what it included and what it left out. It certainly meant the rejection of class struggle and thus of the Marxist idea of a total transformation of capitalist society. Creating a better society through peaceful and incremental change – that was the new Social Democratic creed (Tingsten 1973: 702–705). However, Hansson's speech also meant a severe criticism of the liberal conviction that competition between individuals was a sound principle upon which to build a good society (cf. Fredriksson, Strand, & Södersten 1970: 35–36). Furthermore, Per Albin's oratory showed how adept he had become in using and appropriating popular symbols such as the nation, patriotism, democracy, the family, unity, and others, not all of which were readily associated with the labor movement. His conception of the "people's home," writes Tim Tilton (1991: 142),

not only took a central opposition symbol to convey the Social Democratic values of security, equality, and solidarity, but it equipped Swedish society with a great symbol of the democratic community in opposition to Nazism. Humankind does not live by policy statements and rational choice alone, a fact Per Albin appreciated and utilized by elaborating an extraordinarily evocative and effective political image.

Perhaps most important of all during Per Albin's reign as party leader (1928–1946), the language of the Social Democrats established itself as the political rhetoric of the land, contributing to the SAP's long reign of power and replacing the former liberal rhetoric in the process. During the early 1930s, there was an opening for defining the great rhetorical principles in Sweden, and the Social Democrats seized that opportunity with skill and determination. As noted in Chapter 3, similar opportunities were passed over in the United States. It is clear that although Per Albin's rhetorical conquest included a hefty element of co-optation, one must also remember that he gave the *folkhem* phrase a new meaning by connecting it to ordinary people's lot and desires and the need for government to do something for society's downtrodden. Here is where his vision differed most sharply from that of his conservative predecessors. Rudolf Kjellén viewed the state as a neutral agent, hovering above the petty interests in society and with no obligation to assist any particular class; indeed, the very notion of a "class" was absent from his vocabulary. Per Albin's and his comrades' point was exactly the opposite, namely, that the state should take an active role and intervene *on behalf of* certain classes in society, especially the needy, the poor, and the unfortunate.[14]

The *folkhem* speech indicated that Per Albin was reasonably sure about what the idea contained but not so sure what he should call it. He used *folkhem* and *medborgarhem* ("citizens' home") interchangeably, apparently not sensing which one was the most effective from a rhetorical point of view. When reading the speech today, one comes away with no feeling that the speaker realizes that he has just uttered the word that is going to define Sweden's political debate for half a century to come. He seems to have more or less stumbled upon it in much the same way Franklin Roosevelt rather haphazardly chose the New Deal as the great symbol for his administration.[15] Maybe that is one reason the newspapers gave Hansson's speech such a lukewarm reception, some of them neglecting to mention the key phrase altogether.[16] That Per Albin had hit upon something was evident, however, from the way in which some of his friends and foes reacted to his use of the term. The two leading nonsocialists of the day, liberal Prime Minister C. G. Ekman and the conservative party chairman Arvid Lindman, were among the active participants in the lively ensuing debate, in which everyone tried to frame the issue to suit his own rhetorical purposes (Ekman 1928a; Johannesson, Josephson, & Åsard 1992: 227; Lindman 1928: 18–19).

The Struggle Over the Folkhem *Label*

Communication scholars tend to emphasize certain facts about the nature of political language. One such fact is that language is an important activity in the world of politics, possibly the "most fundamental of political weapons" and even the "central factor in social relations and action" (Edelman 1974: 131; Green 1987: ix). The making of words is an act, something that people do. Furthermore, by its very nature political language is ambiguous and flexible, devoid of precise or fixed definitions. Therefore, the words themselves may evoke several different, sometimes mutually contradictory, meanings and responses. Because of this fact, moreover, political actors are eager to fashion specific meanings for specific labels, particularly the most potent and popular. Thus, the vocabulary of politics is contested terrain, leading actors to engage in arguments, debates, and continuous rhetorical struggles (Rodgers 1987; Spencer 1970: 605). Potentially, a lot is at stake. By shaping the publicly accepted meaning of a key term, a politician or a party can dominate political discourse and define the contours of a whole era.

So it was during the New Deal, when Franklin Roosevelt managed to expropriate the definition of the "liberal" label in U.S. politics (cf. Ch. 3 this volume; Green 1987: Ch. 5). And so it was in Sweden during the depression years, when the Social Democrats took over and framed the meaning of the *folkhem* metaphor. As indicated earlier, there was a stiff competition for the term after Per Albin Hansson had decided to use and co-opt it in the late 1920s and early 1930s. Hansson soon found himself engaged in a rhetorical battle on two fronts: with leading nonsocialists who were unwilling to give up an evocative label they thought belonged to them, and with some of his fellow Social Democrats, who believed that the term was seriously flawed in important respects. His conservative and liberal critics had argued that the Social Democrats could not lay claim to the *folkhem* mantle since their policies were exclusionary and aimed at enhancing the well-being of certain peoples and classes. Only a nonsocialist policy could benefit all classes in society and guarantee security and prosperity in the good people's home (Ekman 1928b; Lindman 1935, 1931, 1928). In fact, the conservatives were so keen on being attached to the label that they published a special periodical in the crucial 1932 election campaign. Fittingly, the paper was entitled *Folkhemmet*, and in the first issue the authors quoted Kjellén's definition of the word, adding that it expressed the most profound aspirations of Swedish conservatism (Hallberg & Jonsson 1993: 45).

A potentially more threatening criticism came from two prominent politicians within Hansson's own party. Ernst Wigforss, perhaps the SAP's leading theoretician and a long-time minister of finance, could not bring himself even to utter the word *folkhem*. His prime objection seems to have been the paternalist connotations that the term might carry; to Wigforss it evoked images of the patriarchal father and thus of the hierarchical structure of the traditional family (Tilton 1991: 128). Journalist and would-be minister of education Arthur Engberg, who for a while competed with Hansson for the chairmanship of the party, echoed similar fears and was appalled to find this old conservative phrase used by his party leader. Although acknowledging that it possessed some rhetorical force, Engberg viewed the concept as contradicting the Marxist principles upon which the party had been founded. The most serious flaw, according to Engberg, was that it obscured reality by overlooking the existence of class struggle in a capitalistic society (Hallberg & Jonsson 1993: 78–79, 121–125; Trägårdh 1990: 42).[17]

Per Albin's response to his critics, particularly those within his own party, was to argue that there was no basic contradiction between the notion of class struggle and the *folkhem* policy the party now pursued. After the introduction of general suffrage, the SAP had emerged as the country's leading political party, representing not only the working class but also, contrary to what the nonsocialists liked to believe, other social groups as well. Because of this development, the party had in effect become a genuine *folk* party that could acquire a popular mandate for its programs only by appealing to all groups in society. This more consensual approach demanded that the old Marxist verbiage be put aside, Hansson implied, and a more inclusive rhetoric adopted. But he insisted that such a change in no way was a repudiation of the labor movement's traditional principles (Hallberg & Jonsson 1993: 38–45, 79–87, 112–121; Hansson 1935: 9, 18, 33–47; Hansson 1943: 13–15).

By the mid-1930s the rhetorical battle over the *folkhem* label was effectively over. Even though the 1932 conservative periodical showed that the opponents had not surrendered without a fight, it was obvious that Per Albin and his allies had emerged victorious; it was their interpretation of the word that became the accepted one in the public's mind. The terminological dispute gradually subsided as the nonsocialists accepted the SAP's crisis measures and later the idea of a welfare state. The internal criticism also faded after the party had made its fundamental policy choice in the early 1930s and pursued a pragmatic strategy of planning (and not socialization) in the economic area. Thereafter, critics both to the left and to the right can be said to have "internalized" the *folkhem* concept and most of the policies covered by that concept.

We can summarize our findings so far by stating that the *folkhem* concept, as it took shape and developed over the coming years, entailed three basic ideological components. The first was an *active government* ready to intervene in the economy and other social affairs, its prime obligation being to ensure a full employment policy in the country. The second was a *general welfare policy* aimed at mandatory national legislation ensuring to the people – all people, rich and poor, employer and employees – basic needs such as health care, vacations, job rights, and the like. The third component could simply be called *corporatism*, meaning a tripartite system wherein government, business, and labor have their separate roles but join in promoting such important common goals as economic growth and social stability. This is the basis of the *folkhem* ideology.

Implementing the Folkhem Ideology

After their victory in the 1932 elections, the Social Democrats managed to get support from the Agrarian Party in exchange for agricultural subsidies and protectionist measures. The so-called Crisis Agreement of 1933, which was later followed by a labor–farmer governing coalition in 1936 to 1939, is one of the formative events in Sweden's modern political history and marks the beginning of the *folkhem* era. Three important results of the agreement are worth mentioning. The first is that it laid the foundation for the SAP's long tenure in office, which was to last without interruption until 1976 (disregarding a few summer months in 1936). Second, the crisis measures established a more interventionist government and a Keynesian economic policy around which there was considerable disagreement at the time. Particularly through the introduction of a new and active labor market policy, government assumed a much more powerful and active role in the economy than it had previously, something the nonsocialists initially opposed but later came to accept (cf. Hermansson 1993: 337–358; Lewin 1975: 285–296). Third, the agreement meant that the government sought to deal with the economic crisis by cooperating with and offering support to the interest organizations involved. Both the labor and farmer organizations benefited from this state–trade union cooperation. Already during the 1930s union membership had increased to a level higher than in other comparable countries. The cooperative pattern thus established constituted an important step toward a corporatist state interest structure in Sweden (Rothstein 1992: 126–135).[18]

Another pivotal event occurred in 1938 when a basic agreement was reached between the leading employer and trade union organizations that institutionalized a collective bargaining system on the labor market. The aim of the agreement was to reduce the number of industrial disputes, which had been abnormally high during the 1920s and early 1930s, and to avoid government interference in the bargaining process (Hadenius 1976: 45–68). The Social Democrats simultaneously made it clear to private industry that they need not fear the specter of socialism or socialization. As long as the economy worked efficiently and the industrialists accepted the policies of social reform, the SAP did not mind leaving the production process in private hands. This was the basis for the historical compromise between labor and capital in Sweden, and it provided the framework for what was soon to be called the Swedish model (Davidson 1989: 135–139; Korpi 1983: 46–50).[19]

With these landmark agreements firmly in place, the Social Democrats could direct their efforts toward the establishment of a welfare state. There was a lot to be done, because the long era of conservative and liberal rule had produced little in the area of social reforms. In 1913 a universal old-age pension scheme had been introduced, but benefits were meager and unemployment insurance and health care coverage marginal to nonexistent (Esping-Andersen, 1985: 152–153). During the latter part of the 1930s, a rudimentary social safety net was introduced through a number of laws, most of which bore the signature of Gustav Möller, the Minister of Social Affairs. However, it was not until the 1950s and 1960s that many of the social reforms often associated with the modern Swedish welfare state were actually adopted. These reforms covered a wide area from education, health insurance, and housing to employment policies, pensions, taxation, and family and child care provisions. In the main the laws were built on the principles of universality and equality. Whereas earlier reforms had been means-tested and directed toward the poor, the post–World War II social legislation was based on universal and equal benefits to all citizens regardless of income (Davidson 1989: 102, 138, 145; Heckscher 1984: 38–40, 53–88).

RHETORIC AND POLICY SUCCESS

By being in the forefront of social legislation, the SAP managed to reap substantial political dividends at the polls. The crown jewel in the party's reform catalog was the supplementary pension plan of 1959, the effects of which made it possible for the SAP to widen its electoral appeal and make substantial inroads into new white collar groups (Svensson 1994: 151–184, 274–281). The politics of social reform proved to be so popular that the opposition parties, after some initial hesitation, offered little if any opposition. Indeed, studies show that during the bulk of the post–World War II period the non-socialists not only accepted the idea of a welfare state but also tried to outdo the government by proposing higher spending on certain social programs such as child care allowances, foreign aid, and other issues. Examples of a principled opposition against the Social Democratic reforms have been few and far between (Uddhammar 1993: 475–485). In other words, during the golden years of the *folkhem* period – roughly from 1950 to 1970 – the opposition parties were unable and unwilling to effectively challenge the rhetorical hegemony of the Social Democrats. When they occasionally did so, as when the conservatives in the 1950s launched the idea of a "property-owning democracy" (*egendomsägande demokrati*) as their new rhetorical concept, it was explicitly built on the achievements of the welfare state and intended merely as a more market-oriented version of the "people's home" (Ljunggren 1992: 130–160). Thus, it was basically flawed and ineffective as a rhetorical counterview. If anything, it reinforced the perception that the nonsocialists were living in the shadow of the ruling party's rhetorical dominance.

It is hard to overstate the extent to which the *folkhem* metaphor has been ingrained in twentieth-century Swedish political thinking. It tapped into some of the most basic values of the country's political culture. It was rooted in the old Swedish factory community, or *bruk*, in which a benign patriarch provided his workers with most of what they needed in terms of housing, health care, and so on (Isacson 1991: 16–19; Larsson 1994: 103–105; Österberg 1993: 141–145). Apart from its egalitarian connotations, the concept also entailed some more novel elements such as democracy, modernity, and citizenship, the combination of which helps to explain its enduring effect. In this regard it represented a clear break with the liberal rhetoric of the past. The Social Democrats of the 1930s were intent on creating a welfare system based on a new relationship between the state and the individual – one in which the idea of "collective progress" was instrumental and the "old rhetoric about the glorious past had to be replaced with visions of a common future" (Löfgren 1993: 181–183).

Despite its pervasive impact, however, the term has been relatively sparsely used in the nation's political dialogue. Reading the relevant texts today, one is struck by how seldom the key phrase itself crops up in political exchanges and debates. This comes out after a study of the important parliamentary debates and other pertinent material since the late 1920s.[20] For instance, Per Albin himself made use of the label at only two SAP congresses (in 1928 and 1944) during his whole period as party leader.[21] The SAP leadership, furthermore, has been fond of using the concept *retroactively* as a rhetorical device for describing the party's past achievements. Thus, it has been much more frequently used in ceremonial circumstances than as a formative concept pointing to the future (cf. Stråth 1992: 205–206). When Hansson's successor Tage Erlander (1946–1969) was asked to summarize the party's history during the 1956 election campaign, for example, he did so by titling the article "From Class Struggle to the *Folkhem*" (Erlander 1956b). The term was given no precise definition; except for the title it was not even mentioned in the text, a good illustration of how the term has worked and been used over the years.

The *folkhem* term thus reached its potency not by being constantly bandied about in campaign oratory or in parliamentary debates but, rather, by serving as a rhetorical *topos* from which parties and politicians could get inspiration when engaging in arguments about the public issues of the day. The reason for this is fairly simple and straightforward. The vocabulary of politics consists of at least two principally different categories of terms: those that are broad and general and designed to be used mainly as guiding metaphors (such as democracy, freedom, equality, and the various ideological "isms" [conservatism, socialism, liberalism, etc.]) and those that are more precise and have some intrinsic practical value and are intended to function in the day-to-day exchange of political debate. The *folkhem* clearly belongs to the former category, whereas terms such as *public sector, wage earner,* and *full employment,* to name but a few, belong to the second. Precisely because they are more general and thus often more abstract, however, guiding metaphors may lose their strength over time, and then the need arises for a new and more appealing label. We now briefly examine the emergence of two such labels in the Swedish case, both of which are variations on the fundamental *folkhem* model.

New Label, Same Ideas I: The "Strong Society"

During the 1950s, Sweden became one of the most affluent countries in Europe. Economic growth was phenomenal, and living standards continually improved. Paradoxically, the prosperous times presented the Social Democrats with an intricate ideological problem. After having been in power for a quarter of a century, the SAP was gradually losing ground to the nonsocialist opposition parties, which now sensed that things were going their way. Higher living standards for working people would inevitably result in *embourgeoisement*, they thought, and a drop in the left-wing parties' voter support. Internally the SAP faced growing criticism for merely administering the welfare state and for having forgotten about its original socialist vision. Critics argued that the party was paying too high a price for its consensual policies.

The ideological problem was general and faced many socialist and social democratic parties throughout Europe in an age of unprecedented economic growth: What was the task of a reformist movement in an affluent society after the basic structures of the welfare state had been put in place? The Swedish conservatives and liberals kept no one in the dark about their preferences. They argued that increasing affluence rendered further public initiatives superfluous; the role of the government was to do less, not more, and to leave increasingly satisfied citizens to provide for their own social needs (Ruin 1986: 235; Tilton 1991: 174–175). It was as a way to turn this idea into an appealing catchword that the conservatives, inspired by Christian Democratic thinking in Germany, launched the phrase a "property-owning democracy."

Prime Minister Erlander responded by turning the nonsocialist argument upside down. People living in a more prosperous society would demand more, not less, of basic social services such as quality education, better schools, housing, roads, and the like. And such services, he maintained, could be provided for only by government, by public money and public solutions. Society had become increasingly specialized and complex, and this development demanded more cooperation and solidarity. Individuals could not by themselves solve the problems of the service state. Erlander spelled out his ideas in a famous 1956 *Riksdag* speech, in which he warned against what he called the "discontent of rising expectations." Such discontent was rooted not in material poverty but in as yet unfulfilled expectations. Erlander was convinced that popular dissatisfaction and demands could be potentially powerful forces in transforming society. In his speech he underlined how important it was for society to try to live up to the demands of the people:

> If one has a secure position it is natural that one will want to give one's children a decent education; it is natural that one will want to acquire better housing; one may even want to acquire a car.... But this focus on the longer term is not just for the individual; it requires society to focus on the longer-term as well: cars require roads, the demand for a good education for children requires investments in research and schools, and the demand for housing requires investments in the housing sector, to consider only a few examples. (For the entire speech, see Johannesson et al. 1992: 269–277; Tilton 1991: 176.)

The rhetorical choice facing Erlander was how to transform this idea into a persuasive and appealing language. The metaphor he eventually chose was the "strong society" (*det starka samhället*). In a series of speeches and publications in the 1950s and 1960s, he spelled out all the good things that society could and should get involved in (Erlander 1954, 1956a, 1962). Interestingly enough, when lauding the virtues of collective action he did not differentiate between "state" and "society," but he did make it clear that a "strong society" demanded and presupposed a "strong government." By obfuscating the linguistic differences – something the opposition parties also routinely did, nicely illustrating the rhetorical dominance of the SAP – he was not only able to make a case for the expansion of the public sector; moreover, as one analyst has noted, the concept of the strong society is "a mystical merging and identification of state and society" (Tilton 1991: 177). By deliberately fusing the two concepts in his speeches and publications, Erlander opted for a particular persuasive effect: Those opposing the public sector would not merely be against increased government activity per se, but they would be questioning "the choices of society itself" (Tilton 1991: 177).

Tage Erlander's choice of terminology should not be interpreted as a repudiation of the *folkhem* ideology. On the contrary, it represented an attempt to continue propagating basically the same ideas albeit with a novel rhetorical twist to suit the new era.[22] The idea of a strong and active *government*, at both the local and the federal levels, which was essentially what Erlander was talking about, was at the very heart of the *folkhem* notion. Like that ideology, Erlander's formulation also entailed a firm belief in economic growth and a fascination with the wonders of modern science and technology.[23] Most important, it espoused the idea that individual freedom and security could best be enhanced through the activities of a democratic state. Erlander, just like Per Albin Hansson, viewed government not as a coercive agent but, rather, as a rational and enlightened instrument that could and should be used in the best interest of the people (Erlander 1976: 104–109). Neither of them acknowledged the possibility that social services could be financed at least in part through user fees, or that they could be supplemented with voluntary arrangements (Lewin 1988: 213–218; Ruin 1986: 233–240).

This is where the *folkhem* concept differs most sharply from the American ideology. In most non-Scandinavian countries, the welfare state was constructed on the basis of a mixture of insurance solutions and charity provisions. The system was primarily aimed at assisting the poor and encouraging individual responsibility. The Swedish and Scandinavian models, in contrast, were based on the principles of solidarity and shared responsibility, going back to a long tradition of state centralism and government intervention. It is a tradition that blends a powerful state with a parliamentary party system and with interest organizations as integral parts of the policy decision-making process. Voluntary associations and private solutions have played a supplementary role at best. This is very different from the American system with its more chaotic and competitive interest groups, weak parties (weakened further by election finance arrangements and the federal power structure), and a strong civil society tradition (Trägårdh 1992: 14; von Beyme 1992: 189–190). As noted in Chapter 3, not even the height of the New Deal produced official U.S. government policy claiming that the individual could reach self-fulfillment and achieve a guaranteed standard of living through the benevolence of an active state.

New Label, Same Ideas II: "Increased Equality"

Economic conditions in Sweden continued to improve during most of the 1960s.[24] In the midst of record economic growth and unprecedented prosperity, however, dissenting voices began to be heard. Rapid economic development did not seem to have produced a more equal distribution of wealth and income. Beginning in the mid-1960s and continuing well into the next decade, a series of mostly left-wing publications appeared that were critical of capitalist society and of the governing party for merely alleviating and not eradicating existing social ills. The notion of an "unfinished welfare state" started to get some attention, particularly after a number of studies had documented the continued presence of islands of poverty and a high concentration of private economic power. Equally important to the critics of the New Left was to highlight the plight of the Third World and the responsibility of Western nations, Sweden included, to come to the aid of poverty-stricken countries around the globe.

The radicalization of the 1960s and 1970s presented the SAP with a different challenge. What rhetorical strategy should be used to accommodate the calls for industrial democracy at the workplace – a favorite motif among some progressive union groups – and a more equitable distribution of wealth and salaries? Just as the *folkhem* concept seemed to have had its day, the "strong society" label no longer could capture the problems and desires of the new era. The solution was to repackage the party's rhetorical message without transforming its fundamental policies. Starting in 1967, a number of party and union officials began to put the issue of *equality* at the forefront of debate and propaganda. A joint party and union group was put together under the leadership of Alva Myrdal, its task being to present a report on the multifaceted equality issue to the 1969 SAP congress (Heckscher 1984: 227–232).

The Myrdal report received favorable reviews by the Social Democratic press, one leading paper calling it "the best and most radical political declaration to have been published by the Party in years." (All sources here are from Åsard 1979: 111–129.) At the opening of the 1969 SAP congress, his last as party leader, Tage Erlander stated that the primary objective for the next decade was to see to it that the ideas of equality put their mark on Swedish society. "To young and old alike, this constitutes the obvious and consistent continuation of our policies." The new motto, plastered around the large conference walls, was "increased equality" (*ökad jämlikhet*). A couple of days later the newly elected party leader Olof Palme followed suit, concluding the proceedings by declaring that the problems of equality would dominate public debate during the 1970s throughout the European continent.

The group behind the Myrdal report made a concerted effort to develop a workable definition of equality. To these writers the old liberal values of equal opportunity and equality before the law were important and necessary, but they were not sufficient. A Social Democratic conceptualization of the term *equality* must also include a demand for "economic democracy," meaning a right for everyone to get a fair share of what is produced in society. This view implied that equality of results was just as necessary an ingredient as the liberal preference for equal opportunity. For this to be realized, Alva Myrdal added, nothing less than a "transformation of society as a whole" was called for.

This may sound more radical than was actually intended. The intention was not to work out some revolutionary strategy, taking the party to new and previously uncharted territories. Rather, it was an attempt to coin a catchy rhetorical phrase that could appeal to critics both inside and outside the SAP, particularly to the young generation drawn into politics by the social movements of the 1960s and the horrors of the Vietnam War. In part, it was also an attempt to placate the dissenting voices of the day. As such, it was fairly successful, albeit for a brief period. It gave the SAP an ideological image commensurate with the past and set the agenda for public debate on a number of different issues. In addition, the label appealed to broad segments of the political opposition; for a while both the Liberal Party and the Center Party competed with the Social Democrats in viewing politics from the perspective of equality (Svensson 1994: 285). Again we see a familiar rhetorical pattern at work, with members of the governing party launching a slogan and much of the nonsocialist opposition following suit trying to imitate what they thought might be a successful rhetorical strategy.

Every slogan is in some sense a product of its time, and that was especially apparent in the case of "increased equality." It resonated against the backdrop of a wave of socialist and Marxist ideas that were affecting societies the world over. However, the label was not met with universal approval in Sweden. Forces on the right feared that the more radical wing of the SAP had gained the upper hand and now determined the party's course. Critics on the left viewed the equality rhetoric with suspicion and as yet another attempt to smooth over the existing injustices caused by monopoly capitalism. Still others ridiculed the slogan on linguistic grounds, viewing equality as an absolute concept and not as something that could somehow be increased or decreased. The phrase as such had a remarkably short staying power. Whereas the *folkhem* concept was potent for twenty-five to thirty years and the "strong society" for another five to ten years, "increased equality" reverberated through the public dialogue for a mere three to five years. It was at the center of the SAP's election rhetoric in the 1970 campaign, but only three years later it had in effect been dropped and replaced by other, more anonymous slogans.

The brevity of the equality interlude indicated that the whole idea of a *folkhem* was beginning to wear thin. Times were quickly changing, and the

economy's downward turn in the early 1970s exacerbated the problems further. For the first time in decades, the SAP seemed to be running out of governing ideas. Gunnar Sträng, a veteran minister of finance, unwittingly captured the state of the party when he said, to the chagrin of young activists,
that the government had already accomplished the "fundamental reforms"
and that little remained to be done in terms of improving Swedish society
(Elmbrant 1993: 34). This development illustrates above all, we believe, the
workings of intervening mechanisms in the marketplace, ultimately resulting
in an exhaustion and devaluation of the political language.

The question is: How can this rhetorical turnaround be explained?

EXPLAINING THE DECLINE OF THE
FOLKHEM IDEA

Something quite dramatic happened in Sweden during the period from 1970
to 1991. The once renowned *folkhem* was gradually discredited and soon was
oddly out of fashion, though more so in some quarters than in others. Social
Democratic attempts at reviving the reliable rhetoric of the past – appeals to
statist solutions, equality, justice, and old-fashioned solidarity – were to no
avail.[25] The SAP's election defeat in 1976 was the first inkling of what was to
come. Fifteen years later, on election night 1991, Conservative Party leader
Carl Bildt basked in triumph after the Social Democrats had suffered a hu-
miliating defeat. To Bildt the election signified the death of the Swedish
model.[26] The international press quickly followed suit with an avalanche of
articles detailing the retreat of the Swedish welfare state (Burke 1994: 53–57;
Elmbrant 1993: 287–288).

About a year before the 1991 election campaign, the official investigation
on power and democracy in Sweden had issued its final report. The authors,
a team of prestigious social scientists, similarly talked about the "end of an
epoch," something they attributed to, among other things, increased polar-
ization and a weakening of the country's consensus culture (Petersson et al.
1990: 389–409). The question addressed in this section is: What accounts for
the gradual decline of the *folkhem* as a governing idea in Swedish national
politics? We offer an explanation by applying the framework of our regulatory model, focusing initially on changes in the *election and party systems* and
later on a discussion of the other pertinent market mechanisms involved.

A good way to begin is to return to our opening remark in this chapter about the pervasive impact of Swedish Social Democracy and its governing ideas. A few facts and figures illustrate the strong position of power the party has enjoyed over the years. At the time of the 1991 election, the SAP had led the Swedish government for fifty-six of the seventy years that had passed since the introduction of general suffrage, representing 80 percent of the time since the breakthrough of democracy in Sweden. For forty years in succession (1936–1976) Sweden had a Social Democratic prime minister. For thirty-eight years, or 57 percent of the democratic time span, the Social Democrats governed alone. In parliamentary elections from 1921 to 1985, the SAP garnered an average of 44.8 percent of the votes. From 1944 to 1991 the figure is 45.1 percent. These are results with few if any international parallels, and they stand out as all the more remarkable if we bear in mind that they were achieved in a multiparty system with proportional elections (Hadenius et al. 1991: 350–351; Therborn 1992: 1–3).

Since the constitutional changes of the early 1970s, however, there has been a noticeable slide in the Party's election fortunes, as evidenced by the Social Democratic losses of 1976 and 1991. The average SAP result in national elections from 1970 to 1991 fell to an average of 43.25 percent, with the dismal 37.7 percent in the 1991 election easily being the worst since 1928. The descent is also evident in changing voter attitudes. For example, the proportion of Social Democratic sympathizers who identified strongly with the party fell to 41 percent in 1988 from 50 percent in 1976 (Bergström 1991: 13). There are several reasons for the SAP's electoral decline, which is historically evident even if one considers the party's remarkable 1994 comeback. With the introduction of the unicameral system in 1970 and a number of constitutional reforms in 1974 and 1975, Swedish electoral politics became much more volatile and unpredictable. The old bicameral *Riksdag*, where the upper house was elected indirectly and for a longer period than the popularly elected lower chamber, had ensured the biggest party (i.e., the Social Democrats) a certain overrepresentation in terms of seats.[27] The revised election system, which first came into effect in 1970, was strictly proportional and gave no seats to parties that did not receive at least 4 percent of the national vote. The significance of these constitutional changes was that weaker and more unstable minority governments were elected and for shorter terms (three years as opposed to four previously). Since 1970 only one Swedish government has been in power for a full two terms (six years); most governments have resigned long before that because of internal divisions or policy problems. In every election since 1968, the ruling parties in Sweden have lost votes in the *Riksdag* (Åsard 1991: 3; Bergström 1991: 23–24; Petersson 1993: 194–195; Ruin 1982: 34–37).

Contributing to the increasing volatility was a worsening economic situation and the rise of new issues and parties. The oil shocks of the early 1970s compounded the problems of stagflation (i.e., the simultaneous occurrence of high levels of inflation and unemployment) and made crystal clear how dependent Sweden had become on trends in the global economic marketplace. In addition, issues dealing with nuclear power and the environment came on the agenda in a major way, blurring the old left–right dimension and giving rise to a new political party in the process. The Environmentalist Party, or the Greens, was formed in 1981, and seven years later it became the first new party since 1918 to enter the Swedish *Riksdag* (Vedung 1988). The Environmentalists survived only one parliamentary term, but in the 1991 election two other small parties entered the *Riksdag*: the Christian Democratic Party, which had been around since the 1960s, and the populist New Democracy Party, which was constituted barely six months before the election. From having been the epitome of what Lipset and Rokkan refer to as a frozen party system (1967: 50–56), Sweden during the 1980s became, in the words of one observer, "a more ordinary West European country" (Bergström 1991: 29). As already indicated in the opening chapter (and as is more fully analyzed in Chapter 6), this development happened simultaneously with a growing voter mistrust of parties and professional politicians. All these trends – in particular the long-term electoral decline of the Social Democrats and increasing voter and party volatility – are indications of a less stable marketplace, making the production of lasting rhetorical visions increasingly difficult.

We now turn to the second mechanism in our explanatory model, namely, changes in the *interest group system*. Scholars regularly emphasize the important role played by the interest organizations for the establishment of the Swedish model. A close relationship between the state and the big interest groups is often analyzed under the rubric of "corporatism." Although the scholarly debate about the precise meaning of this concept has been almost endless, there is virtually no disagreement that by 1970 Sweden – together with countries such as Norway and Austria – had become one of the most corporatist countries in the world. What made this system successful for so long, according to some theorists, was the integration of large, encompassing interest organizations with the state and the intent of these organizations – shared by employer and employee unions alike – to put the interests of society above the interests of a particular group (Lewin 1992: 82–92; Micheletti 1991: 144; Olson 1982: 89–92).

A key element in the Swedish model of corporatism has been to further social harmony and to provide a mechanism for solving conflicts. Michele Micheletti (1991: 148) describes the general outline of this system as follows:

Dialogue between opposing political actors became a Swedish institutional tradition. Established interest organisations still are members or experts of state commissions, which have prepared public policy, and lay boards, which govern many public agencies. Also, they are asked to write replies to public policy proposals. The general Swedish practice has been for the state to legitimise antagonistic interests by incorporating them into government. The key prerequisite for this favourable treatment has been the ability of the interest organisations to argue rationally, present expert opinions and evaluate different policy proposals in a publicly responsible way.

Beginning in the early 1970s, however, this institutionalized system began to crumble as the economy worsened, stagflation took hold, and wildcat strikes spread on the labor market.[28] In late 1969, a big unofficial strike started among the miners at the state-owned iron mines in Lapland, initiating a labor dispute that seriously shook the leaders of the SAP and the union movement. The miners' conflict was followed by a series of wildcat strikes, particularly in 1969 to 1971 and 1974 to 1975, which changed the image of Sweden as a land of labor peace and stability. The conflicts indicated a dissatisfaction among the rank and file with wages and job conditions but also, and more important, with the inability of the union leadership to tackle the problems or even to communicate about the changing times.

In Sweden as elsewhere, the wildcat phenomenon spurred interest in issues related to worker participation and ownership of capital. A widespread political consensus emerged that something had to be done to increase employee influence in companies and to counteract the concentration of capital in the private sector of the economy. During the first part of the 1970s, a series of labor laws were passed virtually without opposition, including those relating to employee representation on company boards, work environment, and worker protection. The reforms were followed in 1975 to 1976 by a push toward economic democracy in the form of so-called wage earners' funds. This broader issue, which was initiated by the Confederation of Trade Unions (Landsorganisationen, LO), the SAP's large blue-collar union affiliate, was much more controversial and soon became the focus of sharp disagreement between the parties and the dominant interest groups.[29]

The proposal for wage earner funds was eventually implemented in a watered-down version in 1983 after a long and bruising fight (Åsard 1985). The controversy over the fund issue was the most visible sign yet that the consensus supporting the Swedish model was on the verge of cracking. The Confederation of Swedish Employers (Svenska Arbetsgivareföreningen, SAF) and other business associations campaigned vigorously against the idea, which they saw as yet another way of increasing the already great power of the trade unions. Furthermore, the employers grew increasingly unhappy with the labor laws and viewed them as a break with the consensual spirit of the past. The SAF's campaign against the corporatist model had begun already in the early 1970s, when the organization embarked on an ideological offensive aimed at better defending and articulating the interests of private business. Feeling outmaneuvered and at a disadvantage in the big marketplace of ideas, the organization began to take more adamant positions on political issues, such as the need for free market solutions, less government intervention in the labor market, and Swedish membership in the European Union (EU). At the same time, it also gave more resources to lobbying (Boréus 1994: 111–134).

Using more sophisticated public relations techniques and an elaborate network of propaganda units, the SAF continued its campaign throughout the 1980s and early 1990s. The final step in this dissociation from the Swedish model came when the SAF simply withdrew its representatives from the lay boards governing most public agencies. The important interest groups are usually represented on these boards, and the idea is that they balance one another (e.g., if the LO has a member, the SAF usually has one too). The employers' withdrawal decision was a demonstration of their alternative strategy to channel resources into public opinion-making activities with decidedly political goals. Other trends toward decorporatization included a decentralization of the system of collective bargaining, which was also actively supported by the SAF. Hence, the employers opted out of a corporatist structure they initially had favored but ultimately had come to view as serving the interests of a Social Democratic state (Elvander 1988; Lewin 1992: 98–101; Micheletti 1991: 154–155).

Thus, both major interest groups in Sweden can be said to have contributed to the unraveling of the corporate model – the LO by going on the offensive and demanding legislation on labor laws and wage earner funds, and the SAF by becoming an ideological sounding board for business concerns and by withdrawing from the corporate structures altogether. The result was a disintegration of a system that for the better part of thirty years had worked rather well. "The general conclusion," writes one scholar, "is that compromise and consensus in political decision-making is emphasised less today than in the past, and Sweden is gradually becoming decorporatised" (Micheletti 1991: 154).

The whole process of decorporatization has opened up the Swedish marketplace of ideas and made it more competitive but also less stable and increasingly difficult to control.[30] Another forum for dialogue and corporatist exchange, the *public commission (remiss) system*, has similarly lost some of its former potency and status. Not only has the number of commissions and their allotted resources decreased in recent years. The commissions, which used to consist of many members who worked in seclusion for a number of years, have also become much smaller and produce briefer recommendations in shorter periods. In addition, they are more tightly controlled by the government and tend to come up with proposals aimed at cutting public spending, not, as used to be the case, increasing it (Johansson 1992; Söderlind & Petersson 1988: 45–50).[31]

Most interesting of all is the diminishing clout that interest groups are able to exercise within the present commission system. Studies show that the number of interest group representatives on public commissions has gone down significantly since the early 1950s. In the 1945 to 1954 period, over a third (34 percent) of all commission members came from various interest organizations. That figure fell to 22 percent from 1968 to 1972 and to just 7 percent from 1985 to 1989. We are witnessing a return to the pattern of the 1930s, when civil servants and parliamentarians dominated the public commissions at the expense of other concerned groups (Lewin 1992: 102–103; Meijer 1969: 109–110). This does not necessarily mean that interest groups in contemporary Sweden play a less significant role or that corporate arrangements are not still alive and well, particularly on the local level.[32] But it does mean that interest groups generally have less direct access to lawmakers and actual policy-making and thus are forced to make their opinions known in other ways – for instance, by relying on advertising and public relations campaigns. To stay competitive in today's marketplace, interest organizations, just as other important actors, have to turn to that great regulator of the flow of ideas in modern societies: the mass media.

So, what has been the role of the *mass media* in all this? Mainly one of reinforcing the tendencies toward increased political and ideological fragmentation. At the turn of the century, most Swedish newspapers were attached to a specific party, arguing for their partisan views both on the editorial pages as well as in regular news reporting. The editors were often members of elected bodies, either locally or nationally. During World War II, for example, 10 percent of the members of the *Riksdag* came from the ranks of newspaper editors. Newspapers were of particular importance for the early labor movement, and many of the leading politicians worked as journalists and editors (Hadenius 1990a: 320–328; 1990b: 35–36).

For a long time, then, Sweden had a partisan press and a weak tradition of investigative reporting. With the advent of radio and television, however, the media in general have adopted an increasingly independent political role. Particularly in the press, there has been a trend toward more independent news reporting and less consideration paid to party lines. Another noticeable change – visible since the mid-1960s – is the emergence of more active and more independent journalists, something that in turn has changed the relationship between the media and the politicians. Elected officials and other people in authority, who in the past were often given a free ride, are nowadays subjected to much closer scrutiny and criticism. With a more fragmented party system, leading politicians, especially party leaders, have also become more dependent on the mass media and more inclined to adapt their messages to the "politics as drama" formula so prevalent in today's media market (Bergström 1991: 22–23; Westerståhl & Johansson 1985: 124–148), all of which has had a profound effect on the parties' rhetorical choices and strategies.

The exhaustion of the *folkhem* metaphor most illustrates the breakdown of the SAP's rhetorical hegemony in Swedish politics. With the onslaught of new issues and movements, a fragmentation of the party system and the media markets, growing voter mistrust and dissatisfaction, more visible and vocal interest groups, and a weakening of the public commission system and thus of the consensus culture, the once stable Swedish marketplace of ideas has become much more open and volatile. Today it is characterized by a cacophony of voices and a lack of a leading or dominant governing vision. No party, movement, or politician has come up with anything resembling a new governing idea for the twenty-first century that is nearly as salient as the *folkhem*. It is symptomatic of this rhetorical void that the 1991 bourgeois coalition phrased its motto negatively – lauding the "end of the collectivist era" – whereas the Social Democrats emerged victorious in the 1994 election on a vague "Sweden can do better" platform.

PART III

RHETORIC AND GOVERNMENT: UNDERSTANDING PUBLIC POLICY AND ELECTIONS

5

Idea Markets and the Policy Process: Tax Reform in Sweden and the United States

> Taxation is a critical arena in the politics of who gets what in society and who pays for it in all polities.
>
> – Sven Steinmo

Tax reform is a good opening case for exploring the interactions among institutions, communication, and policy processes because it discourages ideological claims that competitive markets necessarily produce felicitous results. The U.S. case was notable for the open competition among parties, interests, and the president for definition of a policy situation that was covered extensively (and in some economic detail) by the news media. Yet when the reform had been signed into law, few of the players, whether elites or publics, ended up happy with the outcome. Although some experts pronounced the results impressive, both as a feat of economic redistribution and as an accomplishment of bipartisan politics, few of the leaders responsible concluded that their political capital had been well spent. Perhaps more disturbing, the majority of the public regarded the tax law as an example of the interest group struggles and party politics that had corrupted Washington. The source of the unhappiness, we think, was a generalized inability of any faction to control the rhetorical definition of the policymaking situation, resulting in diminished control over the course of the policy process and its outcome, and decidedly little control over how the process and the outcomes were communicated to the public. Such a competitive idea market may have discouraged political domination by particular factions but without the fruits of Madisonian consensus in the bargain.

This American experience with tax reform illustrates the capacity of poorly integrated or coordinated political institutions to reduce a good idea to hollow rhetoric in the minds of many citizens. Perhaps the greatest irony of this process is that government actually implemented the sort of public preferences observed by Page and Shapiro (1992) in their studies of opinion and policy, yet neither the proceedings nor the results were communicated in ways that led citizens to confer legitimacy on either their government or their representatives. The comparison case of Sweden suggests that different institutional arrangements, particularly involving parties and interest representation, permit different strategies for managing public debates with implications for both the coherence of resulting policies and levels of public support.

THE U.S. TAX REFORM ACT OF 1986

As one might expect from something as close to the political soul as taxes, enduring cultural themes set the tone for public debate from beginning to end. The key question raised by media, party leaders, and citizens' groups throughout the process was whether the new tax plan would be "fair" to average Americans.[1] Yet the grand symbols of fairness and equity that attracted public support in the beginning became hollow by the end of the process – even though the government actually delivered a reform that received praise from many of the experts.

To some extent, the transformation of a potentially successful policy into another example of bad government surely had its roots in the media framing that provided the dramatic tension throughout the unfolding political story: the fear that "special interests" would undermine the new tax law as they had succeeded in capturing the old one. Yet this juxtaposition of fairness with interest group politics was not just a media invention. Politicians had cued this media framing for years by accusing their policy opponents of being captured by special interests. Indeed, as noted in Chapter 3, Ronald Reagan had recently pinned the "party of the special interests" label on the Democrats. Perhaps the resolution of the media drama as the triumph of special interests over public fairness was warranted simply by the intense and highly visible entry of interest groups and their campaign contributions into the policy process (Birnbaum & Murray 1987).

Yet the puzzle still remains as to why this particular episode of interest group politics gave the resulting policy such a bad name. After all, the competition among interests in the battle over tax policy did not deter the government from enacting new law – an interesting contrast to the policy failure following the more effective intervention of interests in health care reform a few years later. The failure to enact health care reform in 1994 was notable for the much more highly coordinated communication campaign by medical interests – a campaign joined by many congressional opponents of reform who were aligned financially with those interests. The various political alignments of parties, interests, and campaign finance thus resulted in quite opposing representations of policy struggles that could easily have been communicated – and decided – differently under different market conditions (e.g., tax reform heralded as a triumph of good government over special interests and the health care failure condemned more widely as the product of interest group corruption).

It is all the more interesting that such different communication outcomes cannot be dismissed as elite manipulation of issues that had little personal relevance to people. Few issues are more personal than health and taxes. Nor are broad categories such as "fairness" and "interests" lacking in cultural or historical examples that might limit their acceptable uses and check their rhetorical abuses. In the matter of taxes, for example, the symbolic categories of "fairness" versus "special interests" go to the core of American culture, from the Revolutionary slogan "no taxation without representation" to the design of a constitution aimed at preventing a government takeover by factions and special interests. Moreover, in the case of tax reform, these symbolic categories cannot be attributed originally to political speech writers or public relations experts but to political unrest at the grass roots toward the end of the 1970s. Polls conducted by a government commission in the early 1970s found that the public rated the income tax the "fairest" of all taxes. By 1980, however, polls showed that it was considered to be the least fair of all taxes.[2] The end of the 1970s saw a groundswell of taxpayers revolts around the country aimed at reducing property and sales taxes at state and local levels, and sending signals to Washington that taxpayers were fed up with government waste and inside deals between public officials and special interests.[3] What is all the more remarkable in this context is that the ultimate passage of a major tax reform was met by such high levels of popular rejection.

Party Politics and the Motives for Reform

Enter Ronald Reagan. Swept into office in 1980 on the promise of cutting big government and restoring traditional American values, Reagan saw in taxes an obvious issue to keep his middle class-populist following in line and away from the Democrats. However, a number of short-term political calculations initially led Reagan away from tax reform and toward a series of short-term tax cuts between 1981 and 1983.[4]

At the time, Bill Bradley was a newcomer to the Senate Finance Committee. Bradley also "saw the populist attraction of tax reform" and sought "a politically palatable alternative to the Republican tax cuts" passed in those early years of the Reagan administration (Birnbaum & Murray 1987: 29, 27). Bradley proposed a broad reform that was to be revenue neutral, that would simplify the rate structure by spreading more taxpayers across fewer brackets, and that could be sold by Democrats at election time by using traditional Republican rhetoric of business growth and free markets (Birnbaum & Murray 1987: 28–29). Bradley enlisted Richard Gephardt to co-sponsor the legislation in the House. However, the Bradley–Gephardt Fair Tax Act was stalled by interest group lobbying efforts and strategic campaign contributions to key members of congressional tax and revenue committees. Thus, parties, interest groups, and political finance arrangements played out early on in ways that encouraged the news media to begin telling a story of wheeling and dealing that blocked reform in Congress. The early failure of the Bradley–Gephardt bill led insiders to regard tax reform as a nonstarter, and the media quickly lost interest in the story.

In fact, another economic story began to receive big play in the press. The first-term Reagan tax cuts left the Treasury with huge revenue shortfalls and the government with a skyrocketing budget deficit. Although these might have been turned into golden political issues for the Democrats in 1984, they were handled in somewhat suicidal fashion by presidential candidate Walter Mondale, who issued a politically fatal call for a new tax increase.

Worried that the Democrats would take a rhetorically more creative approach to tax reform in an effort to win control of the Senate in 1986, and perhaps more worried at how to stop the flow of red ink at the Treasury, Treasury Secretary James Baker saw tax reform as a chance to kill two birds with one stone. Despite some early resistance from Reagan, Baker finally convinced his boss that tax reform was necessary and that Reagan's rhetorical talents could steal the issue from the Democrats and put more voters in the Republican column in the fall of 1986.

Baker apparently failed to understand, however, that the politics behind the rhetoric about taxes had changed, owing in large part to Reagan's earlier involvement in the tax cuts. To begin with, polls showed that public perceptions of tax unfairness had diminished significantly (though not altogether) since 1980 – partly as a result of tangible benefits people received from several years of Reagan cuts.[5] Complicating the communication context further, increasing numbers of people saw the budget deficit as being partly the result of revenue giveaways to big business from the earlier cuts, and they regarded the deficit as a far more important national priority than tax reform.[6] Related to this latter factor was a growing perception that the earlier cuts, although generally fair to the middle classes, had been far too "fair" to big business and the rich.[7] Given this complex public opinion, the political fate and rhetorical management of the original plan were important, because Treasury I (as the original Baker–Treasury plan was dubbed) met with approval by a two-to-one margin in the polls.[8] A much revised Treasury II, however, was soon to appear amidst media reports that both the Treasury and the White House had been besieged by thousands of special interest demands and complaints from wealthy and influential Republicans.[9] With the media setting this dramatic tension between fairness and special interests, it is not surprising that when a substantially revised Treasury II made its appearance following the interest group blitz, the public regarded the plan as unfairly advantageous to corporations and the rich by a two-to-one margin.[10]

This protracted public communication process reflects a remarkable degree of responsiveness between public opinion and the changing content of rather complex policy proposals. A brief overview reveals that policy content moved through at least five stages, beginning in late 1984 with (1) the original Baker–Treasury Department proposal, Treasury I; (2) which was revised into Treasury II, the plan championed by Ronald Reagan; (3) which was then revised substantially in the House of Representatives' bill; (4) which in turn gave way to numerous modifications in the Senate; (5) all of which changed again in the House–Senate compromise bill signed into law by Reagan in September 1986. In this process, the upper individual brackets, or rates, were reduced and some $120 billion in individual income tax revenues were replaced (in an Internal Revenue Service five-year projection) by a like amount of additional increases in corporate income taxes. As the policy process moved toward this result, some provisions of early proposals remained fairly constant, whereas others changed dramatically. For example, early proposals to eliminate taxes for individuals below the poverty level held firm, as did (with only slight modifications) the elimination of deductions for state sales taxes. However, Treasury proposals to end deductions for state and local property and income taxes were killed when the plan went through the

House of Representatives. To cite another change, the Reagan-backed idea of a 35 percent top bracket was cut to 28 percent in the Senate.

The important point is that successive transformations of policy followed the interplay and frequent clash of various regulatory mechanisms in the rhetorical marketplace. Although public support declined as these mechanisms failed to produce a strong, consensual definition of the policy, at the same time the intense market competition helps to explain how a policy that faced so many political obstacles in a system noted for legislative paralysis came into being at all. Above all, these transformations of policy in response to institutional forces show why shaping public opinion is not a simple matter of a great communicator's simply choosing the right rhetoric.

The Great Communicator Meets the Bear Market

Discouraging contextual factors notwithstanding, the Great Communicator (i.e., Reagan) launched his rhetorical campaign on May 28, 1985 with a nationally televised speech calling for

A second American revolution of hope and opportunity, [born of] popular resentment against a tax system that is unwise, unwanted and unfair.[11]

These powerful words were echoed time and again in speeches delivered in eighteen cities around the country by the end of September. A popular and persuasive president reaching out to the people was potentially the media event of the year, and the White House rolled out an impressive array of media management techniques to try to keep the news tracking on the right story line. The local speeches were stage-set to evoke images of small town America and contemporary middle-class life, and sometimes both, as in a speech set in an Oklahoma City high-tech communications plant in which Reagan delivered these lines: "Like the surrey with the fringe on top, our tax system has seen its day." "[The current system has] loopholes big enough for a 747 to slide through." "[Working people] have been taxed up to their eyeballs."[12]

When back in Washington, the Reagan team staged other media events designed to reinforce images of fairness for working people and an end to special interest favoritism. For example, Reagan met with a group of corporate executives at the White House and asked for their help in fighting off "the army of lobbyists" trying to save their favorite loopholes.[13] In all, Reagan briefed nearly 1,000 people at the White House and orchestrated testimonials about the grass-roots support that was building for his plan. Shortly after the senior Republican on the House Ways and Means Committee promised "there is more support building for the President's goal of reform than was anticipated," Reagan took to the road again, promising to convince America that the plan was "profamily, profairness and progrowth."[14]

Although a poll taken the day after the May 28 "second American revolution" speech showed a temporary jump in support for the plan, polls in June, July, and August showed steady erosion, with only 19 percent of the people favoring the revised Treasury II plan as Reagan proposed it and 47 percent supporting passage only after changes.[15] Several factors in the marketplace competed successfully against Reagan's rhetorical definition of the situation. The media again figured prominently by simultaneously covering his speeches and running news analyses contrasting provisions of the actual Reagan proposal with the words he used to describe it. People learned, among other things, that they would lose their deductions for state and local income taxes, whereas the rich would be taxed at only a 35 percent rate (soon to drop even lower). The media also fed back information on the decline of public support by reporting poll results regularly.

The Media War

White House spokesman Larry Speakes slammed the press for undermining the president's message. In an attempt to regain control of the definition of the policy situation, White House speechwriters shifted the symbolic focus, making increasing reference to the impact of the tax plan on the economy, a response to continued media reports that people were worried more about the health of the economy and the size of the budget deficit than about tax reform. The new rhetorical themes built to a crescendo as Reagan made the final speeches of his campaign. Calling it "America's tax plan," he increasingly mixed soft allusions to the American Dream with hard references to economic benefits: "By closing loopholes and making sure that everybody pays their fair share, we can lower tax rates for everybody. With lower personal and corporate taxes and another cut in the capital gains tax, small and entrepreneurial businesses will take off. Americans will have an open field to test their dreams and challenge their imaginations – and the next decade will become known as the age of opportunity."[16] In the final days, the rhetoric even drew on the grand promises of the supply-side economists, promises matched in fantasy by fairy tale references to a child's Christmas story. The closing speech at a Sara Lee cake factory in Chicago included the following juxtaposition of tempting economic payoffs and touching season's greetings:

America's Fair Share Tax is a plan for a growing dynamic nation. Our very conservative, long-term estimates show our tax plan adding three percentage points to our gross national product. That translates into the equivalent of four million new jobs and from 600 to 900 extra real dollars of income for every American family.[17]

Tax fairness will be America's Christmas present to ourselves – and we shouldn't let any Grinch steal our Christmas this year.[18]

Economic bonanzas. American dreams. Money in every pocket. Even Grinches threatening to steal the national Christmas. All delivered in Reagan's inimitable folksy style – his intimate "electronic eloquence," as one observer has put it (Jamieson 1988). The rhetoric matched anything that was orchestrated during the Reagan presidency. The crowds appeared, the news cameras rolled, and people cheered. But something was wrong. As a Republican Senator from Idaho put it after a speech there: "They were cheering. But it was for him, not for tax reform."[19]

In short, the Great Communicator delivered his best rhetorical sales pitch, but the public was not buying. The sheer entertainment value of the Reagan performances was not enough to keep images of fairness from falling on deaf ears. And the exhortations to join the peoples' fight against the special interest villains (who in another Reagan image had tied the economic damsel in distress to the railroad tracks) met with skepticism, cynicism, disbelief, and simple disinterest. In one news story after another, the predictions were anticlimactic: The President's tax plan would die from lack of popular support, or "death by boredom" as one account put it.

What went wrong? The answer, we think, lies neither in Reagan's rhetoric nor in the lack of popular interest in a major and credible change in the tax system, but in the workings of the larger rhetorical marketplace that pitted Reagan's rhetorical claims against persuasive arguments from political opponents and competing interests that the tax plan was anything but "a second American revolution." The blunted impact of the rhetoric was not owing only to media scrutiny of the proposal but to the kind of information cueing that resulted from institutional and media interaction in this particular situation.

There is growing evidence that attentive publics attend to cues provided by party and institutional elites who make the news (Zaller 1992). In addition, it is clear that in the U.S. media system these cues rise or fall with journalistic norms that filter political content in the news according to patterns of political conflict among elites along Washington news beats (Bennett 1989, 1990; Hallin 1985). This means that the opposition rhetoric of the Democrats in the early years, when Reagan won the Great Communicator title from the press, was less partisan, less antagonistic, and less unified when the party was in a weaker electoral position in the early 1980s. Following the Democratic rebound in campaign financing (Bennett 1996b) and the desperate resolve not to lose control of Congress, the party mobilized to go public with opposing claims about tax policy. Interest groups tried to get their ideas into the news as well, adding to the volume of noise surrounding both Republican and Democratic definitions of the situation. Thus, the media coverage that undermined the Reagan rhetoric was driven less by a liberal or critical press than by routine reporting of growing rhetorical opposition between the political parties and among Washington-based interest groups.

The Democrats Challenge the Great Communicator

The Democrats saw tax reform as an issue they could not avoid. If they resisted or ignored it, Reagan could blame them for its failure, pin the special interest label on them, use taxes as an issue to increase the Republican hold on the Senate in 1986, and, some feared, narrow the Democratic balance in the House as well. On the other hand, the Democrats could gain little from attacking a popular president whose tax reform message, although not universally believed, was not universally condemned either.[20] As a result, the Democrats evolved a "good cop, bad cop" rhetorical strategy in which they supported Reagan's efforts to promote tax reform while criticizing many specific elements of his proposal. This enabled the Democrats to address and perhaps to reinforce the ambivalent leanings in the opinion polls while gently undermining Reagan's own words. Contrast, for example, House Ways and Means Committee Chairman Dan Rostenkowski's support for Reagan's campaign with the subtle reservations expressed by other leading Democrats:

Rostenkowski: "[If President Reagan leads the charge for tax reform, it] ought to be done, and it can be done."[21] "[Reagan must] bang the drum loudly [for tax reform.]"[22] "If the President's plan is everything he says it is, he'll have a great deal of Democratic support."[23] "[I will support him] as much as I can. I've made no concessions to anyone. No promises to anyone."[24]

New York Governor Mario Cuomo: "[The Reagan plan is] dynamite for rich people."[25]

House Speaker Tip O'Neill: "[If the President's plan is enacted], the working poor will still be paying more taxes than they did before he took office."[26]

Representative Richard Gephardt (co-author of a Democratic tax bill): "The loser clearly is the middle class."[27]

Evidence that this rhetoric was part of a party strategy comes from a number of sources. As a top Rostenkowski aide put it, "If we turn on his plan, Reagan will destroy us."[28] On the other hand, as Representative Barbara Kennelly of Connecticut said, "If the President is 100 per cent behind tax reform, he'll get most of the credit. We Democrats have to be careful that we can campaign in 1986 on tax reform as a plus. The public will be aware of what happened, and we will need to be able to hang our hat on something that has passed. Our goal is that we prevent the Republicans from making this a realignment issue."[29] Or as Mary Rose Oakar (Ohio), secretary of the House Democratic Caucus explained, the rhetorical strategy of faint praise for Reagan, although emphasizing potentially unpopular points of his program, "... will come across well to the ethnic regular guys at the neighborhood tavern whom the party has been losing lately."[30] She added that if the party handled the issue properly by making it "their" issue, they could also reclaim lost middle-class support in 1986 congressional races. Which, it turns out, they did.

Interest Group Noise

To the volume of tax rhetoric in the news that resulted from party competition was added a chorus of voices from interest groups that used advertising to get their messages directly to the public. In most cases the aim was similar to the Democratic Party strategy: Be nice to the president, but raise doubts about his tax plan. However, because these were special interests talking, their rhetorical strategy required keeping their interest labels deep in the background while creating messages that might raise doubts about reform in more general terms. Tax reform, as perhaps no other issue in the Reagan era, illustrated the power of interest groups to define issues directly in public debates. Communications methods included direct mail campaigns, advertising, news conferences, appearances on public affairs shows, and buying endorsements from celebrities. Although the point of opposition to the tax plan differed in each case, the cumulative message added up to much the same thing: There is something objectionable to every American in tax reform. Among the efforts designed to get out this message were the following:

The National Association of Manufacturers, along with dozens of other business groups, sent their memberships analyses of the economic impact of Reagan's plan.

The life insurance industry ran a national television ad campaign to alert American workers that they would be taxed on fringe benefits such as employer-paid health plans. A coalition of interest groups, including labor unions, later joined in getting this message to a broad audience. (The coalition included the unlikely pairing of groups like the AFL–CIO and the U.S. Chamber of Commerce.)

National charities mobilized over 37,000 local chapters to put the word out at the grass roots about lost deductions for charitable contributions. Meanwhile, prominent charity spokespeople put out the same message through the national media.

The National Restaurant Association warned of huge losses in jobs and local tax revenues if business meal deductions were cut.[31]

Lost jobs, less charity, lowered value for employee benefits, cuts in community tax bases – all were strong messages not likely to be traced directly to the particular interest groups that put them out. The rhetorical images used to convey these messages were also effectively constructed, as illustrated by a television ad in which a flock of birds identified as the Treasury descended on a loaf of bread representing workers' fringe benefits. The birds pecked at the loaf until it was nearly gone, while a voice proclaimed that taxing fringe benefits "is for the birds."[32] These messages mobilized millions of people to object to various provisions of the Reagan plan without forcing people to identify themselves with the special interest villains. At another level, however, the intense media coverage of the huge interest group mobilization gave the impression that the special interests were swarming around the issue.

More Noise: Parties, Election Strategies, and Campaign Financing

By the time the House of Representatives began its deliberations on the final tax bill near the end of 1985, the marketplace had generated a range of competing rhetoric, a phenomenal supply of evidence pro and con, and something resembling a media dialogue among the players and between them and the public through the reporting of opinion polls. As a combined result of the media attention, the involvement of so many players, and in particular as a result of the development of party rhetoric based on electoral strategies, the final showdown in Congress on the eve of an election year brought all these market forces to bear on the final resolution of the issue. As Dick Gephardt, the author of a leading congressional tax bill said, while looking ahead to the decision-making process at the end of the rhetorical campaign: "This is going to be the biggest political brawl Washington and the country has [sic] ever seen."[33]

The Congressional showdown also brought Political Action Committees (PACs) and campaign financing squarely into the picture. Whereas interest groups used both lobbying and direct national rhetorical appeals to mobilize public pressure, the PACs were able to apply added pressure where it was felt most acutely: in the political bank accounts of members running for reelection. The entry of PACs into the tax reform marketplace was crucial because of the rhetorical tension created between parties and PACs. PAC forces pushing against tax reform threatened to undermine party discipline by converting party members into electoral entrepreneurs (leaving party rhetoric with little coherence), feeding what cynical voters understood as corrupt political motives coming out of Washington. Pushing from the other direction, party leaders on both sides saw the balance of electoral power in Congress hinging on the cohesiveness of tax reform rhetoric and on the plausibility of that rhetoric as an account of what the parties eventually would do.[34]

Despite the attempt at party discipline, PAC pressures made defection from the party rhetorical programs tempting to many individuals. According to one report, nearly all thirty-six members of the Ways and Means Committee came to the decision with at least one provision of the old tax code they wanted to protect.[35] The financial pressures to defect from public party rhetoric in the privacy of the committee room were considerable: Members of the House panel received more than $6 million in campaign funds from special interest PACs aimed at securing tax benefits. The scenario in the Senate was even more dramatic, with PAC contributions totaling nearly $11 million given to the twenty members of the Finance Committee. And these interests were by no means easy to reconcile, with oil industry PACs putting more than $500,000 on the political line, the insurance industry $855,000, and labor unions more than $1.3 million.[36]

With these two market forces so squarely opposed, it is not surprising that the chairman of House Ways and Means went public in a series of speeches prior to the final decision, trying to prepare the public rhetorically for a less than perfect outcome: "The reality is that tax reform, like all massive changes in policy is negotiated – not dictated. We don't work in blacks and whites. We work in shades of gray. Compromise is the price of reform. Like it or not, tax reform ends up in a series of compromises."[37] And compromises there were, reflecting both the competing forces in the marketplace and the growing feeling that public confusion might translate into voter disarray on the issue in November.[38] Playing into these complex market forces, the House panel members hedged their bets and passed a reform that:

1. Lowered tax rates across the board, but more for the rich than the middle classes.
2. Shifted more of the load back to corporations but not as much as a fairness-minded public wanted.
3. Closed some loopholes but left many others open, with still more merely reduced in size.

Rostenkowski admitted during a House floor debate, "It is not the bill any of us would have written in sanctuary."[39]

Reluctantly accepting the House measure as being better than abandoning the issue to personal and perhaps party defeat, Ronald Reagan reentered the picture, first by pushing House Republicans to support Democrats in passing it, and second by lobbying wayward members of his party in the Senate.[40] As the Senate battle raged, however, the special interests appeared to be winning, leading a former senator to observe: "I can tell you there's little to choose between a lion's den and the Senate when it comes to tax reform."[41] Indeed, at one point during the heat of the Finance Committee wrangling, the members were reported to be giving away $2 billion a day. Pressed hard from the White House and with his newly won leadership sorely tested, committee chairman Robert Packwood proposed the radical idea of starting over. He closed committee doors and presided over a deal that dropped a number of corporate loopholes in favor of an even lower bracket for upper-income earners.

Media Redux: The News Drama Plays Out

Another market mechanism came back into play at this crucial juncture: The news media simplified the noisy rhetoric from the various factions by framing the dramatic conclusion of the story in terms of government fairness versus special interest politics. In the absence of a clear alternative political framing coming from the actors themselves, this was the easiest story to tell. The political stage could hardly have been better set for news drama. For the first time in Senate history, a floor debate would be held under the light of television. There was tremendous pressure to accept the committee recommendation without adding too many amendments that would be interpreted by the viewing audience as more concessions to special interests. The nightly news juxtaposed shots of lobbyists waiting in the hallways with scenes of senators moving onto the floor. The interpretive context was clear, as Senate Majority Leader Robert Dole warned a group of Republican colleagues prior to the debate: "I wouldn't want to be offering any tax breaks."[42] At this point, tax reform was in Dole's words "unstoppable," and key senators appeared to be more concerned with how they looked on television than whether there was any more room at the margins to play off the party rhetoric of fairness against the campaign benefits flowing from the PACs. Sensing that victory was at hand, Reagan stepped back into the spotlight and invited a group of senators to a White House breakfast before the floor debate. Signaling that the political process was nearing an end, Reagan for the first time was not selling his plan. Instead, he offered acting advice to camera-shy senate heavyweights: "Learn your lines. Don't bump into the furniture. And in the kissing scenes, keep your mouth closed."[43]

And so, the "gang of 535"[44] as the *Wall Street Journal* described the tax reform congress, brought their versions of the Reagan, Gephardt, Bradley, Rostenkowski, Packwood, Treasury, interest group, PAC, Republican, Democrat, media-inspected, public-suspected tax bill to conference. If there were gaps between the final product and the rhetoric that ushered it through virtually every corridor of the political system, they were glossed over by the celebratory rhetoric of key players jockeying for political position in the bill's aftermath. Packwood heralded the Senate version as "the most radical tax bill that this Congress has seen in a half century."[45] Treasury Secretary Baker proclaimed that lowering the top tax rate from 70 percent to 28 percent was an "extraordinary achievement."[46] Rostenkowski said, "The political process works. This tax bill brings a sense of justice to the way we tax income."[47] But something of the obligatory tone of all this jubilation was given away by Reagan spokesman Larry Speakes who said "By and large, the bill is one we like very much and think it is historic and all that."[48]

There were a few negative reactions (e.g., Gephardt) and a sour pro-nouncement from House Speaker-to-be Jim Wright about the revenue disas-ter that would flow from the bill,[49] but the rhetoric of praise and self-congratulation carried the compromise legislation through both chambers and on to the president. Yet the week Reagan sat down to sign the bill into law a national poll showed only 19 percent supporting the new program, 16 per-cent opposing it, and a whopping 65 percent of the public expressing no opin-ion. That was not the kind of opinion formation on which clear or legitimate public policy depends.[50] Although he pronounced the obligatory words of fairness, equity, and victory for the American taxpayer, Reagan's rhetoric had an "and all that" quality similar to the language used earlier by his press sec-retary. Reagan's subdued tone suggested that the interplay of so many market mechanisms had denied any group a clear victory over either the rhetorical definition of the situation or the content of the actual policy. This would be-come neither the Republican vehicle for party realignment nor the means of pinning the special interest label on the Democrats, as Reagan had attempted to do since 1980. As the polls made clear, neither party could argue persua-sively that its efforts had advanced dramatically the cause of tax fairness.

In the end, the rhetoric of "revolution" was tempered by the modest real-ity of the results. Yet without the full engagement of the spectrum of market forces, there might not have been any results to speak of. As one lobbyist saw the unfolding process, its most remarkable feature was the fact that reform continued to go forward at all against the resistance of powerful interests and the "yawning indifference" of the public: "The progress of 'tax simplifica-tion' resembles what Dr. Johnson said about a dog walking on its hind legs: 'It is not done well, but you are surprised to find it done at all.'"[51]

As the political players walked quietly away from the issue, a final market adjustment took place: The most tangible measure of all that rhetoric became available to millions of Americans on the bottom lines of their tax returns. As a collection of polls analyzed by Phillips (1990: 247) shows, most of the "no opinions" turned into negatives. Among the national poll results two years later were the following:

- "Reform" made the system worse by a 55 to 31 percent margin. (ABC News/ *Washington Post* survey, March 1988)
- 67 percent found the new law more confusing than the old, resulting in an 85 per-cent overall agreement that the tax law is too complicated. (*USA Today*/CNN polling, April 1988)

- 66 percent regarded the new law as unfair, 39 percent found it less fair than the old one, and only 13 percent thought it was fairer. (Gallup Polls in February 1989)
- 58 percent said they paid more taxes under the new law, and only 22 percent said they paid less. (ABC News/*Washington Post*, early 1988 polling)
- 60 percent said the reform benefited the rich, and 78 percent agreed that it benefited special interests. (*USA Today* poll, no date)

In light of this opinion formation, there was little more rhetorical advantage to be gained from the issue. Gone from the national scene was the rhetoric of fairness, along with the electoral posturing, the finger pointing, and the credit taking. As the media played public opinion back into the marketplace of ideas, silence became golden.

THE SWEDISH TAX REFORM ACT OF 1990

Sweden is often regarded, sometimes justifiably so, as a more highly regulated society than the United States (Kelman 1981: Ch. 5). If this is true, how does this regulation affect the Swedish marketplace of ideas? Is Sweden more entangled in regulatory mechanisms and thus less likely to be open to new ideas and demands from the public? Judging by the tax reform issue and our election studies, the answer is both yes and no. The Swedish tax reforms of 1989 to 1990 involved an astounding array of actors trying to influence the debate and the policy outcome. In the early stages, the idea market was very competitive, rivaling the U.S. case. When the tax issue entered its final decision-making phase, however, a very small group of elite politicians, mainly top Social Democrats and Liberals, effectively closed the market and made the crucial decisions as to the final formulations of the proposals. As soon as a parliamentary compromise had been reached and the leading politicians decided to stick by it, come rain or shine, it did not matter what the outside world said. At that stage, the issue had been settled and the marketplace was closed. Although the policy results resembled the U.S. case in many ways, closing the market before losing control of the definition of the issue enabled the Social Democrats to present a clearer policy that eventually met with greater public approval – despite initial negative public reaction to preempting debate on the issue. Before we analyze these market dynamics more closely, consider how the decision to reform the taxation system in Sweden came into being and how various regulatory mechanisms engaged with the issue.

The Political Context

Sweden had long occupied a top position concerning the level of taxes and public expenditures in the OECD countries.[52] In the 1980s the progressive state income tax, for instance, ranged from 30 percent at the lowest level to about 90 percent at the highest.[53] In addition, Sweden has a national value-added tax on most products, flat rate (proportional) local income taxes, and flat rate social security taxes (Haskel 1987: 225; Steinmo 1989: 504). Less well known, perhaps, is the fact that the Swedish tax system as a whole is not particularly progressive and that capital income is relatively lightly taxed. By comparison, the United States has had a system that taxes capital income more heavily than earned income. When all taxes are considered, the United States relies substantially more on redistributive individual and corporate income taxes than do countries such as Britain or Sweden (Steinmo 1989: 502, 504).

Since the dawning of parliamentary democracy, the nonsocialist parties in Sweden have advocated lower taxes. In more recent times, they have focused on the need for lower marginal taxes. The Social Democrats have regularly opposed this, arguing that lowering the marginal tax rates would unduly favor the rich. Beginning in 1987, however, three major public commissions were established with the aim of reforming the income and corporate taxes as well as the system of indirect taxation. The most important of the commissions dealt with a reform of the income taxes and consisted of party representatives only. For once, the interest groups were confined to voicing their opinions from without, not from within.[54]

Why was it suddenly deemed necessary, after years of stalling, to act on the tax reform issue? Two reasons, one domestic and one international, were particularly decisive. First, tax policy always reflects the shifting ideological values and sentiments in society. What people think about taxes is quite important for the conduct of public policy (Hadenius 1986). The decision to embark on a major tax reform in Sweden must in part be viewed against the backdrop of a general right-wing trend at home and abroad, a trend affecting both elites and the public at large. But it was also in part a reaction against the market excesses of the 1980s when Sweden, firmly under Social Democratic rule, witnessed the birth of a new millionaire every day and growing income inequalities on the labor market. The result, not surprisingly, was a gradual decline in the faith and legitimacy of the whole tax system akin to what had happened earlier in the United States (Elvander 1989: 163).

Second, it also became necessary to act because of developments in the vital sphere of international economy. During the 1980s, many Western nations reformed their tax systems, several of them after having been inspired by the American debates and proposals. Sweden was no exception. Being a small nation heavily dependent on the world economy, Sweden, it was argued, could no longer maintain a tax system that differed fundamentally from that of other leading countries. Accordingly, the directives to the commission on income taxes, for example, show clear signs of having been influenced by the 1986 U.S. tax reform (Södersten et al. 1990: 9–13).[55]

Parties, Interests, and Election Strategies in the Media Age

By this stage of the policy process, most of the key players in the Swedish policy debate had been identified. The political parties finally concluded that a comprehensive tax reform was long overdue and that the way to go about it, in typical Swedish fashion, was to refer the matter to a public commission. This was done in full cooperation with major interest groups, some of which had championed the idea of a tax reform for quite some time. Referring issues to a public commission ensures that they will be thoroughly investigated but also that they will be clothed in technical language, buried in endless committee meetings, and thus withdrawn from the open marketplace at least for a while. It gives the power players some breathing space, which was exactly what the Social Democrats wanted at the time.

Enter the mass media in the 1988 election campaign. In every campaign, the Social Democrats pick a main adversary, usually one of the three nonsocialist parties, or all of them. This strategy traditionally gave the Social Democratic leadership (until their loss in 1991) an opportunity to determine the pattern of conflict in a campaign, which is tantamount to determining how the election will be covered in the media, an absolutely crucial aspect of any modern campaign (Åsard 1989: 80–81; Asp 1988: 9; Gilljam & Holmberg 1990: 56–57). In 1988, the Liberals were chosen as chief adversaries. Prime Minister and Social Democratic party leader Ingvar Carlsson criticized the Liberals for supporting positions to the right of the conservatives and particularly for their proposal to lower the marginal tax rates to 50 percent for the majority of all wage earners. This was described as an unjust giveaway to the rich. The government, instead, favored "fairer taxes," Carlsson said, without specifying what that meant or how it could be achieved.[56]

The Liberals were subjected to harsh criticism by Social Democratic candidates all across the country. Other candidates, both from the left and in the center, quickly followed suit. The media, which are always interested in attacks and conflicts, gave ample space to the tax issue in general and to the criticism of the Liberals in particular.[57] Prime Minister Carlsson went to great lengths in describing the Liberal view as "unjust" and "right-wing," both epithets in the Swedish political vocabulary. In a further attempt to portray the chief opponent's tax proposal as being on the fringe, he publicly announced his doubts as to the possibility of reaching a compromise with any of the nonsocialist parties. A more likely outcome was a purely Social Democratic reform, he said, perhaps supported by the Communists.[58]

The prime minister's rhetoric on taxes is interesting because it was intended to appeal to voters on two levels: (1) as a statement of fact, and (2) as an expression of solidarity with the less affluent members of society. Carlsson wanted to convey the impression that the Social Democratic position on taxes was vastly different from that of the Liberals; this was the *logos* underlying his message. But he also appealed to the listener's *pathos* by choosing highly salient enemy symbols. The Liberal party leader Bengt Westerberg did not take this criticism lightly. In a series of speeches, he attacked the ruling party for using "sleazy campaign tactics" unworthy of a free and democratic society. The rhetoric used was just as heated as that of Prime Minister Carlsson. Westerberg warned that, because of their behavior, the Social Democrats had "burned all bridges" and thereby ruined every chance of cooperation in domestic affairs for a long time to come. If the government were allowed to continue after election day, Westerberg predicted, no new initiatives would be taken on tax reform.[59]

A Rhetorical Reversal: Saying One Thing to Get Elected and Another to Govern

Yet in November 1988, just two months after the election, the government startled everyone – including the Liberal Party leader – by issuing new guidelines for a reform of the national income taxes. The guidelines turned out to be strangely similar to what the Liberals had been proposing all along. In presenting the new proposals, the government also in effect issued a repudiation of the whole tax system in Sweden. This system was now said to function exceedingly badly, to undermine its own credibility, and to create greater economic injustices in society. At an accompanying press conference, Treasury Secretary Kjell-Olof Feldt and trade union leader Stig Malm took a leaf out of Ronald Reagan's book, condemning the current tax system as "rotten" and even "perverted." What had been considered as basically sound just a few weeks earlier was now presented as hopelessly inadequate and outdated.[60]

Two alternative tax scales were presented by the treasury secretary, the most radical one calling for a flat rate income tax of up to the 200,000 Swedish kronor (Skr) bracket and a 50 percent tax for incomes above that level. Furthermore, the proposal included a substantial drop in the taxation of additional incomes. A person making 250,000 Skr a year would see the marginal tax rate go down from 72 percent to 50 percent, whereas people in the 160,000 Skr category would get to keep 70 percent of their extra earnings as opposed to only 40 percent previously. The government's turnaround took virtually everyone by surprise. A Social Democratic member of the income tax commission later wrote: "Sweden was indeed witnessing the dawning of a new world."[61]

The media complicated the political picture at this point by emphasizing the political reversal of the Social Democrats and underscoring the gap between earlier rhetoric and actual policy, creating a public relations muddle that was only made worse when the prime minister announced that the government's proposal was "light years apart" from what the Liberals had advocated during the election campaign.[62] Unjust. Right-wing. Light years apart from the mainstream. The problem with this language from a rhetorical point of view was mainly that it appeared to be inconsistent or contradictory, offering no unifying rhetorical theme to invite the public to see the logic of the new position.

Treasury Secretary Feldt, the government's foremost spokesman on the issue, mentioned no fewer than three arguments in support of a sweeping reform: the bankruptcy of the old system, the need for a fairer tax system without any loopholes for the rich, and the need for a uniform taxation of capital and individual incomes.[63] The message, besides containing more than one thought, was hard to reconcile ideologically with its party source and was difficult to get through. According to a poll published in December 1988, 40 percent of the public were positive toward the proposed reform, 30 percent were negative, and 30 percent had no opinion on the issue.[64] These results indicated that a substantial part of the population was still uncertain about the effects of a reform and that elected officials had a lot of explaining to do.

Up to late 1988 the idea market remained wide open, allowing all sorts of ideas and actors to participate in the debate. No one was able to control the rhetorical situation, perhaps because at this stage anyway none of the actors was trying very hard to do so. Seemingly content to let commission politics grind out a working national consensus, no one, not even the prime minister or his secretary of the treasury, embarked on a big rhetorical campaign à la Ronald Reagan to educate and arouse a seemingly detached audience.

The situation began to change in June 1989, when the income tax commission published its voluminous, 1,500-page report, including suggestions for a new law. The report, which closely adhered to the government's November proposal, clearly did not accommodate some of the key interests, and its impact was anything but consensual. There was an avalanche of critical comments, and the key parties and groups rushed in trying to protect their interests and getting as much attention for their causes as possible.

Four of the six parties in Parliament were openly critical of the commission's conclusions, albeit for varying reasons. The Moderates – formerly the Conservatives – opposed them because they did not signal any change in the total tax burden in society, which now suddenly was an overriding goal for a party that had previously focused very hard on the necessity for lower marginal taxes. The Center Party, the Communists, and the Environmentalists did not like the measures because they gave too much to the rich and too little to the common people. Only the Social Democrats and the Liberals seemed fairly content, even if some dissent could be discerned from within their party ranks.

Interest groups from all sectors of society also reacted promptly to the report. As was the case in the United States, public relations drives were launched in the media in an attempt to directly influence public opinion. In addition, lobbying activities continued with the commission members who were now engaged with drafting the law. After the measure was later signed and enacted into law in June 1990, the Social Democratic chair of the income tax commission, Erik Åsbrink, gave a vivid and amusing description of how a meeting with a typical lobbyist usually proceeded:

First of all they voiced their support for the reform, stating how much they endorsed its basic principles.... When this ritual ended, however, there was always a big "BUT." ... Industry "x" from region "y" representing group "z" was actually in great trouble. In addition, the industry in question was totally unique, making an exception from the basic principles an absolute necessity in this particular case. They reassured me that the risk for other companies to follow suit and demand the same special favors was virtually nil.... If, on the other hand, an exception was not made in this unique case, the consequences not only for the industry but also for the region, the group and for the entire nation would be disastrous.[65]

Although the commission system in Sweden undoubtedly kept interest groups from having the same kind of an impact as in the U.S. case, some of the most important labor organizations and business associations continued to wage a public rhetorical battle, complicating both the legislative process and its eventual legitimacy. The government's problem from a corporatist point of view was how to contain the potential damage within the interest group system while securing the cooperation of the most influential groups. The media did their part to keep this political pot boiling by covering the debate from the "who wins, who loses" perspective. Most journalists seemed interested in the bread-and-butter issues only, overlooking – with few exceptions – the broader implications of the reform. For them it was a matter of short-term financial gains, not of long-term economic consequences. This narrow perspective added to the sponsoring parties' problems in publicly discussing the issue.

Closing the Marketplace to Protect the Policy

The fall of 1989 was a critical period in the policy process, with public support and understanding still at stake and interest groups still not neutralized by the commission process. At this point, the government shifted political strategies from an effort to forge public consensus to the new goal of imposing a swift settlement. The new strategy could most accurately be described as *closing the marketplace*. Because the Social Democrats were a minority government, dependent on other forces inside and outside of Parliament, they could no longer sustain the loss of public opinion capital and had to make a choice as to the actors they would align with.[66] It was decided at this point to close the idea market by inviting certain actors into the deal and purposely to exclude others.[67] A corporatist deal was struck that excluded all the minor interests.

The prime minister played out his strategy by making use of another feature of corporatist Swedish politics, the famous "Haga talks." The name refers to the castle outside Stockholm, where government and interest groups occasionally meet to discuss current issues. On October 3, during the opening of the new parliamentary season, Ingvar Carlsson invited all party leaders and representatives of the major interest organizations to a summit

meeting at Haga. The sole item on the agenda: tax reform. The first meeting
was soon followed by another one, after which the Moderates and the employer associations predictably dropped out of the negotiations.[68] After a
third encounter, the number of active participants had narrowed to five, all
representing the broad middle ground in Swedish political life. The government's strategy seemed to be working.

The final agreement was hammered out in close collaboration among top
officials from the Social Democrats, the Liberals, the big blue-collar Swedish
Confederation of Trade Unions (LO), and its white-collar counterpart
Swedish Organization of Salaried Workers (TCO). It was a classic case of
corporatist decision making, Swedish style, in which a few key actors tried to
settle the issue outside of the fiercely competitive idea market.[69] This they
succeeded in doing, to the amazement of political pundits in the media. After
a dramatic final round of negotiations, in which TCO chairman Björn Rosen-
gren – at the prime minister's direct urging – intervened and pleaded with
the Liberal leader not to leave the bargaining table, an agreement was
reached and presented with great fanfare on November 7, 1989.[70] The "tax
reform of the century," as it was often called, meant that:

1. About 85 percent of the adult population would pay only a local income tax of
   30 percent.
2. People making over 170,000 Skr a year would pay in addition a 20 percent national income tax.
3. Corporate taxes were lowered to 30 percent.
4. Indirect taxes went up across the board to make up for the Treasury's revenue
   losses.[71]

The architects of the reform, like their U.S. counterparts, heralded it as
a great achievement. In the long run, they promised, everyone would be a
winner.[72] Gone was the rhetoric of "right-wing proposals" and "sleazy campaign tactics." Instead of "burning bridges" the Liberals and the Social
Democrats seemed to be building them. But taking the issue off the public
market had its price in terms of popular confusion and suspicion. The
prime minister's earlier statements came back to haunt him in the media.
Did he still consider the Liberals to be his chief political opponents? After
all that had been said and done, did he still regard the Liberals as standing
to the right of the Conservatives? Carlsson brushed these questions aside,
saying in effect that campaign rhetoric was one thing and reaching broad
agreements in the national interest was quite another.[73] It was a brush-off
that he may have regretted in 1991.

CONCLUSION

Whereas the chorus of elite, party, and interest group dissent continued to fuel public confusion and mistrust in the United States, public disfavor in Sweden turned out to be a short-term phenomenon directed more at the pre-emption of public debate than at the policy itself. Unlike in the United States, the interest groups in Sweden were unable to continue undermining the rhetoric supporting the reform, partly because with the closing of the market there just wasn't much rhetoric to undermine. Although Ronald Reagan tried very hard to win public acceptance of his tax plan, the Great Communicator failed, leaving a trail of dashed metaphors and empty symbols in his wake. In comparison, the Swedish reformers simply withdrew from playing the public opinion and voter markets, and ceased efforts to construct a convincing public tax message. This sent conflicting signals to the public, as evidenced by an early poll released in December 1989, which showed 40 percent still support-ing the tax reform, but the number of displeased had jumped from 30 percent to 48 percent in one year. Those having no opinion dropped to just 12 per-cent.[74] This opinion formation, as noted earlier, was more in response to the political methods of the political elite than to the results of their policies. Over the next two years, as media attention turned to other issues and the effects of the new policy were felt at street level, support for the tax reform increased markedly, in contrast to the U.S. case over a similar period. A national poll in June 1991 showed that support in Sweden increased to 50 percent and that disapproval dropped from the 48 percent recorded in 1989 to a modest 23 per-cent.[75] Recall that in the U.S. case at the time of signing 65 percent withheld their opinions, but over time, opposition grew steadily, with 55 percent think-ing the reforms worse than the old system, 67 percent finding the new law more confusing, 66 percent saying it was less fair, and 78 percent feeling the real beneficiaries were the special interests.

The two case studies show how policy results are affected by specific mar-ket conditions operating in different societies. To put it simply, the effect of rhetoric on both the content of policy and on public acceptance of that poli-cy can be explained by how market mechanisms regulate the interplay of ideas. In the case of national tax reform, the following differences and simi-larities were detected in the two countries:

1. In both cases the key actors had great problems creating a compelling argument for reform, although owing to quite different market conditions.

2. The U.S. idea market was overall more open and competitive than the Swedish one. Yet early public frustration at the market closure in Sweden was quickly replaced by increased support and reduced opposition to a generally clearer, more sweeping reform policy. In the U.S. case, the chaos of the largely unregulated debate produced an initial wait-and-see attitude that was replaced with strong disapproval of the policy and little lasting party commitment.

3. The power of interest groups (magnified by election finance practices) to define issues and to influence the policy process was more evident in the United States than in Sweden, despite or perhaps because of the corporatist nature of Sweden.

Both case studies show how policy results and public reactions are affected by specific institutional arrangements that constrain communication about policy deliberations. Neither case of reform resulted in the kind of policy that tax experts would have devised if driven by the sheer force of economic ideas. To the contrary, the focus on middle-class concerns reflected party election strategies (that ironically in both cases met with little success among voters). Whether the issue is taxes or health care, it is clear that the ideas for policies are not simply generated by ideologues or experts. Although expert consensus about simpler, more efficient revenue systems surely figured into the legislative equations in both cases, the eventual policies departed (particularly in the American case) from ideas grounded mainly in economic theory. These cases illustrate that policies are also shaped by rhetorical choices anchored in electoral strategy, interest pressure, campaign finance, and the flow of media information. These market forces can have major effects on policy substance, symbolic representation, and public acceptance. In this perspective, policy takes on an important symbolic dimension, and political rhetoric becomes the currency of the public realm – the creative political capital that lends power its institutional vocabulary, its cultural acceptability, and its humanly inventive possibilities. Other cases offer further insights about how much and what kinds of regulation in public debates produce the most felicitous policy results in the marketplace of ideas.

6

The Marketplace of
Ideas in Elections and
Campaign Rhetoric

Campaigns are the conversation of democracy, and the one that just concluded was angry, deeply personal, powerfully ideological and exceedingly negative.... Many experts worry that negative advertising reached new highs – or lows – in the 1994 [U.S.] campaign and only insured that the voters would remain angry and cynical about their politicians... Still, many scholars and politicians argue that incremental reforms are unlikely to truly change the nature of the political debate. Campaigns do not happen in a vacuum, they say. "Why should people expect politics to be any different from the rest of the culture?" asked Representative Barney Frank, Democrat of Massachusetts. "It's not as if politics is deteriorating but everybody's watching Shakespeare " Mr. [Thomas] Mann also noted that anger and cynicism are not unique to the United States. "I worry a lot about the fraying of the civic culture, but we have to understand what is going on around the world," he said. "There's a lot of undifferentiated animus toward elites, suspicion of government and politics and an unwillingness to strike out." Angry times, in other words, breed angry campaigns. What is less clear, however, is how the cycle ever ends.
– Robin Toner

The four regulatory mechanisms referred to throughout this book have clear implications for elections. During the course of an election campaign, parties and candidates, according to traditional democratic theory, present – or should present – their views and positions on a broad range of issues and face each other in open debate. In an ideal electoral marketplace that is devoid of market disturbances among the regulatory mechanisms, the free flow of ideas ensures that the voters are well informed about the issues and alternatives and thus are able to make an enlightened choice. The mass media are instrumental in ensuring that ideas, issues, and candidates are widely and fairly covered to enable the electorate to choose between competing viewpoints. Ideally and theoretically, at least, election campaigns should enrich the public dialogue and strengthen the democratic process.

In the real world, as we all know, it does not work that way. Just as the economic marketplace produces monopolies and other market anomalies, so does the political marketplace create disturbances that impede the free flow of ideas and distort the electoral process. Campaign promises that have been made are not kept for a variety of reasons – often because they are so moralistic or so grandiose that they have little application in the real world of government. The mass media, which are supposed to be the great watchdogs in society, often fail to perform their duties properly, thus making it much more difficult for voters to make up their minds (Patterson 1993). Interest groups intervene by supporting or opposing certain actors and have little concern for the impact of that support on the whole of the polity or the coherence of policy. The consequences of such market disturbances can be severe, leading, for instance, to sloganeering and empty rhetoric, and – in what is perhaps a worst case scenario – to the withdrawal of a growing number of voters from the electoral arena altogether.

Our question in this chapter is: How do similarities and differences in our regulatory mechanisms help to explain patterns of electoral politics in two nations that are experiencing similar electoral trends but present challenges for ordinary institutional comparisons? We explore this question by applying our framework for comparing the rhetorics used in recent Swedish and American election campaigns.

THE DECLINE OF ELECTORAL RHETORIC

As discussed in the opening chapter, a common complaint among journalists, academics, and voters is that the electoral marketplace in many Western democracies has changed from being a forum for heated debate and a comparatively lively exchange of ideas into one dominated by highly stylized and circumscribed issues and quite streamlined rhetoric (Bennett 1996b; Phillips 1990). This strategic political rhetoric is constructed by pollsters and media consultants to win short-term public support rather than to articulate long-term governing programs. Elections are arguably the place for fine-tuning the governing ideas of parties or regimes to the evolving preferences of voters and the problems of changing societies. However, what we find increasingly is a combination of mechanical or ritualistic pronouncement of slogans, attacks, or party labels while the work of attracting voters is increasingly done by short-term images created by marketing research on voter moods. The result, as noted by Toner in the opening quotation of this chapter,[1] is a vicious cycle of voter cynicism in which elections fail to clarify the guiding principles that bind voters to parties or parties to programs, resulting in voters becoming increasingly suspicious of parties, candidates, and their promises.

The causal sequence here is particularly interesting. Changes in institutional regulatory mechanisms in both Sweden and the United States (explained later) have produced changes in the language of elections. Despite the negative effects of these communication patterns on voters and on the capacity of elected governments to make policy, both marketplaces have experienced difficulties in correcting their dysfunctional electoral communication. For empirical case studies illustrating the development of a more closed or unresponsive electoral marketplace, we have chosen the candidate and party rhetoric in the post-1988 Swedish and American election campaigns, viewed in the context of evolving historical trends (Åsard 1989; Page & Shapiro 1992: 383–398). In both countries 1988 was a watershed year in which market disturbances became increasingly evident, as illustrated most dramatically by the U.S. case, where we observe the then-highest recorded modern levels of public discontent with politicians coupled ironically with the highest recorded levels of victories by incumbents (98 percent in the House of Representatives). In Sweden the ruling Social Democrats managed to stay in office despite rising voter discontent that saw the Labor Party eventually lose power to a Conservative-led coalition in 1991. Even this apparent market adjustment in Sweden has not resulted in the kinds of changes in public debates that one might expect, a point to which we return later.

Earlier election campaigns on both sides of the Atlantic showed signs of a narrowing of the idea markets. The post-1988 campaigns were special, however, because Madison Avenue–style marketing strategies, personalized and emotional rhetoric, and growing voter distress all seem to have become institutionalized in a way that had not previously been seen. The reason, quite simply, is that these communication strategies succeed in winning elections at the considerable price of reducing the capacity to govern afterward. Parties in both systems began to trade what might be called their "governing ideas" for rhetoric designed primarily to win short-term support from many voters. The implications of this rhetorical shift are numerous, ranging from abandoning traditional constituencies and declining voter loyalty to the conclusion among campaign managers – particularly in the more advanced case of the United States – that voter decline is less a problem than an advantage (Bennett 1996b). All of which pointed to signs that voter inputs may matter less in modern electoral markets even as they are affected adversely by various regulatory factors.

CHANGING ELECTORAL RHETORIC IN SWEDEN

Eloquence has not been an essential part of the Swedish political culture. In Sweden there is nothing remotely similar to the traditional American acceptance speech or to the grand oratory that is sometimes displayed in the British House of Commons or the French Chamber of Deputies. Politicians in contemporary Sweden simply do not seem to regard eloquent speech making as an important part of their ordinary day-to-day activities. Doing things, such as attending meetings and conferences, conferring with party regulars or members and, above all, continuing the routine business of governing, have long been regarded as being much more pertinent and valuable than just saying things.

However, the fact that there is no great tradition of political oratory in Sweden does not mean that important rhetorical choices have been historically absent from the public dialogue. During the early stages of parliamentary democracy in Sweden, for instance, the rhetorical and ideological differences between the parties were clear and indisputable, making it meaningful even to talk about a liberal rhetoric or a conservative political language. Today it is questionable whether such generalizations make any sense, considering the shrinking range of the idea market and the vast changes that have occurred in politics and in society since the 1920s (cf. Boheman 1970: 155–158).[2]

The growth and development of the Social Democratic Labor Party (SAP) is an illustrative case in point. In the late nineteenth and early twentieth centuries, just after the formation of the Swedish labor movement, two different rhetorical styles or strategies competed against each other within the party. The first one was general, abstract, and impersonal, a sort of administrative language that turned out to be highly effective at regular party meetings and conventions. The second strategy was much more concrete, personal, and agitational, tailor-made for arousing the masses and increasing party membership. There wasn't much competition, however. As the party grew in size and came closer to taking on governmental responsibility, the agitational style became less appropriate and gave way to the more administrative language (Josephson 1991). This tendency was later reinforced as the party's propaganda reached beyond traditional core constituencies and came to include the concerns of much broader segments of the electorate.

Consequently, the Social Democrats of today no longer talk about "the working class," as they used to do in days past; instead, they make appeals to the much more diverse group of wage earners in society. What we are talking about here is probably one of the most important changes in Swedish political life since the end of World War II: *the gradual disappearance of a class-based rhetoric in favor of a centrist and more neutral political vocabulary aimed at the growing groups of independent and undecided marginal voters.* All the major parties in Parliament today share a basically common view on vital issues such as welfare spending, social services, and security and defense policy (Jerneck, Sannerstedt, & Sjölin 1988: 169–194; Uddhammar 1993). The differences that remain deal largely with the means, not with the ends, something party officials are not always eager to expose. Upholding the illusion of a fiercely combative idea market seems to be a common concern shared by representatives from all the established parties.[3]

The new and more diffuse rhetoric of the center is characterized by, among other things, generalities, a lack of a historical perspective, increasing sloganeering, and a less argumentative style (Åsard 1990: 5–7; Svensson 1990). Nowadays it seems more important – and electorally more rewarding – to focus on short, media-adjusted messages than to engage in substantive arguments and debates. The aim of the new rhetoric is to appeal to as many undecided voters as possible, particularly to the voters in the center who are considered to be vital to the outcome of any election. As the 1988 and 1992 elections in the United States illustrate, a similar tendency has developed there, with the ironic result that few voters, including middle-class groups, are satisfied with their choices.

However, this growing trend does not mean that the days of party competition in Swedish politics are over. As recent elections have shown, party competition is still alive and well, but it is now a competition more over selected issues and leadership abilities than over ideology. In the U.S. case, discussed later, there is much more competition between individual candidates supported by their handlers and media consultants. The contemporary American election – always something of a character test – has subordinated both character and issues to the strategically developed electronic image. By contrast, strategic communication in the more party-oriented Swedish system involves the decline of ideology and the appropriation of the opponent's key issues.

The Dawn of Strategic Communication in Sweden

The 1988 Swedish election campaign was notable for its lack of divisive issues and for the mostly low-key tone of the debates.[4] However, the campaign did not lack controversy altogether. For example, the Social Democrats chose to single out the Liberals as their chief opponents in the campaign, thus giving the party faithful an enemy to focus on. Some of the Liberal proposals – especially the party's pledge to cut taxes – were regarded as easy and convenient political targets. True, all the traditional parties – including the Social Democrats themselves – campaigned on platforms supporting different degrees of tax cuts, but no one spelled it out in such detail as the Liberals. Their proposal included lowering the marginal tax rate to 50 percent for all people working full time (with the ultimate goal of reducing those taxes to 40 percent in the coming years).[5] This was a good symbolic issue for the Social Democrats and provided the party activists with a golden opportunity to criticize the Liberals for being unjust and right-wing, labels that had found some resonance among the public and set the tone for much of the ensuing debate. Branding the liberal proposals as unjust had the additional advantage of providing the government with a useful symbolic foil to its own rhetorical theme of fairness, thereby implicitly strengthening the claim that the Social Democrats, despite frequent criticism to the contrary, still stood up for the common man against continued attacks from the right.

More typical of the campaign, however, was the government's attempt to depoliticize the election and the debate, chiefly by co-opting certain issues and avoiding others. After the murder of Prime Minister Olof Palme in the winter of 1986, the Social Democratic leadership began to develop what came to be called a "strategy of silence" as a method of dealing with the rival opposition parties. One controversial issue after another – drugs, social services, the European Union, among others – was politically defused and disappeared at least momentarily from the public dialogue. The aim in essence was to cool off the debate and disarm the opposition by simply co-opting some of their strong, or leading, issues.[6]

The one topic around which most of the debate centered was a cluster of environmental issues such as algal bloom in lakes, acid rain, and mass deaths of seals in Swedish coastal waters (Gilljam & Holmberg 1990: 19–20). All the parties focused on the environment as a leading issue, knowing perfectly well that it was sure to catch the attention of the media and also that it was of great concern to many people. An August 1988 poll showed that no less than 75 percent of the electorate thought that the environment was by far the most important issue in the campaign (Bergström 1988: 20; Gilljam & Holmberg 1990: 21–22).[7] The Environmental Party, or the Greens, previously a rather insignificant political force, benefited from the heavy media exposure and became the first new party to enter the Swedish Parliament in some seventy years (Gilljam & Holmberg 1990: 19–25; Wörlund 1989).

It could be argued that by focusing on such a popular issue the electoral marketplace was working smoothly. Or was it? Although the parties did address environmental issues, they by and large failed to show the voters that there were differences among them or that they had actual proposals to back up their policy aims. Again, the Social Democrats are a good case in point. When presenting the party's election platform in August 1988, Prime Minister Ingvar Carlsson put the environment on top of the issue agenda. Describing it as "the great challenge of the 1990s," Carlsson tried to convince the audience that the party was seriously concerned with these matters and that it was ready to take far-reaching steps in dealing with them. What followed, however, was a list of very general and noncommittal statements, again emphasizing the importance of the issue but offering very little in terms of substantive proposals or policies.[8] Much the same strategy – high-pitched rhetoric and little policy substance – also characterized the messages of the other parties. There was also a startling similarity on other matters, particularly regarding campaign promises and rhetorical themes. It is interesting to note, for example, that both the Social Democrats and the Center Party – and, among the smaller parties, the Communists and the Greens – championed fairness issues as a rhetorical strategy, sensing that this theme would resonate among substantial sections of the electorate.

In sum, the 1988 Swedish election campaign was characterized by:

1. A great similarity among the parties in their selection of issues and promises.
2. A vagueness in offering concrete proposals and policy choices.
3. An attempt – especially by the Social Democrats – to depoliticize the debate and keep complex and controversial issues at bay.

All these tendencies support our general thesis of a shrinking idea market. Even the fact that the Social Democratic leadership chose to attack the Liberals on the tax issue does not contradict this basic tendency; on the contrary, it seems to strengthen it. Going on the offensive rhetorically has become just another way of glossing over the lack of a more specific policy agenda and thus another method of putting symbols before substance (even though the distinction between the two is becoming increasingly difficult to uphold). One indicator of this trend, as explained in Chapter 5, was that after the election the Social Democrats proposed a tax reform virtually identical to the Liberal plan they had criticized during the campaign.

Beyond Issues: From Stability to Uncertainty

Despite a loss of three parliamentary seats in the 1988 election, the Social Democrats managed to remain in office. Since that election, however, Swedish politics has not been the same. Stability and one-party rule have been replaced by instability, rhetorical flexibility, and what seems like a regular turnover of government. The results of the 1991 election cemented this pattern. In an effort to capitalize on the popular ideas of the day, the Social Democrats moved further to the right, making it even more difficult for their core voters to support them. This market adjustment did not prove successful since most voters preferred "the real thing" when given a choice between a Social Democratic copy and the original.[9] A majority of the electorate was not convinced by the government's revised rhetoric and instead opted for something new (Gilljam & Holmberg 1993: 11–21). However, the resulting Conservative-led coalition was unable to maintain its initial momentum and lost the 1994 election soundly after having failed to find a convincing rhetoric to match its (unpopular) policies. These outcomes nicely illustrate the current volatility of the electoral market and the difficulties now facing parties and candidates when they try to satisfy an increasingly skeptical electorate.

The SAP's main rhetorical theme in 1991 was "Sweden is unique." This was a *topos* designed to assure voters that the party was *the* guarantor of the world-famed welfare state and that opting for any of the nonsocialist parties would be a big gamble. It was the language of a party in government bent on protecting what it had already achieved, not one that aimed for new or radically different agendas. About three years later, however, when the SAP was in opposition and enjoyed the support of between 45 and 50 percent of those

surveyed in various opinion polls, party strategists settled on a vastly different slogan for the upcoming campaign: "Sweden can do better." This was the
rhetoric of a movement eager to get back into power and continue the politics of reform. It was also a choice of words which indicated that the party's
marketing experts had been looking across the Atlantic to find a suitable role
model for ways to run campaigns and win elections.[10]

Preparations for the 1994 campaign started in the late fall of 1991, when
campaign coordinator Bo Krogvig attended a meeting of the International
Association of Political Consulting (IAPC) in Sydney, Australia.[11] Krogvig
came back from the meeting convinced that strategy was the all important
thing and that the key to success was to connect the party's policies with the
everyday concerns of ordinary people. It was vital, in other words, to establish a connection between campaign rhetoric and policy programs. Spreading his message to party activists across the country, Krogvig stressed the necessity of focusing on just a few select issues, such as jobs and social welfare.
Equally important, he thought, was to focus attention on only two of the
party's leading candidates – party leader Ingvar Carlsson and party secretary
Mona Sahlin. Viewing politics as a great smorgasbord, Krogvig feared that
the more the SAP offered voters in terms of issues, slogans, and candidates,
the more diffuse its message would become.

The party strategists also shared a conviction that candidates and campaign
workers alike needed to improve their skills in marketing their policies to the
public. This required more knowledge of how the media work in campaigns,
and more reliable and substantive information about voter attitudes. This belief led to the hiring of three American campaign consultants and pollsters
who had been active in U.S. politics for a long time. One of the consultants
was an expert on opinion polling and the use of focus groups. Another had
considerable experience in conducting opposition research (i.e., mapping out
the strategies and positions of the political opponents). The third offered advice concerning local opinion polling and voter contacts. The use of these
consultants got wide media coverage during the campaign and was criticized
by some for unduly "Americanizing" the Swedish election.[12] The SAP's own
marketing experts, for their part, toned down the importance of the consultants and insisted that their role had been mainly advisory in character and
that they had not been involved in deciding overall campaign strategy.

However, an indication that the SAP campaign team had indeed been
inspired by a well-known U.S. example was the creation of a Bill Clin-

ton–like "war room" at the party headquarters in Stockholm, from which the campaign was being run. What the party strategists had learned from the successful 1992 Clinton campaign was not only how useful it was to rely on sophisticated opinion polling and extended interviews with focus groups but also how significant it is in today's politics for a party to be able to set the media agenda. One of the teams placed in the SAP "war room" thus worked exclusively with the task of researching the opponents and launching counterattacks against any criticism coming from representatives of the other parties. The goal was to predict 90 percent of the opponents' attacks and to have prefabricated press releases ready for instant media distribution.

But not everything went according to plan. The original idea was to present the party as the responsible alternative and not to promise more than could realistically be delivered. Forced by market actors beyond its control, however, the Social Democratic leadership decided a few weeks before election day to present a tough austerity plan for reducing the enormous national budget deficit, an issue that had become central to the campaign. This meant proposing some long-expected tax increases but also, and more important, a series of cuts in popular welfare programs sure to affect many if not most of the prospective voters. The publication of the plan got huge media attention and had three effects: first, it transformed the SAP from an opposition party to a government-in-waiting, moving the then governing nonsocialist coalition to the sidelines; second, it put the Social Democrats in the unenviable position of having to defend cuts in programs that they had once enacted and that enjoyed strong cross–party support; third, and most dramatically, it caused the party to drop in the polls from a high of around 50 percent at the beginning of the campaign to the middle to low 40s. A proper market adjustment at this point would have been, one could speculate, to rescind some of the most unpopular proposals, particularly the one promising to introduce a qualifying day (no pay for the first day of sick leave) for working parents who had to stay home attending to sick children. That did not happen; apparently the calculus was that flip-flopping on such a vital issue as the economy would have caused the party to lose more credibility than sticking by the original proposal.

The final 45.2 percent was the best result for the Social Democrats since 1982. There is little doubt that the party could have done even better had it opted for a more populist platform and dropped some of the more provocative elements in the austerity plan. It is particularly interesting to us, however, that when the new SAP government started to put its economic proposals into legislative action, as it had promised it would do, voters registered their disapproval by abandoning the party in droves and moving to the left (benefiting primarily the Left Party and the Greens). Ten months after the 1994 election, the SAP had dropped almost as many percentage points in the polls. This development cannot be explained simply as a disconnection between campaign rhetoric and government performance. It apparently confounded many voters in 1994 that the Social Democrats promoted two somewhat contradictory rhetorical themes, one inviting the voters to believe that everything would get better if they were returned to power ("Sweden can do better"), and another specifying in some detail the tough economic measures that had to be enforced to deal with the massive budget deficit. Apparently, many voters were receptive to the former theme but did not listen to or believe in the latter. Part of the problem is that the image campaign dominated the election until the party was pressured by opponents to take a position on the budget and government spending. The late-developing issue must have seemed to many voters to be merely a necessary rhetorical calculation in response to an issue that received media attention because certain business leaders and the opposing parties took stands on it.

Events following the 1988 election generally illustrate the exhaustion of traditional political language. We seem to have arrived at a stage at which the old ideological slogans and traditional party catchwords are increasingly difficult to market effectively. No matter how hard candidates try, people have a difficult time seeing the connection between words uttered and policies implemented. The magic once attached to words such as *freedom, justice,* and *equality* fades when voters sense a growing gap between what is said and what is actually being carried out. Hence, the common complaint in recent years from old-time Social Democrats is that they no longer "recognize themselves" in the party's policies (cf. Hårsmar 1991: 289). This is a dilemma facing all the major players in the party system, not just the SAP, and underscores the need for new visions and fresh governing rhetoric.

The SAP's victory in 1994 was probably less a result of voters being impressed with the party's platform or ideas than a repudiation of the policies and rhetoric of the incumbent nonsocialist government. The party's 1994 image campaign centered around the "we can do better" theme thus proved to be more successful than its "Sweden is unique" campaign of three years earlier. But the SAP's inability to come up with more enduring visions and platforms may undermine its goal of establishing another long-term era of Social Democratic rule. All of this would suggest that the rhetorical exchanges between candidates and voters may be more effective in terms of registering short-term citizen discontent than in building voter consensus and party commitment to the agenda of government. The ideas exchanged in the political marketplace these days may be better suited to getting politicians elected than to helping them form coalitions and maintain the public support necessary to govern.

Voter Response to the Decline of Rhetoric in Sweden

During the 1970s, 1980s, and early 1990s, the Swedish electorate changed in ways that indicate how attentive citizens are to the interaction between language and institutional contexts. Among the most important changes were a decline in class voting; a rise in issue voting; a sharp decline in party loyalty (the proportion of voters that identifies with a particular party either strongly or weakly dropped from 65 percent in 1968 to 48 percent in 1991); an increase in swing voters; a growing voter mistrust of parties and politicians, contributing to a gradual decline of party strength; and a drop in voter turnout, albeit not a huge one, from 91.8 percent in 1976 to about 86 percent in 1988, 1991, and 1994 (Gilljam & Holmberg 1990: Chs. 4–6, 9–12; Gilljam & Holmberg 1993: 169–184).

What are we to make of these significant changes in the electorate? Obviously, they mirror even more fundamental structural and institutional changes in Swedish society that have occurred during the past three decades, too many to be detailed here (Petersson et al. 1990: Chs. 1, 11). What is interesting from our perspective, however, is that the trend toward a more shifting, independent, and skeptical electorate has occurred at the same time as politicians have exhibited a growing failure to communicate with the voters. The more vague the politicians have been in addressing the issues, the more negative the response from the voting populace. Consider the signs of mounting voter discontent. In 1968, 37 percent of the voters concurred with the statement: "The parties are interested only in peoples' votes but not in their opinions." In 1991, the figure had risen to 68 percent. Similarly, in 1968 46 percent agreed that "Those [politicians] who are in the *Riksdag* and make decisions do not show much consideration for what ordinary people think."

Twenty-three years later 70 percent shared this view (Gilljam & Holmberg 1993: 170). Thus, a majority of the Swedish electorate today has little confidence in politicians generally. These results are by no means unique to Sweden; a similar trend of growing voter discontent has swept most Western nations since the late 1960s, including the United States.

The tension in the Swedish system arguably reached its peak in the post–1988 elections and triggered important, although not stable adjustments in rhetoric in subsequent years. Voter turnout in the three elections from 1988 to 1994 was the lowest in twenty-four years. Even among those who did participate, there were clear signs of a lack of commitment or interest. In 1991, for instance, 51 percent of the voters complained that the campaign contained too much "party bickering," and 36 percent thought that too much attention had been focused on the party leaders. A mere 6 percent said that the campaign had been "factual and informative" (Gilljam & Holmberg 1993: 27–31). These signs of voter dissatisfaction indicate that the political marketplace was not working very well.

Explaining the Market Disturbances in Sweden

How have the regulatory mechanisms operated in the Swedish marketplace to create the present state of affairs? The question is complicated, but we will suggest an answer by analyzing the mechanisms one by one, beginning with the party system and, more specifically, with the pivotal role played by the Social Democratic Party.

The power wielded by the SAP in Sweden has been truly astounding. With the support of a strong trade union movement, the party has been able to put its distinctive mark on Swedish society for more than sixty years. No other party has been nearly as successful in influencing policies and setting the agenda for political debate (Therborn 1992: 1–5). The SAP has made use of two strategies in exercising its political power. One is class mobilization, built on organization and close collaboration with the trade union movement. The other is coalition politics, aimed at forging alliances with other social groups and parties. Both strategies have been important, the former because it provided the labor movement with a strong mobilizing capacity among the working class, the latter because it enabled the SAP to reach necessary compromises and deals with various opposition parties (Petersson et al. 1990: 200–202).[13] Furthermore, the labor movement early realized the need to cooperate with private industry in order to secure economic growth and better living conditions for working people. In the late 1930s, a "historical compromise" between labor and capital was thus formed, setting the agenda for decades to come (Korpi 1983).[14]

To a considerable degree, the supremacy of the Social Democrats has also been a hegemony over language. The most striking example is the success of the *folkhem* metaphor, which has already been discussed. The concept was more widely used after a landmark speech in 1928 by the then party leader Per Albin Hansson. As explained in Chapter 4, the future prime minister used the old image of a home to project the Social Democratic vision of a society characterized by equality, cooperation, and togetherness. Suffice it to say here that Hansson's 1928 speech reflected the dual rhetorical strategy we have described: one being conflict-oriented, the other more conciliatory. Already in this early statement, Hansson chose to address "the people" rather than "the working class," a rhetorical twist designed to appeal to much broader strata in society, as it eventually did. No single political metaphor during the twentieth century has been so universally acclaimed and used across the Swedish political spectrum as that of a *folkhem*.

The ascendancy of Social Democracy in the 1930s rested on an alliance of workers, farmers, and private domestic industry. The alliance was highly pragmatic, signaling that the SAP did not hesitate to put practical policies ahead of ideological principles. Thus, when the Social Democrats came to power in the fall of 1932, they decided to cope with the severe economic crisis not by making use of traditional socialist methods, such as nationalizing major industries, but by adopting a Keynesian economic policy, leaving the basic features of the market economy intact. Slowly but surely the Social Democrats came to accept the principles of the market economy, in practice and eventually also, although more grudgingly, in theory. This was a triumph for the nonsocialists. During the 1950s and 1960s, however, when the Social Democrats had firmly established themselves as the governing party, all the nonsocialist parties – including the Conservatives – accepted the basic principles of the welfare state, a clear victory for the SAP. When these two ideological concessions had been made, Swedish politics and national debate were fundamentally affected.[15]

For decades the SAP was also remarkably successful in keeping its working-class base intact. According to election surveys, 81 percent of the blue-collar workers voted for the party in 1956. Roughly three manual workers out of four still voted Social Democratic in the 1988 election. In 1991, however, the figure had dropped to 61 percent (Gilljam & Holmberg 1990: 224–225; Gilljam & Holmberg 1993: 199–200; cf. Lewin et al. 1972: 168–171).[16] As the employment structure changed and the country moved into being a postindustrial society, however, the working class decreased numerically whereas the middle classes steadily grew. In 1956 blue-collar workers accounted for 54 percent and salaried employees for 23 percent of the electorate. By 1985, the former figure had dropped to 43, and the latter had risen to 38 percent (Elvander 1980: 133–140; Holmberg & Gilljam 1987: 185). This was a decisive change, meaning that the SAP could no longer rely on blue-collar votes only; now it also had to mobilize white-collar voters in order to win elections.

Herein lies the crux of the matter. To maintain its grip on power, the SAP needed to win a greater share of the white-collar vote. And to do that, it had to adjust its policies and rhetoric accordingly. The victory on the issue of a new pension system in the late 1950s helped to initiate a new political coalition between the working class and white-collar employees. Between 1956 and 1960, support for the SAP among lower-echelon white-collar voters increased from 37 to 42 percent. Blue-collar support stayed virtually the same (Esping-Andersen 1985: 106–110). The point is that this change in voter support, which was later solidified, also necessitated a change in rhetorical practices. What was left of the old class-based language had to be further toned down, thereby accelerating the convergence of ideas in the marketplace. Soon after the pension issue had been settled, says one observer, the SAP "abandoned its 'little people' rhetoric and began to label itself the 'wage earner party'."[17]

The ability to pursue several cross-class alliances simultaneously has been a key ingredient in the SAP's electoral success, as evidenced most recently by its strong showing in the 1994 national election. In contrast, the nonsocialist parties have been unable so far to establish similar viable alliances or to introduce competing rhetorical visions in the marketplace. Their main difficulty has been the inability to reconcile policy differences among themselves – that is, to abstain from emphasizing their own party platforms and to focus on the common objective of winning elections. The development of postwar political rhetoric in Sweden is not only a result of changes in the *election and party systems*, however. The other elements of our explanatory model – interest groups, campaign finance, and the mass media – have also contributed to the spreading of a more centrist political language. In particular, *interest groups* and *campaign finance* have long played an important role in Swedish political life, whether we are talking about business associations backing the nonsocialist parties or trade unions supporting the Social Democrats. Both the nonsocialists and the SAP used to rely heavily on financial contributions from their respective backers. Up to the early and mid-1970s, the Liberals and the Conservatives in particular accepted substantial economic support from various business quarters. The SAP, for its part, has long relied on the employee unions to help fund its campaigns. For example, throughout the 1950s, no less than 90 percent of the party's campaign chest during election years emanated from union contributions. This monetary link no doubt disciplined party rhetoric at election time.

With the introduction of *public financing of parties* in 1965, the situation changed dramatically. According to the new law, parties were entitled to public money in proportion to their seats in Parliament. One of the strongest arguments for such a reform was that it would enable the parties to stop accepting contributions from powerful interest groups and thereby minimize the dependency problem. The effects of the reform have been considerable. Public (i.e., tax) money now provides the main source of income for all parties in Parliament. The nonsocialists doubled their resources when the 1965 law was enacted and soon phased out business contributions altogether. The SAP's economic funds, meanwhile, tripled in election campaigns and increased eightfold during nonelection years as a result of the reform, enabling the kind of spending necessary to hire marketing analysts and media consultants of the kind used during the 1994 election campaign.[18]

What we have witnessed during the last couple of decades, then, is a gradual dissolution of the ties between parties and interest groups in Sweden. Not that the ties have been dissolved completely; the SAP still accepts trade union contributions, and the nonsocialists do not mind it when business groups intervene politically on their behalf – for instance, through lavish advertising campaigns.[19] But the relationship between parties and interest groups is generally much looser now than it was, say, fifteen or twenty years ago. The significance of this change for the production of rhetoric is that it has made parties more *independent*, both financially and politically, enabling them to focus more effortlessly on the task of structuring language to please the all-important middle-class voters.[20]

As the parties' dependency on special interest groups has decreased, the importance of using the *mass media* has visibly increased. For the parties, the media have become essential tools of communication, especially during competitive election seasons. Starting in the 1940s and accelerating in the 1950s and 1960s, politics was gradually given more air time in the Swedish broadcast media. The parties' old propaganda channels – election rallies, newspapers, and leaflets – declined steeply in importance, a tendency that has continued during the past two decades. With today's emphasis on the media, the relationship between politicians and voters has become more distant and indirect. Political messages are directed less and less toward selected core groups and more and more toward the elusive middle-class audience.

The 1994 election was probably the most mass-media–dominated ever, with party leaders concentrating their public appearances at press conferences and other staged events and with media consultants playing a significant role in laying out marketing strategies (Bengtsson & Nilsson 1994).[21] The traditional speech, previously the most important rhetorical form, thus continues to decline in importance. It is important to recognize that these market mechanisms often operate independently, with media pressures driving party responses as much as the other way around.

To sum up, it seems reasonable to hypothesize that the following events have occurred in the Swedish case:

- The range of ideas between the established parties has narrowed significantly in the post–World War II period.
- The exhaustion of traditional political language has made it harder for people to differentiate between the parties, contributing in turn to increasing voter frustration and a weakening of party loyalty.
- The introduction of public financing in the mid-1960s has not only strengthened the parties financially but also helped to cut their dependence on powerful interest groups.
- Instead of the interest groups, the mass media and the methods used by parties to control them have now become the prime regulators of party and candidate rhetoric in the electoral marketplace.

In the end, we are left with a convergence of ideas and rhetoric produced by the parties with little regard to demands from many sectors of the consumer market, leaving voters increasingly unhappy. The changing media situation in Sweden – especially the advent of political advertising on commercially owned radio and television – is likely to reinforce these tendencies even further. The swing to a Conservative-led coalition in 1991, the rise and decline of a populist New Democracy party between 1988 and 1991, and the

SAP's return to power after the 1994 election all suggest an unstable marketplace in which language is less constrained by party loyalty and power relations than by short-term media appeals to disenchanted voters.

CHANGING ELECTORAL RHETORIC IN
THE UNITED STATES

The rhetorical and ideological ranges of American party politics have probably never been as broad as they once were in Sweden. Both Republicans and Democrats have long subscribed to the basic tenets of classical liberalism with its emphasis on individualism, free enterprise, and the limitation of governing powers. In addition, a two-party, winner-take-all system further blunts rhetorical differences, driving parties and candidates to the center of the rhetorical spectrum where they often try to outdo each other in claiming allegiance to safe "American" symbols of patriotism – defense, freedom, family, and God (Page 1978: 153). Many observers have suggested that the two parties simply represent different wings of a broadly consensual ideology of "Americanism" (Hartz 1955: Ch. 5).

All of this said, the parties displayed notable differences in their policy rhetoric in most of the elections between the mid-1930s and the mid-1970s. On economic matters, the Democrats favored free trade and protections for domestic labor, and the Republicans became identified with trade protectionism and a relatively unregulated domestic labor and wage market. The Democrats favored welfare programs against Republican opposition. The Democrats also advocated federal involvement in many areas of the economy and state government, whereas the Republicans opposed most regulation during this era of so-called cooperative federalism. These and other differences were salient enough in the 1930s to trigger a major voting realignment that made possible a thirty-year period of unprecedented Democratic dominance in social, economic, and foreign policy (Burnham 1970).

Beginning in the late 1960s, however, and accelerating in the 1970s, these rhetorical differences began to dissolve for reasons discussed in the next section. Traditional party differences on economic issues narrowed to the point at which the 1980s saw the Democrats campaign without jobs programs and related prolabor rhetoric, while adopting fiscal and monetary policies that differed little from those of the Republicans. Meanwhile, the Republicans took over traditional Democratic positions favoring free trade as they abandoned protectionist monetary policies. On the social front, the Republicans found an audience for sharp attacks against welfare along with coded racial rhetoric pitting civil rights against individual liberties. In response, the Democrats increasingly backed away from traditional liberal rhetoric in these areas. The emergence of candidate character, along with symbolic or valence issues such as crime, patriotism, government spending, and tax breaks increasingly dominated elections after Walter Mondale's disastrous attempt to campaign in 1984 on a program of fiscal responsibility through new taxes.

Having little programmatic rhetoric to offer in the absence of clear or broadly popular party visions, candidates increasingly turned to public relations experts to figure out how to reach growing numbers of disenchanted voters. The result was a vicious rhetorical cycle. Rather than building broad party coalitions, the rhetoric of the 1980s and 1990s aimed increasingly at creating short-term emotional links between individual candidates and individual voters. Rather than addressing a broad spectrum of society, the new political rhetoric tended to address the short-term emotions of independent, centrist voters who would make the numerical difference in winning the next election. Rather than risking dialogue and clarification, candidates opted for short, largely visual appeals backed up with few words. Traditional speeches gave way to soundbites – short, emotive bursts of language designed to echo the themes of political commercials and to provide verbal captions for visual images of the campaign on the nightly news. And lacking much in the way of positive proposals to offer the voters, candidates turned increasingly to negative attacks on each other. To summarize the gradual changes in rhetoric from 1930 to the early 1990s, political language shifted from a focus on governing to a focus on getting elected – from building social support for parties and their governing ideas, to creating emotional support for individual politicians who, the voters increasingly told pollsters, had no ideas.

Negative Communication: Read My Lips – No New Ideas

The 1988 campaign was regarded by many observers as a rhetorical watershed in which traditional party positions were displaced by "hot issues" developed through focus group and marketing research aimed at media strategies (Gronbeck 1990; Jamieson 1988, 1992; Manheim 1991). A sign of the times in 1988 was that with all candidates and parties fully committed to the new political communication, the average length of a candidate soundbite on the TV news plummeted to 9.2 seconds, marking a steady decline from more than 40 seconds in 1968 (Hallin 1994: 133). The tenacity of this structural change in rhetoric was revealed in the 1992 campaign when several television news organizations attempted to increase the length of reported candidate statements. For example, CBS mandated candidate quotes of at least 30 seconds but was unable to enforce that norm because speechwriters, candidates, and their handlers had adopted such firm commitments to shorter statements about their ideas.[22]

The best fit within this shrinking rhetorical space was the "dirty" rhetoric that Jamieson (1992) has described in detail. In 1988 Republican imagery was centered around attacks such as ads about the Willie Horton prison release, and a steady flow of personal attacks by George Bush on the character of Democratic candidate Michael Dukakis. At the same time, the Bush campaign effectively confused the debate on issues by positioning its candidate squarely in traditional Democratic territory as the "education candidate," the "environmental candidate," and the "jobs candidate." A study by Hershey (1989) found that, as the campaign progressed, even these issue positions were increasingly abandoned in favor of emotional images and negative attacks.

Candidate Marketing: Illusions for the Disillusioned

An important sign of the instability of this rhetorical marketplace is that such formula rhetoric may work in one election but not in the next. The negative rhetoric of the Bush campaign in 1992 was as keyed to negativity and personal attacks as in 1988, but other conditions had intervened to reduce voter responsiveness to such appeals. Few candidates have been as subjected to press criticism and personal attacks from the opposition as was Clinton in 1992, but the voters had become inoculated against such rhetoric and demanded more positive ideas, particularly in the area of solutions for a deteriorating economic situation.

The Clinton campaign (with its headquarters motto "The Economy, Stupid") addressed the economy with promises of jobs and tax remedies. In addition, a positive image of Clinton as "The Man from Hope" emerged from marketing research both to contextualize the economic promises and to counter the personal attacks that made the pejorative nickname "Slick Willie" one of the ten most repeated phrases in the print and broadcast media during the July–November period of the campaign (Miller & Pavlik 1993: 67). The "Man from Hope" image was developed in a marketing research effort that was so secretive and technologically sophisticated that it was termed "The Manhattan Project" (after the atomic bomb project) by campaign insiders (Bennett 1995). In important respects, the Republican marketing triumph of 1988 was equaled by the Democratic marketing success in 1992, and the ineptitude of the Dukakis campaign to devise a counterrhetoric in 1988 was matched by the disorganized Bush management team of 1992. Such are the fates of campaigns that must capture vast and unpredictable publics with technologically complex short-term rhetorical strategies.

However, in 1992 there were also some positive signs of market adjustment to the numerous strains between voters and candidates in 1988. Like the 1991 Swedish case (with the emergence of a new party, New Democracy, and a shift in the governing coalition), the American marketplace adjusted palpably to voter demand with the entry of Ross Perot, who ended with a stunning 19 percent of the vote. Among the signs of market adjustments in 1992 were the greater levels of satisfaction with discourse on issues; far larger audiences for (and satisfaction with) the candidates' television debates; increased turnout (up modestly from 50 percent in 1988 to 54 percent in 1992, with the largest gain of nearly 20 percent in the disaffected 18–24-year-old youth vote); and the third candidacy of Ross Perot that accounted for many of these changes, particularly the sharper definition of issues that tends to emerge in three-way races (Page 1978; Pomper 1989, 1993).

However, as in the Swedish case, the market adjustments proved to be far from stable. Indeed, there was considerable instability in the U.S. case of a third candidate without an official party structure and no hopes for converting a substantial 19 percent support level into legislative power. Even the popularity of candidates' debates on issues was an unstable market adjustment. Although these debates during the campaign undoubtedly elevated the levels of the discourse on issues, there was no mechanism for ensuring their institutionalization in future elections. To the contrary, candidate campaign managers (particularly for Bush) nearly sabotaged them, and press organizations were often at odds over the formats (Patterson 1993: 236–237).

If one looks still deeper beneath the surface of the rhetorical shifts in 1992, a number of persistent problems in the underlying institutional regulatory mechanisms give cause for continued concern. For example, despite high levels of voter discontent and large numbers of contested legislative races, the rate of incumbent victory in Congress was 90 percent. The large freshman class (that was a result of many retirements) failed to live up to promises to push campaign finance reform, with many new legislators quickly discovering the benefits of incumbency backed by PAC financing. For all the promise of change, the 1992 elections set new records of campaign spending and PAC financing. Finally, the Clinton victory, although a masterpiece of political marketing and strategic rhetorical construction, hardly changed the unstable relations among voters, parties, interests, and governing ideas. Clinton received the shortest honeymoon period in modern history and suffered defeat of his first economic initiative (a jobs program), and encountered considerable resistance on budgets, health care, and other major issues. Political commentator Kevin Phillips summarized the political mood following the 1992 election with the blunt understatement, "Voter disillusionment is clearly widespread."[23] This assessment would seem to provide no reason to change his earlier pronouncement following the 1988 election: "From the White House to Capitol Hill, the critical weakness of American politics and governance has become woefully apparent: a frightening inability to define and debate emerging problems. For the moment, the political culture appears to be brain-dead."[24]

The Ultimate in Strategic Communication: The 21 Percent Landslide

For the optimist, this critical condition of the national political intelligence may have seemed to be improving with the dramatic reversal of party power in 1994. The Republican landslide of 1994 was proclaimed to be a rebirth of popular ideas by those, like Newt Gingrich, who composed the party's "Contract with America" that called for congressional votes on a balanced budget amendment to the Constitution, and welfare reform, among other things. However, as noted in Chapter 1, the overwhelming majority of voters revealed that they had never heard of the contract. Fully 60 percent of those who voted regarded the election as a repudiation of the Democrats, and only one in six said it was an affirmation of Republican ideas. Like much of the rhetoric in the American electoral process these days, the symbolism of the "Contract" is more easily understood in campaign-based strategic terms of winning and losing than in any longer-term significance of building stable coalitions of voters united behind policy agendas.

What the Republican platform of 1994 offered the party was an opportunity to nationalize a midterm election and force the Democrats to put on a national campaign despite a weak president and a poor legislative track record after two years of Democratic Party control of government. The Republican strategy made many Democratic candidates – who were running on local issues and claiming little or no affiliation with their party or president – look as if they were hiding from the issues and from their own record. Thus, although 1994 was notable for its complete reversal of party positions in Congress and the White House in just over a two-year span, the prospects for stabilizing a national policy agenda or creating enduring understanding between voters and parties were not enhanced.

Immaculate Conception: No Parties, No Ideas,
No Government – Just Candidates

The Republican landslide of 1994 came wrapped in contradictions, paradoxes, and ironies. There was the contradiction of an election that promised (really, this time) to clean up the mess in Washington, while setting an all-time congressional campaign spending record and reaching new levels of negative campaigning. Then there was the paradox of an election called a landslide when the winning party was supported by only 21 percent of the eligible voters. Finally, there was the irony that the struggle between the two political parties had become so intense at a time when many observers and most voters considered the two parties to be hopelessly weak and ineffective, if not politically dead.

These and other contradictions of the new American politics can be seen most clearly in election contests between dinosaur parties that seem unable to settle on agendas that appeal to more than bare voting majorities. Leadership has become a battle of images among politicians whose personal ambitions (and marketing strategies) often compete with the good of their own parties. Issues in such fragmented and calculating politics are often the symbolic sort that move voters emotionally in the short term without leaving much of a lasting mark on social problems in the long run. All these add up to a system that is rapidly undermining the basic assumptions of democracy itself.

Perhaps the most troublesome development of the new politics is a reversal of the very idea of elections and representation. Traditional assumptions about democracy describe a system in which representatives are sent to government to push for issues that won them votes in the last election. We are now approaching a system in which promises from the last election are routinely sacrificed to strategic calculations about how to win the next one. Issues that matter to people – health care being a good example – often become chewed up in calculations about how to make opponents in government look weak and ineffective in the eyes of their former supporters. The irony is that playing politics with important issues makes all sides look bad. Perhaps the ultimate irony is that these same politicians campaign against the very ills of government that they have helped to create. This political world has become a dizzying play of symbols in the news and advertising, with the Capitol being condemned most vigorously by those who most want to work there. As one top campaign consultant described the symbolic uses of the Capitol building in 1994 campaign ads: "It rattles, it shakes, it opens up, money is poured into it; it's clear that it has become demonized."[25]

In this upside-down world, where parties may regard issues more as opportunities to defeat each other than as means of delivering government to the people, one might even ask why parties bother to contest elections at all. The obvious answer in the new American politics is that parties remain the strategic mechanisms for handing out power to individual members who still need political bases from which to reward their financial backers and continue advancing their careers.

The unexpectedly quick return to gridlock following the Democratic sweep of power in 1992 in part reflected the fact that the political fortunes of individual members of Congress depend less on loyalty to party or president than ever before. Congressional careers today develop through the efforts of individual politician–entrepreneurs who attract financial support from organized interests, deliver government services to states and home districts, and proclaim their allegiance to parties and presidents when it seems politically expedient to do so. During the 1994 California Senate race, for example, Democratic incumbent Dianne Feinstein recognized Bill Clinton's appeal to wealthy liberals by embracing him at a Beverly Hills fundraiser that produced nearly $1 million for her expensive campaign against Republican challenger Michael Huffington, who was spending a sizable portion of his personal fortune to get elected. Yet Feinstein also withdrew as a legislative sponsor of the Clinton health plan after polls showed that the president's name on the plan caused public support to "sink like a rock," as one health care analyst put it.[26] Another example of the absence of party loyalty was provided by the congressional campaign brochure of Georgia Democrat Craig Mathis, which according to one observer offered "prospective voters no clue as to whether Mr. Mathis is a Democrat, a Republican, or some kind of hybrid."[27] As *Time* magazine observed, the casual observer of the 1994 campaigns might "suppose that no one is a Democrat – especially the Democrats."[28]

In fact, in the 1994 elections, the president's pollster Stanley Greenberg advised Democratic candidates to emphasize their own records rather than their ties to the president or the party. He even issued a memo advising candidates how to respond to Republican attacks that they were liberals, Democrats, or Clinton supporters. In his "Strategic Guide to the 1994 Election," Greenberg advised candidates to make campaign issues of "their accomplishments and their agenda to help people at home." Greenberg continued, "There is no reason to highlight [your accomplishments] as Clinton or Democratic proposals."[29]

Typical of the new electoral politics, this advice echoes a similar warning issued in the 1990 midterm election by Edward Rollins, then chair of the Republican congressional campaign committee. President Bush had damaged his popularity by agreeing to a tax hike that toppled his famous 1988 campaign pledge: "Read my lips. No new taxes." Rollins bluntly told candidates that inviting President Bush to help them campaign or otherwise identifying with him could "fatally wound your campaign."[30]

Bill Clinton geared up his 1996 campaign by staking out his own independent position on balancing the budget – a move that angered congressional Democrats, who accused the president of going his own way and undermining the party position. It is hard to imagine Clinton subordinating his own political fortunes to the solidarity of a party that had made his legislative life so difficult and had squandered its first solid grasp of governing power in more than a dozen years.

The New Washington Power Game

The conventional wisdom in Washington today is that political clout is directly linked to media images and public approval ratings. In the view of CNN pollster and pundit William Schneider, Washington is a town of individual political entrepreneurs who rely less on parties for their political support than on their own media images, along with the popularity of visible politicians like the president.[31] Consider, for example, the decision of Representative Lee Hamilton (D–Indiana) to vote with those who temporarily blocked the president's 1994 crime bill at a crucial moment in both Clinton's and the party's effort to make good on campaign promises from the election.

Hamilton, a key player in Washington and a prominent member of the Democratic party establishment, defected from the party leadership on a key election-year issue with this explanation:

> The basic nature of American politics has changed. I don't get elected because of what Bill Clinton thinks or what the House leadership thinks. The electorate makes up its own mind. That inevitably means that presidents have a lot less clout with Congress than they used to have. All presidents, I mean.
>
> It's also true that when a President is riding high his influence goes up, and when a President is in the dumps the way Clinton is, his influence declines.[32]

The electoral marketplace is characterized by chameleon candidates, disappearing parties, and fears of voter backlash against incumbents – particularly those who proclaim that government might be a useful means of solving society's problems. Such changes in the relations among voters, candidates, and parties described throughout the book signal new patterns of power in the American political system.

The key question is: How did all this occur?

The Negative Equilibrium in the United States

In this brief review, we can consider only several of the historical turning points in modern American politics, along with how they engaged market regulatory mechanisms in ways that changed the production and distribution of language in the electoral marketplace. Political communication has been fundamentally altered by changes in parties, campaign finance, and interest group politics.

If there was a single fateful event in the slide of the Democratic Party in presidential politics, it was probably the signing by Lyndon Johnson of the civil rights laws of the mid-1960s. Johnson himself recognized the political perils involved. After signing the Civil Rights Act of 1964, he remarked to an aide, "I think we just delivered the South to the Republican Party for a long time to come."[33] Although the subsequent election in 1968 was complicated by the third-party candidacy of George Wallace, the landslide Republican victory of 1972 over liberal Democrat George McGovern seemed ripe with the possibility of a Republican realignment. Continued Democratic support for civil rights, welfare, and federal interventions in state politics fueled the successful Republican rhetoric of race, morality, states rights, and free enterprise. Traditional Democratic voter support began to erode, particularly in the South. Democratic party identification, once at 47 percent of the electorate in the 1950s, began a steady slide that reached lows of just above one third of the electorate at the beginning of the 1990s.[34]

The great puzzle, however, is not so much why the Democrats lost voters but why the Republican realignment never materialized. Or to put the question slightly differently, why did so many voters who abandoned the Democrats choose to remain independents? Although the Republicans picked up some strength at the beginning of the 1970s, the path to large-scale realignment was blocked first by the historical event of the Watergate scandal of 1972 to 1974 and then by the restructuring of the electoral marketplace in its wake.

With both parties suffering credibility gaps by the mid-1970s and large numbers of voters staying put as independents, the crucial regulatory mechanism of the party system was destabilized. Next, the Democrats temporarily seized the political initiative and damaged a second regulatory mechanism by passing a series of *campaign finance reforms* that set in motion changes in the other mechanisms regulating the marketplace of ideas. A series of Federal Election Campaign Acts during the 1970s limited individual campaign contributions, created partial public funding of presidential elections, and permitted limited candidate and virtually unlimited party funding by PACs, something that at the time appeared to be a modest loophole. Although they had existed as means of labor union support for the Democrats since the 1940s, PACs were elevated by the new system to being the main method for corporations and interest groups to channel money to individual candidates, parties, and directly into independent campaigns for and against candidates and issues (Alexander 1992: 23–47; Sabato 1985: 3–27).

Although having some positive effects on the electoral process, the new finance laws gave a third regulatory mechanism, *interest groups*, more direct leverage in the electoral market than had ever existed before (Malbin 1984). Business interests, along with groups promoting issues from the environment to abortion, quickly realized the opportunities for funding parties and, more important, individual candidates who supported their causes. Parties already weakened by their inability to respond to the historic challenges of the 1960s and 1970s now were challenged by more independent voters to forge new rhetorical visions – a task made all the more difficult because individual candidates were less disciplined as party members owing to their personalized sources of funding (Bennett 1996b: Ch 4).

It became increasingly clear as this system emerged that potential campaign promises and party policies were filtered through the interests of campaign contributors and increasingly independent individual candidates, further moving the rhetoric of elections away from parties and ideological visions and toward individual candidates who had little to offer voters beyond advertising themes and personal images. In one view (Ferguson & Rogers 1986), the competition between Democrats and Republicans for the same campaign money created an ideological right turn among the Democratic leadership, who grew increasingly out of step with large numbers of still-liberal voters. Another view (Domhoff 1990) is that the financial pressures were far less organized and ideologically coherent, producing instead simple party fragmentation. In either case, the rhetorical results were a decline in policy differences that voters regarded as meaningful and a growing emphasis on candidate images and the marketing methods required to create them. Election campaigns became increasingly run by marketing experts relying on Madison Avenue image techniques to replace broader social appeals that were being driven out of circulation by the campaign finance process.

Of course, selling candidates like soft drinks or soap detergents had been going on in limited ways for at least thirty years (Diamond & Bates 1992). But the wholesale use of these techniques combined with the massive intrusion of special interests behind the scenes were more recent developments, and they met with little approval from the electorate. Or, as a leading advocate of reforming the recently reformed system put it:

We've always experienced individual cases of corruption and impropriety in government. But today we have a system of institutionalized corruption. The rules themselves allow activities to take place legally that are improper and corrupting.... Washington insiders argue that the American people don't really care about Washington's ethics mess. They're wrong. But what's happening is even more dangerous than what they perceive as indifference on the part of the American public.

The American people are moving beyond outrage to a state of deep cynicism. They are reaching a state of "no expectations" about our government leaders. And in a democracy, that's a red flag alert. There cannot be a fundamental erosion of ethical values at the seat of government without grave consequences for the nation. (Wertheimer 1989: 45)

These facts place a slightly different interpretation on the Reagan Revolution, along with the failure of the long-predicted Republican realignment, the successful Democratic defense of Congress, and the style of the emerging political rhetoric in general. To begin with, the Reagan rhetoric was successful but within the narrow limits of a shrinking voting population. Those who responded to the rhetoric of race, morality, abortion, and states' rights were enough to keep the Republicans in the White House, but the so-called landslides of 1980, 1984, and 1988 were produced by fewer than 30 percent of the eligible voting population. The point is that the rhetoric of the new right rallied only a minority of the potential electorate, leaving the prospects for a Republican realignment dashed by a combination of nonvoters and split-ticket voters who voted Democratic for Congress. Meanwhile, the Democrats were unable to produce a competitive rhetorical program at the presidential level, relying instead on increasingly individualized campaigns, pork barrel politics, and constituent service delivery in home districts to strengthen their hold on Congress. An economic downturn, a disorganized Republican campaign (buoyed by false confidence in early polls), and an effective marketing effort for Bill Clinton in a three-way race turned the presidential tide in 1992. Yet the voter coalitions and the party governing agendas appeared no more stable or predictable when one looked ahead to 1996 and beyond to 2000. The 21 percent landslide of 1994 was hardly a party realignment. In an age without coherent political parties, the very idea of a realignment becomes meaningless.

The limits of rhetoric in the modern era speak to the evolution of a marketplace increasingly unresponsive to consumer (i.e., voter) demand. As Entman (1989) has explained so clearly, the peril of contemporary communication is that it constructs a democracy without citizens. This is not just an accident of the passive relationship between the receiver and the sender of electronic messages; it is becoming a basic operating assumption of those who create the messages in the first place. With its emphasis on market research and images aimed at the short-term emotions of strategically targeted voter groups, the logic of the emerging rhetoric is not geared to expand the voting ranks, much less to develop broad governing visions. As Paul Weyrich, one of the chief engineers of the Reagan Revolution, put it in a moment of candor: "I don't want everyone to vote. Our leverage in the election quite candidly goes up as the voting populace goes down" (Ferguson & Rogers 1981: 4).

The production of rhetoric designed for small numbers of centrist voters creates little incentive to use language that might strengthen party identification, sharpen ideological differences, or increase voter turnouts. All the market regulatory mechanisms have contributed to this communication pattern: (1) the loss of *party* cohesion, (2) which has been magnified by changes in methods of *election finance*, (3) which results in increased *interest group* influence on individual candidates, and (4) all leading individual candidates to rely heavily on advertising and marketing methods, along with the techniques of press management in order to control their images in the *media*. Although we could begin at any point in this vicious cycle, we summarize this alignment of institutional effects on communication as follows, starting with the media:

- The increasing reliance on television advertising drives up the costs of campaigning, producing more reliance on the PAC finance system.
- Individual candidates need large sums of money to run competitive races and so become dependent on the interests that finance campaigns, giving those interests tacit veto power over rhetoric that might restore voter interest and confidence.
- Narrowing the range of rhetoric further discourages voters, making them harder to reach, which reinforces candidate reliance on marketing and drives up costs.
- The costs of campaigning, combined with the personalized finance system, give a huge advantage to incumbents who can use office and power to attract money, which helps to explain why incumbents are reelected despite the unpopularity of their rhetoric.
- Unpopular rhetoric leads to increased reliance on television advertising and press management techniques, thus reinforcing the cycle.

These are the dynamics of a market that has settled into a negative equilibrium, unable to restore the production of competitive, favorably regarded communication on a stable, long-term basis. This market analysis also suggests various regulatory solutions to stimulate the production of more satisfying ideas in the electoral system. Reforms could be achieved by changing the rules or laws affecting the operation of the regulatory mechanisms (e.g., prohibiting paid television advertising, providing public financing for legislative races, and dismantling the PAC system). Such reform possibilities highlight the reasons the regulatory model is useful. It is the market and not just individual psychology that governs the production and effects of rhetoric. It is unreasonable to expect the efforts of individual candidates or voters to bring about meaningful changes. In fact, given the regulatory constraints operating in the current market, both individual candidates and voters are behaving rationally. For their part, adrift from party ideologies and pressed by financial supporters, candidates use the communication methods still available to them to get themselves elected. Voters either boycott elections, or if they decide to vote, they make the best sense of the symbolism they are given. The irony is that the sum of these rational individual responses to a poorly regulated market leaves both parties and voters collectively worse off. For these reasons, changing the communication between individual actors depends on changing the rules and market incentives governing the production and exchange of ideas in the marketplace itself.

CONCLUSION

It is not surprising that changes in society are reflected in changed public demands and political loyalties. The key question, however, is how do leaders and parties adjust to new political circumstances? In both Sweden and the United States, to varying degrees, the response has been to rely on technologies of polling, marketing, and media management to secure short-term voter support. Bombarded with fragile images and promises that dissolve upon election, voters understand they are being manipulated and become ever more distrustful. The growth of cynicism, in turn, sends parties and candidates in search of new short-term appeals.

This vicious cycle has begun to change the nature of electoral rhetoric. If it is an exaggeration to speak of the end of rhetoric, it is no exaggeration to talk about the end of certain assumptions about public discourse long held by citizens and communication scholars alike. Perhaps most important, it is no longer reasonable to assume that political communication between candidates and voters is governed by stable ideological (or at least principled thematic) exchanges that are cued to parties and linked to responsive institutional power arrangements. In this increasingly atomized or personalized election process, it is not even clear that voter dissatisfaction will somehow condition the way candidates communicate. The strategy behind contemporary rhetoric is actually enhanced when voters abandon the political process. Rhetorical battles are fought these days for smaller numbers of centrist voters (precisely the ones with the least party loyalty), and so the loss of large numbers makes the job of targeting and test marketing easier. The spiral of short-term, strategic communication means that parties lose support from their loyal cadres who no longer hear familiar words or commitments to ideology (or do not believe partisan rhetoric about issues when they hear it). At this and every turn in the emerging communication process, the language of politics wears away memory, undermines loyalty, and raises doubts, even as it influences last-minute decisions to vote this way or that.

The market of ideas, no longer regulated by voters and ideological or policy-driven parties, becomes regulated by other mechanisms. Those factors (e.g., the media, interests, finance) have always been part of the regulation of idea markets, but in recent years they have been working more independently of (rather than in concert with) the traditional (party and voter) bases of elections. In the U.S. case, organized interests, campaign finance mechanisms, and media technologies increasingly determine election results independently of voter wishes and past party traditions. In Sweden, successful efforts to set the media agenda around centrist positions drives voter preferences to the margins, leaving little room for the marketplace to adjust.

PART IV

MAKING DEMOCRACY WORK

7

Reinventing Communication by Reforming Institutions

This black mood is no monopoly of America's. Britons are feeling sleazy; the French are having another bout of *morosité;* Italians ask whether they will ever get a clean-handed government, even Japan, for once, wonders where its politicians are taking it. The G7, with maybe a half-exception for Germany, is the Grumpy Seven.

– The Economist

Our analysis of language, institutions, and the decline of governing ideas in the United States and Sweden has been guided by three basic propositions. The first is that ideas and language matter in political life – that they have consequences and often shape public policies as well as public attitudes and political actions. It is likewise clear that ideas and the rhetoric used to convey those ideas mobilize support or opposition around particular policies, however well or poorly conceived those policies may be. Second, we have taken the marketplace of ideas as a point of departure and proposed a way of understanding how rhetoric is produced, used politically, and exchanged for political support in two very different polities. In all idea markets, the keys to production, valuation, exchange, and consumer satisfaction are the kinds of institutional regulatory processes at work. We outlined four broad regulatory mechanisms that can be found in various configurations in all liberal democracies: electoral and party systems, campaign finance practices, interest group systems, and mass media. Third, we contend that the institutional forms and interactions among these regulatory mechanisms constrain the production, distribution, and valuation of ideas in elections and public policy debates. The uses of this framework for comparative analysis were illustrated with case studies of the following:

1. The rise and fall of two important governing ideas: the New Deal in the United States and the *folkhem* in Sweden.
2. The United States (1986) and Swedish (1990) tax reforms.
3. The candidate and party rhetoric in recent American and Swedish national elections.

Our primary interest has been to understand how governing ideas are produced in different political systems and how these systems respond to the decline of ideas and the growing disjunctures among parties, leaders, publics, and the agendas of governments. This perspective offers a new comparative approach to the often ignored intersection of language, institutions, and mass political communication. Using two very different political systems such as those of the United States and Sweden may seem like a daring enterprise from a comparative point of view. However, we are convinced that our approach has yielded valuable results precisely because the two cases are so different. Above all, using a comparative approach has enabled us, to quote an often used book, "to go beyond description (what? when? how?) towards the more fundamental goal of explanation (why?)" (Hague & Harrop 1982: 7).

What we have found, generally speaking, is that the institutional mechanisms that regulate public communication in our two cases tend to work against the revitalization of governing ideas and spirited debates on public policy. Although it is clearly more developed in the United States than in Sweden, the drift our cases reveal toward what we have called a negative equilibrium in the marketplace is characterized by unstable communication environments, a decline of party loyalties and voting participation, along with a widespread loss of faith in politicians and their rhetoric. The lack of guiding visions and the reluctance of parties and leaders to engage in searching national debates accentuate the spiraling discontent of publics and the fragmentation of traditional forms of governing powers. The rhetoric of candidates and leaders alike often encourages citizens to seek private gain from government rather than common good. Societies become pockets of isolated and often suspicious groups easily led by the languages of personal economic interest, racial animosity, and mistrust of others. These failures of the political imagination further undermine the possibility for broad visions of society that might promote identification across groups and mobilize support for enduring agendas of political action.

The first of our three case studies on the rise and demise of governing ideas shows how public discourse has eroded over the years and how the processes of communication have changed. The New Deal clearly defined a new role for government in the United States. At the same time, the evolution of an ideologically independent response to the conservative (classical liberal) tradition was stunted by an unwieldy Democratic party that appealed to an ever-expanding coalition of interests and a shifting collection of financial backers. The intellectual strains of these divisive factors (along with media coverage that dramatized them) made it possible for the Republican opposition to sustain a conservative ideological agenda that was severely challenged by the economic and social crises of the 1920s and 1930s. The *folkhem* idea in Sweden continued to develop through a solitary party that prospered under a system of cohesive finance arrangements and a corporatist interest group process. As a result, the governing ideas of the Social Democrats were instrumental in cementing a culture of consensus and structuring both election rhetoric and policy debates in much of the post–World War II period. For reasons discussed later in this chapter, both visions became hard to sell rhetorically, and they eventually fell into considerable disrepute. However, it took much longer for that to happen in Sweden than in the United States, and the Social Democratic agenda has retained some political strength, indicating that the flow of ideas operates differently in the Swedish marketplace.

The second of our case studies explored the interplay of institutions and ideas in the policy process by analyzing the politics of tax reform in the two countries. If our first case study is an example of communication as *agenda setting*, the second one could be labeled communication as *policy choice*. The tax reforms were quite similar in substance but led to very different public opinion responses. The more easily controlled and eventually closed Swedish idea market produced a more sweeping tax reform that attracted more public support than did the less regulated American market. Ronald Reagan's failure to win public support for his tax plan was caused primarily by his inability to control the various institutional mechanisms that were engaged by the issue and that generated competing ideas all the way through the policy process. By contrast, the Swedish reformers in the end simply withdrew from playing the public opinion and voter markets and ceased efforts to construct a convincing tax message. Such a rhetorical strategy was not available to their American counterparts. These cases both show how grand political symbols such as fairness can become confounded and deflated as they move through various institutional contexts. The comparison also illustrates the importance of different institutional designs for regulating such nonverbal aspects of mass communication as noise levels, the timing of actions, and the unified endorsements of authorities.

Our third case study, dealing with candidate–party rhetoric in recent national elections, illustrates how short-term communication strategies have replaced governing ideas as the basis for exchanges between voters and leaders. In both the United States and Sweden, leaders and parties, to varying degrees, adjust their messages by relying on technologies of polling, marketing, and media management to secure short-term voter support. The growth of voter cynicism, in turn, sends parties and candidates in search of new (and even emptier) short-term appeals. This vicious circle has begun to change the nature of electoral rhetoric, leading to more personalized messages and negative attacks. Thus, the marketplace of ideas is increasingly regulated by mechanisms that pull at the coherence of broad governing visions. Important national differences in the rules for party representation, the methods of campaign finance, and the political uses of the media affect the capacity of parties and candidates to respond meaningfully to voter demands and distress. These differences in the institutional regulation of electoral discourse reveal different patterns of market adjustment and suggest alternative strategies for election and party reform.

Both the United States and Sweden, then, have been experiencing surprisingly similar political communication patterns and problems. In both societies, the core institutions of politics and the media have been limiting the terms of national debate and thereby adversely affecting the production of ideas in the marketplace. At the same time, our approach also helps to clarify the fact that the two nations face different kinds of institutional limitations, which in turn lead to differences in policy outcomes as well as in levels of public satisfaction. Among the key differences found in these studies are the following:

- Our case studies show that the U.S. idea market is overall more open and competitive – or at least it is less coherently regulated – than the Swedish one.
- Because of this unregulated competition, however, the American idea market has produced less sustainable governing ideas, a less sweeping and popular tax reform, and higher levels of political fragmentation and voter frustration. The extent to which the political process has fragmented in the United States since the early 1960s, with accompanying effects on communication and rhetorical practices, probably has no parallel in any modern democracy in the world (cf. Dahl 1993: 447–448).

- Despite being more closed and controlled (although less so in recent years), the Swedish idea market over time has produced more lasting governing ideas and witnessed a dramatic overhaul of the tax system, which eventually resulted in a high level of popular support. In addition, the range of viewpoints in the Swedish electoral arena is still comparatively wide, which makes it possible for new parties and movements to air their views and to be incorporated into the public dialogue (as shown by the fact that three new parties entered Parliament in the period from 1988 to 1994).

- Governing ideas in a society dissipate faster and meet with stiffer opposition in a less regulated communication system than in a more regulated marketplace. The reason is that the coordination, or rationalization, among the institutional mechanisms that shape political communication is much looser in an unregulated system than in a more regulated one.

- However, both systems have great problems in reforming themselves as well as in generating and sustaining new political ideas, a point that we expand upon below.

A general conclusion that follows from these results is that not only do ideas and rhetoric matter in the political life of nations; they are also shaped by a nation's political institutions. Whether idea markets function well or poorly depends on how their constituent regulatory mechanisms are integrated and whether some mechanisms dominate at the expense of the others. In the U.S. case it seems clear that the combination of weak parties, strong pressure groups, and a more reactive, drama-oriented media system encourage personalization and negativity in public communication while discouraging the deliberative communication necessary for ideas to develop into positive governing agendas (Fishkin 1991; Patterson 1993). In the Swedish case, the combination of fairly strong parties and interest groups, coupled with a publicly financed election system and media, points in another and less ominous direction. But it is the way that these combinations have developed in each culture that makes them unique and that helps to explain the different outcomes detected in this study.

What is perhaps most puzzling about these two systems is that they have taken such different political paths and yet have arrived at similar sticking points. The differences dramatize the basic problem that must be overcome if reforms are to happen in these faltering democratic orders: The very institutions that have disrupted the communication links between citizens and their representatives also are the basis of maintaining political power in each system. When parties and politicians in both nations were confronted with the prospect of reinventing themselves at the risk of losing power – a state of affairs that emerged earlier in the United States than in Sweden – they

turned to short-term, marketing-based communication strategies to maintain their positions in government. Understanding how two such different
systems arrived at much the same general point is essential for thinking about
reforms that might restore the legitimacy of government as the engine of
popular ideas.

POWER VS. IDEAS:
TWO PATHS TO DEMOCRATIC INSTABILITY

Perhaps the major difference in the Swedish and the American experiences
since the 1930s is that the Social Democrats in Sweden have been largely able
to realize their governing vision in ways that fundamentally transformed society. Neither of the American parties has had anything approaching such
policy success – each leaving a legacy of unfinished agendas and compromises that became symbolic targets for social division and political blame.
Our framework helps to explain both how the Swedish case became more
fully realized and why political processes in both nations now weigh against
new ideas as actively as they once encouraged them.

The assertion that the *folkhem* vision was largely realized must be qualified
by noting that some policy sectors in the Swedish Social Democratic regime
were more fully developed than others. For example, Rothstein (1986) cites
the greater attention to and allocation of political talent to labor policies than
to education. It is interesting that his analysis points more to political choices
and resource allocation within the ruling party than to limits imposed by regulatory institutions on the scope of the overall party vision or its appeal to
voters. The fact remains that the Social Democrats were able to put their ideas
into action in such systematic ways that even opposition parties subscribed to
many of them (Tilton 1991). The ironic result is that the successful implementation of so much of the party's governing agenda moved large numbers
of Swedes out of the lower classes and into middle-class conditions, resulting
in a declining base of support for the original ideas.

The quest for power, however, continues after agendas are fulfilled. The
same institutions that enabled government to implement the Social Democratic program now have the task of keeping the party in power even though
its rhetoric consists more of slogans and issues stolen from opponents. Recall
here the rhetorical evolution outlined in Chapter 6: from the *folkhem* vision,

to more isolated issue positions within that vision, to stealing popular issues from opponents, to broad slogans such as "Sweden is unique," and "Sweden can do better." As this evolution has occurred, the uses of institutional power bases (from interest group mobilization, to campaign finance, to the management of the media, to the party's own considerable electoral and bureaucratic organization) have all grown increasingly at odds with the rhetoric about what the purpose of governing should be. Perhaps the greatest irony of all is that the post-1994 party confronted the task of downsizing the welfare state that it had built in earlier years.

By contrast, the Democratic Party vision for American society fell far short of policy realization, even as it went through successive revivals under such names as New Deal, New Frontier, Great Society, and New Covenant. Much of the reason for this, we believe, is that a coherent intellectual alternative to conservatism was never fully achieved in the United States (recall the analysis in Chapter 3). The single principle of government activism born of the New Deal and sustained through a long period of Democratic Party rule was not separated ideologically – or, recalling the *folkhem*, even metaphorically – from the underlying conservative principles of individual freedom and free economic enterprise. The result was a self-limiting tendency built into both the policy agenda of Democratic politics as well as into the communication between liberal politicians and voters. Meanwhile, the absence of a fully independent political challenge gave the Republicans little incentive to reinvent their basic governing vision – turning instead to more divisive concerns about how to accommodate religious and moralistic agendas within it.

Although the incomplete American break with conservatism can be traced to the pragmatic origins of the New Deal, more surprising is the subsequent failure of liberals to articulate a broader, more independent set of ideas, as their lone tenet of activist government came under attack repeatedly from the Truman administration on. The rhetorical path taken instead, as indicated in Figure 3-1 (page 73), was simply to add more promises and programs to appeal to party constituencies that were more diverse and poorly integrated. The rhetorical whole became considerably less than the sum of its parts, leaving party leaders with little to say in defense of Ronald Reagan's outrageous charge from the 1980s that the Democrats were the real party of the special interests in America. Even when the Democrats gained power in the White House in 1992, the divisions and party paralysis on such crucial issues as health care and labor policy sent them to stinging defeat in Congress just two years later. One of their own leaders pronounced the 1994 election to be the final judgment on the fragile governing vision born of the New Deal and embattled ever since. According to Al From, president of the Democratic Leadership Council (DLC), the New Deal finally ended in 1994: " The old New Deal coalition is gone. It's dead. It's Humpty Dumpty" (White 1995: 1).

It is interesting that From cited Humpty Dumpty to refer to the language that once held the coalition together. We cannot imagine a more appropriate metaphor. It is equally interesting that Bill Clinton addressed the DLC after the 1994 election and acknowledged the importance of "fighting for ideas," yet his recommendation was not for an encompassing thematic vision to enlist society's diverse groups in common purpose. He endorsed, instead, a top-ten list to match the points (introduced by marketers) in the Republican Contract with America:

> We've got to engage the Republicans in a spirit of genuine partnership and say, you have some new ideas; we do too; let's have a contest of ideas.
>
> The best thing [the DLC] can do is what you have done – put out ten new ideas as a counterpoint to the Republican contract. That is the best thing you can do. Let's stand on that. Let's fight for those ideas. (White 1995: 24)

As might be expected, the Democratic top-ten list was quickly forgotten, and Clinton's New Covenant had a hollow ring to it. Perhaps the motives in both cases were so transparent as to defy higher principle. The clear political objective, far from rallying the nation's warring social factions around a project of national renewal, was merely a marketer's goal of winning the middle-class vote. After acknowledging that "Everybody knows that all is not well with America," Clinton went on to acknowledge that "everybody" really meant the middle-class burghers whose political outlooks he characterized as being at the lowest levels of personal psychology: "I'm doing everything I can – I'm working a longer work week. I can't afford a vacation anymore. I'm paying more for health care. I may lose my job tomorrow. My kid could get shot on the way to school. And all my money is going to people who misbehave" (White 1995: 24).

Some Democratic Party intellectuals have proposed reinventing the party around more powerful and enduring visions, such as the restoration of community and family (see Bennett 1996b: Chs. 2, 10). However, the inability to achieve consensus within a diverse and internally fragmented political organization has left the task of communication with the public to pollsters, marketers, and image consultants. Hence, the chosen strategic focus on person-alistic rhetoric aimed at stereotypical middle-class psychology.

Meanwhile, the Republicans have appropriated the core vocabulary of cul-tural symbols (family, community, flag, and freedom) as their own. The con-temporary rhetoric of the conservative movement, from Ralph Reed to Kevin Phillips to Rush Limbaugh to Newt Gingrich, has managed to cast govern-ment itself as the reason for the demise of family, community, and freedom in America. Yet, the narrowly conservative definition of these core symbols (along with what many people perceive to be a mean-spirited attitude on the part of the right) has limited their popular appeal to not much more than the symbols of the Democrats. The ironic result is that, despite having taken the symbolic high ground, Republican communication has come to depend on marketing and short-term communication strategies as much as that of the Democrats. As noted earlier in this chapter and in Chapter 6, the Contract with America was less a coherent program of ideas that captured the popu-lar imagination than a top-ten list of marketing ploys. The party's determi-nation to run through the list in its first 100 days in power further illustrates the tunnel vision with which governing ideas are viewed by politicians these days – even by the more ideologically coherent of the two American parties.

If the endurance of traditional Republican principles can be attributed to the failure of a strong challenge from the Democrats, the reasons for the Democratic shortcomings are less apparent. It is too easy to say that the American culture is resistant to socialism and leftist ideas. As the case of Sweden illustrates so well, however, an alternative to conservatism need not have been framed rhetorically in blatant ideological terms such as socialism (which was, after all, the charge that was continually lodged against the lib-eral wing of the Democratic Party from the New Deal onward). Rather, fol-lowing the example of the *folkhem*, the American left might have contem-plated a symbolic regime based on some image of community and family. As noted in Chapter 3, the failure to develop a coherent rhetorical program – whether ideological or metaphorical – had to do with the fragmenting effects of interests and campaign finance and the difficulty of sustaining media focus against the more easily framed Republican definitions of Democratic actions. It is telling that at the moment Lyndon Johnson signed the Civil Rights Act into law – marking the greatest Democratic Party achievement of the era – he feared for the very survival of the party coalition.

The importance of a broad and easily grasped set of ideas cannot be un-derestimated. To return to the central point, the crucial difference between the Swedish Social Democrats and the American Democratic Party is the difference between a party that realized its political agenda and one that did not. As a result, the Social Democrats must resort to strategic communication because its former audience has been largely satisfied – a factor that urges greater caution in the Swedish reform proposals to be discussed shortly. By contrast, the Democrats in the United States never provided a vision that was coherent enough to hold the attention of a popular following long enough to implement the vision. Meanwhile, the Republicans never experienced the intellectual challenge needed to expand their vision to appeal to a strong governing majority. Thus, from the new Nixon to the Reagan Revolution to the landslide of 1994, the GOP has operated increasingly with marketing strategies that assume limited popular participation and interest in politics. In short, the Democratic agenda has been exhausted short of fulfillment, and the Republican agenda has if anything grown more divisive and exclusive since the 1970s, leaving both American parties dependent on strategic communication to maintain power. The key to resolving the dilemmas – more in the American system than the Swedish – is to reform the institutions that are currently being used to maintain power for its own sake, thereby blocking the market operations that might generate new directions for government.

INSTITUTIONAL REFORMS AND COMMUNICATION CHANGE

Because the communication problems in the United States are more developed and their effects on the health of democratic participation are more acute, the required institutional reforms are more extensive. The pattern in the American case is one of nearly complete breakdown of integrating linkages among parties, interest groups, finance, and media. The Swedish case, by contrast, requires perhaps less drastic reforms aimed primarily at discouraging strategic communication that prevents an otherwise more coherent set of political institutions from adjusting to new political conditions.

Institutional Changes in the United States

In light of the analysis throughout the book, it should come as no surprise that campaign finance reform looms as the major reform needed in the United States.

Not only would finance reform reduce the chaotic pressures that pull candidates away from party positions, but it might also check the power of interest groups in the legislative process. Accompanying reforms of the lobbying process would help to assure the latter result. When Congress became embroiled in a dangerous ethics war during the closing years of the 1980s, calmer heads negotiated a cease-fire, for it quickly became apparent that nearly everyone could be taken down by ethics charges. One marvels at the rich array of creative financing programs the members had worked out: breakfast clubs, free air travel, honoraria, dubious book sales, huge bankrolls of unspent "campaign" contributions, questionable investment opportunities, lobbying services for clients with little or no base in a member's home district, and the list goes on. The representation system itself seemed to be undergoing a transformation from one based in geography and votes to one anchored in high finance and influence.

Reforms in campaign finance must affect all levels of politics from the president and Congress to local offices. Since we are talking about a system of influence, it will do little good to correct one part of the problem without attending to all of it. Electing a president with his or her own ideas for a change will have little consequence if Congress throws up a wall of special interest resistance to putting those ideas into action. The same parallel applies to state and local politics.

The dilemma of finance reform is that the parties that maintain their power through the finance system are in charge of changing it. If finance reforms of the mid-1970s and early 1980s helped to create the new American politics, the political advantages of that same money machine have kept elected officials from dismantling it in recent years. The story of recent finance reform efforts follows much the same plot, no matter which party has just won power on a promise to clean up the mess in Washington: foot dragging, weak measures, lack of party solidarity, and much posturing and moralizing for the benefit of the media.[1]

The most frustrating characteristic of the many failed reform efforts is that even if they had been passed, they were all too weak to make much of a difference in the election system that underlies the governing crisis. Research by Krasno and Green (1993) shows that none of the reforms proposed in the past decade would have seriously altered either the incumbent advantage in elections or the huge emphasis on the monetary alliances that have warped political priorities. For example, their models indicate that spending limits of

$300,000 in House races would have to be set in order to give challengers much of an assist against the incumbent's advantage. Yet current incumbent spending averages are over $500,000, and the spending limit proposed in the Democratic bill that passed the House during the 103rd Congress was $600,000. The Republican landslide of 1994 was produced with cash infusions that would have chafed under serious limits, illustrating the reasons for popular skepticism about the idea of "politician, reform thyself." We suggest ways to press for serious reforms. What kind of finance reform would make a difference?

- First, eliminate PAC contributions to political campaigns. Contributions to party organizations might be permitted, but state and national parties should be severely restricted in soft money spending during the several months prior to election day. (Soft money is the virtually unregulated and hard to monitor funding of party activities that are not directly tied to particular candidate contests.) Let party-building activities take place between, not during, elections.
- Next, set spending limits on campaigns, and index those limits according to the office and the size of the district. To observe Supreme Court rulings that political finance is a form of free speech, set spending limits on those who voluntarily accept public funding. In conjunction with the other reforms that follow, it is possible to imagine spending limits set at half or even a third of current spending averages.
- Finally, create a system of public funding for both congressional challengers and incumbents. It would be possible to modify various European models, as we note later. How would federal moneys be allocated? Under the most obvious scheme, funds could be given to parties in proportion to their strength in Congress or, at state levels, in the legislature. Party nominees would then be granted shares of the party fund based on the numbers of voters in their districts. This would encourage greater ideological or issue linkages between candidates and party organizations, and it would encourage parties to run better candidates against incumbents in the other party. Fancier schemes could include incentives based on some measure of party and candidate performance in the last election.

Although no system of financing is perfect or free of corruption, a financial index based on some linkage between party programs and voter support is preferable to the current system in which candidate and party bank accounts are indexed directly to PAC and private investor support. This system would be all the stronger if the two-party dominance of American politics could be gradually replaced by steps toward a proportional representation system. Such a system, as noted later, would invite a government reform party to emerge and challenge the existing parties in ways that might produce more meaningful reforms. A government reform party with a national political standing would be more likely to keep these issues on the political and media agendas than current citizens movements and public interest groups are.

But, the critics will argue, the costs of serious finance reform are too great. How can the government afford to back large numbers of political aspirants, many of whom stand no chance of ultimate victory? To put this question in perspective, the costs of financing the entire slate of national candidates, including challengers, in a presidential year would amount to about 1 percent of the annual defense budget – even if current high levels of campaign spending were allowed to continue. Leaving aside the questions of what the national tax priorities ought to be and what dollar value should be placed on democratic competition, there is another, more expedient answer to this criticism. The cost of campaigning could be lowered by over half through one very simple move: Eliminate the enormously expensive practice of paid political advertising on television and radio. This could be done in ways that would also end the Madison Avenue–style candidate marketing that is so damaging to the spirit of democracy.

This brings us to our next proposal: Regulate political advertising on commercial radio and television. Under the present system, the political commercial that reaches the television screen or the rush hour "drive time" radio program does little to stimulate democratic dialogue. To the contrary, the practice of candidate marketing sets in motion an antidemocratic syndrome. Rather than promoting dialogues between candidates and voters that might result in new political initiatives, political advertising of the sort that dominates American campaigns short-circuits the very chances for such communications. Skipping the stages of dialogue, reason, feedback, and debate, marketing techniques probe the subliminal mind of isolated segments of the voter market for images and themes that produce quick psychological responses. The resulting interactions between candidates and voters defy the clear understandings on which stable consensus and programs of action depend. Moreover, the practice of scientifically targeting small voter blocs and then aiming the bulk of campaign content at them violates the spirit of broad democratic involvement. Any practice that turns citizen withdrawal from voting into a good thing rather than a cause for alarm should be outlawed as being unhealthy for the principles on which the whole system rests. Alas, cultural taboos about free speech permit no such direct solutions.

Although it is probably unconstitutional to ban broadcast political advertising, regulations could impose requirements for free access, thereby undercutting candidate reliance on expensive advertising to get messages across. One solution is to empower the Federal Communications Commission to include elections more centrally within its sphere of public service broadcasting. In particular:

- Networks should be required to donate set amounts of public service air time to candidates and parties during elections.
- The time issued (and used by candidates) should be in blocks of five to fifteen minutes – perhaps with an added requirement that candidate statements fill the bulk of that time.

These two reforms would simultaneously cut the costs of campaigning and require candidates to actually say something in the space allocated to them. (Further encouragement could be added by requiring candidates to appear live or in press interview format in a substantial percentage of the spots.) More important, these reforms would help to set in motion the right kind of electoral dynamic: Free air time would cut the costs of campaigning while making strict spending limits more realistic. An additional ratcheting down of spending beyond the costs of air time would further discourage expensive marketing research.[2]

In addition to creating a short-term rhetoric based on appeals to personal emotions rather than common public interest, the inroads of political marketing have thoroughly corrupted the news as a source of political information. Image campaigns rely on crossover image placement in both advertising and news coverage to create message saturation and authenticity. Staging news events as part of comprehensive campaigns of strategic communication feeds the worst tendencies of contemporary journalism (Manheim 1991). As Entman (1989) and Patterson (1993) have argued so persuasively, part of the breakdown in American political communication surely lies with the media and their abandonment of critical reporting.

Thus, reforms in the journalistic profession become part of our recommendation. There are some promising signs that the press is struggling to define a new election journalism. For example, the focus on political advertising has increased, and many newspapers have added "adwatch" analyses to their election coverage. Another promising move, pioneered among others by R. W. Apple, Jr. of the *New York Times*, is the use of focus groups with a broad range of citizens to sensitize reporters to public concerns. Several other innovations might be considered that build on the idea of a critical dialogue contained within news reports:

- The leading national news organizations could stake their prestige on creating a national agenda reflecting a synthesis of public opinion and the views of bipartisan experts on the major concerns of the day. This agenda could then be used as a reference for analyzing candidate responsiveness to the national interest. Instead of framing the campaign story as an often baseless horserace, journalists could compare candidates on how well they were responding to the items on the national agenda.

- Creating national agendas and evaluating candidate credibility might break down candidate ability to control the content of campaign news coverage, while opening up other aspects of the press–politician relationship. By responding pointedly to poor showings against their competition, politicians might actually turn idle promises into more serious issues in the eyes of voters and experts alike. Moreover, if broadcast advertising were regulated, candidates might have to say something substantive just to stay even with each other in precious media exposure.

- The pressure on candidates to discuss the national future could also be increased by holding real political debates. As currently conceived, the debates scarcely deserve that name. Candidates do not really engage each other on adversarial terms; instead, they respond to reporters' questions that are usually based on the candidates' own agendas. A debate system in which candidates are permitted to go at each other could provide revealing glimpses of candidate character, along with insights about their ability to function under real pressure. The debates could become opportunities for the media to pressure candidates to address an independently constructed issue agenda (if the press is willing to construct such an agenda, that is).[3]

Changing the ways in which campaigns are covered and public debates are presented is not likely to be a high priority with media organizations that are comfortable with big profits, smooth and relatively standardized news production routines, and the ease of traveling in a pack with other news organizations (see Bennett 1996a). There are notable weaknesses in the standard "free speech" reasons offered by media executives when explaining why they can't change their approaches to news coverage.

Also at issue is the curious set of norms the American press has adopted to define its role. Politicians' personal failings and scandals are fair game, not to mention great fun. The press froths at the chance to catch a candidate in a gaffe or indiscretion. Yet breaking from the pack and deciding independently what really matters blurs the neat distinction between news content that emanates from the candidates themselves (scandals and gaffes conform to this rule) and content that is injected into the news from the editorial desk. This old distinction between reporting and editorializing still holds powerful sway and accounts for the ability of campaigns to control media coverage to a remarkable extent. Surely journalists could draw a distinction between an editorial, which is an in-house opinion, and an agenda of national priorities constructed from the opinions of experts and the public. Few of us want to hear personal opinions passed off as news analysis, but an analytical standard constructed from an intelligent definition of public opinion would give people a useful tool for evaluating candidates and locating themselves in the ongoing debate.[4]

Finally, we propose our most sweeping recommendation: the gradual development of a proportional representation system in elections. The communication problems discussed thus far add up to one common conclusion: The political parties in America are moribund; they no longer serve the purpose of organizing competing national agendas and pushing their members to support those platforms. With the collapse of the parties and the rise of a political star or personality system, the marketplace of ideas has fallen into disorder. One mechanism that might stimulate new life in the national political dialogue is a limited proportional representation rule in deciding races for Congress. (For obvious reasons, such a scheme would take root first in the House and later, if at all, in the Senate.) What would this system look like?

- First, it would be less European in look than the typical parliamentary process in which the executive and the cabinet are forged from the balance of power in the legislative body itself. An American system could keep an elected president, while restoring a better representative balance between the people and Congress.
- The goal of making Congress more accountable to the grass roots would be advanced by a simple proportional representation rule granting House seats to parties whose candidates won at least 10 percent of the vote both locally and nationally. Say, for example, State X has twenty House seats up for election, and the New Ideas party wins 20 percent of the vote in that state and qualifies nationally by winning 12 percent of all the votes cast. In this result, four seats from State X would go to New Ideas. Those representatives would join winning party candidates from other states with qualifying vote margins to form a New Ideas bloc in the House.

Imposing a national qualifying percentage minimizes the chance of elevating isolated state or local movements to national power, while favoring idea-based movements with nationwide appeal. Beginning on a limited scale, the introduction of multiple-voice blocs and parties into the power structure would not disrupt the day-to-day workings of government any more than the current party disorientation has already thrown the system into a state of near-paralysis.

The intent of this shift in the representation process is to give voice to political initiatives – such as a credible campaign finance reform – that are now eliminated or diluted by a winner-take-all system in which the two leading alternatives either fail to differ significantly or fail to act upon their differences when they gain power. The important advantage of more parties is to introduce more ideas into public debate. Given what we know about the press, well-articulated and controversial viewpoints from government officials make the news. The newness alone of this system would attract press attention. With the publicity granted to incoming idea groups, existing parties and incumbents would face stiffer competition, and voters would be given a chance in subsequent elections to reward parties whose platforms continue to make sense, while punishing those who fail to compete.

If the public is interested in opening the party system to more competitive grass-roots ideas, the first move might come from states that offer direct popular initiatives and referendums on their ballots. State legislatures could thus become the experimental proving grounds for proportional representation schemes. Successful reforms in a few model states could lead the way for a national constitutional amendment. Even if this initiative were to get off the ground, however, it would be unlikely to go very far without major campaign finance reforms that would make parties with new ideas competitive nationally. With or without a restructuring of the representation system, campaign finance reform remains the key to restructuring the marketplace of ideas in American politics.

Institutional Reforms in Sweden

As the practice of strategic communication has taken hold in Sweden also, contributing to greater instability and to the exhaustion of any lasting governing vision, the need for changes in the political marketplace has become apparent. However, the institutional reforms that we have in mind for Sweden are less sweeping and far-reaching than the ones that we have proposed in the U.S. case. The reason for this is only partly that the problems now confronting the American communication process are greater and in some instances have reached crisis-level proportions. Equally important is the fact that Sweden is currently undergoing vast external as well as internal changes, the effects and direction of which are difficult to assess properly at this stage. The 1994 EU referendum campaign discussed later illustrates an awkward trend, however, and brings the need for institutional changes to the fore.

Our first set of reforms is aimed at *strengthening the party system and revitalizing the democratic dialogue between leaders and voters.* Recent studies have questioned the vitality of Sweden's political parties. Although voter participation is still high, the parties have gradually lost members since the beginning of the 1980s. The members who remain – predominantly middle-aged and older males – are not as active as they used to be. Also, parties today function primarily as machines for getting people elected and not as agents around which public issues are discussed and solutions proposed.

Ironically, this development has occurred at the same time as the old Swedish parties have been challenged by an array of new parties, both nationally and locally. Since 1988, three new parties have entered Parliament, and during the 1990s alone, twenty-eight new national and more than 200 local parties were registered around the country (Rothstein et al. 1995: 57, 60). One of Sweden's problems today may be that there are too many parties fragmenting the body politic and raising the noise level to sometimes unhealthy proportions. Parties formed with the sole purpose of promoting a single issue or candidate are often divisive and make it more difficult to view politics as a collective enterprise aimed at arriving at solutions for the common good.

What could be done to counter this development?

- First, tougher rules for the registration of political parties should be introduced on the national, regional, and local levels. The current system is simply too lenient, stating that in order to get on the ballot a party need get only 1,500 registered members nationally, 100 locally, and 50 regionally. We propose that those numbers be raised to 15,000, 1,000, and 500, respectively. Such a change would signal to new potential parties and candidates that to compete they must have some support among the electorate and that entering the political arena entails something more than just producing catchy soundbites and populist single-issue solutions.

- Second, we believe that it is time to end the peculiar practice of letting parties that have been voted out of Parliament keep most of their public financial support during the term following the election. There is no sound reason why a party that has lost the confidence of voters and may be supported by only a tiny fraction of the electorate should be able to hold on to the taxpayers' money for a full term after a defeat at the polls, as the present rules stipulate.

A related reform aims at *incorporating more people into the political decision-making process, particularly on the local government level.* Since World War II, the number of ordinary Swedes elected to various local government positions has decreased dramatically, going down since the early 1960s from almost 200,000 to just about 40,000 today. These cuts have been made in the name of greater efficiency and higher governmental potency, but the result is a democratic void that local party organizations have been largely unable to fill. At the same time, the number of appointed local civil servants has grown substantially. Studies indicate that voters are still very interested in local issues, as witnessed by the proliferation of new local parties. The drawbacks, however, are that some groups – particularly young people and immigrants – are not included in the democratic dialogue and that politics has increasingly become a profession practiced by a select few.

There is a rather simple solution to this democratic problem:

- Increase the number of elected local government officials to around 200,000. There is no reason local institutions such as schools, day-care centers, and hospitals, for example, should not be governed by elected bodies composed of laypeople who may be either party members or political independents. The link between citizens and their local governments could thereby be strengthened and the democratic debate further enhanced (cf. Rothstein et al. 1995: 61–68).

Such a reform is particularly important today, bearing in mind the concerns that have been raised about increased bureaucratization and a widening communication gap between citizens and leaders after Sweden's entry into the European Union.

Another area in need of reform concerns *campaign finance practices during elections.* One might assume that all is well since Sweden, contrary to the United States, has a system of public financing of political parties. After the introduction of this system in the mid-1960s, there has been little debate on the subject and even fewer incidents of misuse or scandal. Beginning with the 1995 EU parliamentary election, however, the electoral system has been gradually changed by way of allowing a greater element of candidate voting on the ballots. Voters can now state their preferences not only for a party but also for a specific candidate (although to get elected that candidate needs to receive a minimum of 5 percent of the party's votes; in addition, the party needs to get at least 4 percent of the national vote). Candidates are thus expected to present themselves not only as Conservative, Liberal, Social Democrat, Leftist, or Environmentalist but also as exemplary human beings worthy of representing the people in elected parliamentary assemblies. This is a potentially important change that highlights an often forgotten fact about campaign finance practices in Sweden: There is currently no legislation whatsoever regulating either spending or contribution limits or funding from corporations, unions, or other donors. Nor are there any rules requiring parties or candidates to make public accounts of incomes and expenditures during election campaigns.[5]

Even if the emerging electoral system in Sweden in all likelihood will be much less candidate-oriented than the one operating in the United States, the changes now underway illustrate the need for stricter legislative control. If the trend toward a more candidate-oriented system continues, as we predict that it will, current campaign finance practices must be regulated in some way – that much we have learned from countries where similar systems already exist. The following reforms are urgently needed:

- At a minimum, Sweden needs a law stating that all funds raised by or given to a party or candidate during the course of an election campaign must be publicly accounted for. A full accounting of both incomes and expenditures should be made to a nonpartisan election commission.
- Second, spending limits should be set on campaigns, and those limits should be applied to parties and candidates alike. Ideally, the whole issue of campaign finance reform should be discussed and analyzed in a broad parliamentary commission, the purpose of which should be to come up with a series of concrete proposals and reforms.

It is important to enact legislation before a new electoral system has been cemented. Only by doing so can we hope to avoid the spread of corruption and maintain the legitimacy of the political system.

Furthermore, *the public commission, or remiss system, needs to be reformed and revitalized.* As shown in Chapter 4, the public commissions have lost much of their former status and importance. During the height of the Swedish model, the commissions played a pivotal role in collecting facts, analyzing issues, and proposing new policy solutions. That is no longer the case. The commission system still exists, but its much diminished role today illustrates the breakdown of the old corporatist model as well as the higher level of political conflict in Swedish society (Micheletti 1995: 120–122).

Perhaps the most useful role played by the commissions has been to function as a forum for public discussion and an open airing of the issues. Can any of those functions be restored? What specifically could be done to revive consensus politics in Sweden? Although it may be unrealistic to imagine a return to the "good old days," a revival of the commission system is both possible and desirable and some of its leverage could be restored by making more effective use of the existing system. Specifically, we propose the following set of reforms:

- Reinstitutionalize the practice of using public commissions whenever important issues and problems are brought on to the political agenda. The commissions should, as a rule, consist of representatives from both parliamentary parties and interest groups. Recent studies have indicated that the possibilities of reaching consensus solutions increase if groups operating outside of Parliament are allowed to participate and work within the commission system (Hermansson 1993).
- Abolish the rule which says that commissions cannot propose solutions entailing increased public spending. Even if such proposals are put forward, it is up to Parliament and the government to make the final call.
- Raise to four years the maximum time in which a commission must complete its work by issuing a final report. The current maximum of two years is simply too short and makes it virtually impossible to penetrate complex issues in depth.

Such reforms would most likely broaden the democratic debate and increase popular participation in the process. Even more important, they could facilitate the return to decision-making by consensus in Swedish politics. Inviting interest groups back to the commission system could have the additional advantage of reducing the growing practice of lobbying and expensive media advertising campaigns.

That brings us finally to *the rules guiding the operations of the mass media,* the last of our reform areas in the Swedish case. Before the advent of commercial radio and television in Sweden during the 1980s and 1990s, citizens got most of their information about politics from newspapers and from the coverage provided by the Swedish Radio Corporation (SR). Although the SR had in effect a monopoly on broadcasting, voters usually had no problems getting information about current issues or about the views of different parties. The many programs devoted to social and political issues – as well as the direct encounters and debates between party candidates during election campaigns – ensured that the interested voter was at least reasonably informed.

The commercialization of the Swedish electronic media has broken the monopoly of the SR, which in itself is a positive development. But it has also fueled concerns about private monopoly tendencies, with a few media tycoons dividing up the market and thereby actually narrowing public debate rather than diversifying it. Other effects of the commercialization of Swedish media are an increased personalization of news and more of a focus on controversial and emotional "human interest" stories. A recent study demonstrates that this pattern has now spilled over into public television's news coverage as well. Over the past decade, television news stories have been presented in shorter segments and with a greater emphasis on entertainment, crime, and assorted trivia. This is true for public and privately owned news organizations alike, even if there are still differences between the two (Asp 1995; Rothstein et al. 1995: 37–42).

To counteract some of these tendencies, we propose the following:

- Keep political advertising out of both public and commercial radio and television. As of now, paid political ads are still not allowed on Swedish radio and television (the only exception being commercial radio), and we think it is important to keep it that way. Political ads on television, in particular, invite candidates to spend their money attacking their opponents rather than presenting their own solutions and visions for the future.
- In addition, stricter rules must be introduced for granting and selling concessions for new radio and television channels to enable people and groups with limited financial resources to participate in the public dialogue. Until now, new radio and TV channels have been auctioned off to the highest bidder, allowing some big media giants to become even bigger. In particular, powerful newspaper owners should not be permitted also to own and operate new radio or television outlets.
- In addition to the usual debates and question-and-answer programs in the media, parties and candidates should be given some free air time during election campaigns to present their platforms and programs. This has occasionally been done in the past but seems lately to have lost out to programs controlled and led by professional journalists.

The issue is not private versus public ownership of the media but, rather, the enforcement of guidelines and rules ensuring a vibrant debate in the interest of the common good. Market forces alone cannot be counted on to enforce such rules. Just as in the cases of parties, local decision-making, campaign finance, and the public commission system, a healthy dose of government regulation is required to reinvigorate the Swedish communication process.

CONCLUSION: DEMOCRACIES WAITING FOR IDEAS

During the time that we have been at work on this book, many of the conditions and problems that we have discussed seem to have become worse, not better. After the initial euphoria and epochal changes that followed the collapse of communism in Europe and the Soviet Union, signs of crisis in those political systems are evident almost everywhere. With few exceptions, opinion polls show that voters all over Western Europe and the United States are angry with the leaders and parties that have dominated politics for decades. There is a widespread sense that conventional politics is increasingly corrupt and that its practitioners have been in power for too long.[6] Our analysis of parties maintaining power in the absence of ideas suggests that the voters may be right. In growing numbers, voters are turning to what we have called *amateur politicians,* outsiders whose prime asset is that they have no previous experience in politics and no public record to defend. Incumbency is gradually becoming a liability, "professional politician" a dirty word.[7] The recent wave of proposals in the United States for congressional term limits is only one sign among many of a widespread distrust of elected officials.

American voters seem to be the angriest of them all. Before the 1994 midterm elections, a *Time*/CNN poll asked a sample of the U.S. electorate the question, "Are officials in Washington out of touch with the average person?" Eighty-four percent answered yes, and only 15 percent no. When the same people were asked, "How could the federal government be improved?" 29 percent thought the best way was to "replace politicians," whereas 61 percent said "change the system" – a sign that the time may be ripe for more serious reforms. By a clear 4 to 1 margin, or 76 to 19 percent, those surveyed also wanted national referenda on important issues affecting the nation.[8] Given this widespread discontent with the elite establishment, it came as no big surprise that the midterm elections themselves resulted in a political earthquake, yet it was based on negative rhetoric rather than popularly supported governing ideas.[9]

However, as Britain's *Economist* magazine promptly reminded its readers, the Americans had no monopoly on democratic disorder (see the epigram at the opening of this chapter).[10] And on and on it goes. In Austria the extreme right Freedom Party won a stunning 23 percent of the vote in the 1994 October national election. Its party leader Jörg Haider called for a ban on all immigration (except for political refugees) and defended Kurt Waldheim and Adolf Hitler's employment policies. In Italy polls showed Gianfranco Fini, leader of the postfascist National Alliance, surpassing popular (and soon deposed) Prime Minister Silvio Berlusconi as the country's most popular politician. In municipal elections in Belgium, extreme right parties did well in the depressed industrial belt and became the dominant force in Antwerp, the country's second largest city. The startling success of these xenophobic and extreme right parties was interpreted by one analyst as reflecting "the failure of traditional ruling parties in those countries to defuse the growing anxieties of voters who feel that their jobs, personal security and future well-being are now imperiled."[11]

The underlying issue, as touched upon in our opening chapter, seems to be worry about mounting unemployment and faltering economies. Equally evident is the confusion about the purpose and future of Western societies after the end of the Cold War. Bill Clinton's call for a rhetoric aimed squarely at the middle-class taxpayer is at best a stop-gap communication strategy. Such substitutes for ideas do little to distinguish parties or candidates in the minds of voters, and they do less to solve pressing national problems.

Communicating intelligently about current problems and future concerns is no less a daunting task for a small nation than it is for a large one. What should be the proper role for a country such as Sweden in a new and changing Europe? What would be the likely effects on the nation's economy, social welfare system, gender policy, and jobs and employment prospects should Sweden decide to join the European Union (EU)? What would be the effects if the country were to remain as a nonaligned and independent country outside the Union? Those were some of the issues dealt with in the November 13, 1994, Swedish national referendum on whether to join the European Union. The result was a clear but narrow victory for those advocating Swedish membership: 52.3 percent of the electorate voted yes, as opposed to 46.8 percent who voted no. However, the EU debate and the way that the whole issue has been handled domestically in recent years are a perfect illustration of some of the key communication trends and problems that we have been trying to pinpoint throughout this book.

In the early 1990s, the issue of increased cooperation in Europe – first in the European Economic Community (EEC), then in the expanded European Union (EU) – had been in the public domain in Sweden for at least three decades. Ever since the beginning of the 1960s, the official Swedish position had been that the country could not become a member of the EEC because of the neutrality and nonalignment policy that the country pursued. That policy would be severely compromised, the argument went, should Sweden opt for full membership. Cooperation in the form of trade and economics was acceptable (not to say necessary), but closer political and foreign and security policy cooperation with other countries was considered potentially dangerous for the way Sweden was perceived in a polarized world that still had a Cold War mentality. This view was widely shared by the parties in Parliament and by a big majority of the general public.

During the height of an economic crisis in November 1990, however, the then Social Democratic government hastily produced a crisis package that included a point stating that acquiring membership status in the EEC was now a desirable goal for the Swedish government. Overnight, more than thirty years of persistent arguments and objections to EEC membership were rendered obsolete. This may or may not have been a necessary turnabout to accommodate actors in the economic market; that is not the issue. What is important is that the sudden flip-flop on this very significant issue happened without any debate either internally or externally, which means that it caught most of the public off guard and caused considerable surprise as well as some confusion.

In May 1991, Prime Minister Ingvar Carlsson formally applied for Swedish membership. Negotiations with the EU bureaucracy soon followed, a process that was to last for almost three years. Then it was decided that the issue would be put before the electorate in a national referendum, only the fifth one in the nation's history. Note the order of things: first a membership application was handed in (without much prior debate), then extensive negotiations began, and last, when the process was already well underway, it was decided to seek the voters' approval by having a national vote on the matter. At first, voter approval looked like a virtual certainty, with polls showing over 60 percent of those interviewed favoring membership. But as the referendum grew closer and the debate started to heat up, it became clear that the issue was tremendously complicated and that the parties and leaders had not prepared the public for the referendum through an extended debate. The voters' growing confusion and uncertainty were evidenced by the fact that a sizable minority – at one point amounting to a third of those surveyed – said they did not know what to think or refused to take a stand on the issue.

In most parties there was no debate to speak of – certainly not in the SAP, the biggest of them all. There was a failure of leadership and a wish for a quick fix. The issue not only dealt with material, or bread-and-butter, issues such as jobs, the economy, and future employment prospects; it also entailed more delicate and sensitive issues such as national character and the country's relation to its European neighbors. For several reasons, the parties and leaders did not try to engage themselves or the public in a debate about these matters until very late in the referendum campaign. One reason was that once the membership application had been handed in there was a near unanimous view among the elite politicians that, although the order of the steps taken may not have been perfect, now that it was done they were all for it (with the Left Party and the Greens as the only major opponents). No great debate emanates from a near unanimity of views. Another reason was that the issues involved *were* complex and sensitive and that almost all parties who supported a yes position – in particular the Social Democrats, the Center Party, and the Christian Democrats – were split down the middle. As a result, the party leadership did not want to impose their views too forcefully and risk an upheaval in their own ranks.

The debate thus started very late and heated up only during the last few weeks of the campaign. Perhaps most striking was the lack of a leading vision on both sides of the issue. Those arguing for no thought that Sweden should be a model in the old sense and an example to the world. Those saying yes (*Säg ja till Europa*) did so with jobs and economics influencing their decisions: Don't let us be outside Europe. No side argued for its position on the basis of a strong governing idea for the future.[12] The 1995 election for the European Parliament displayed a similar lack of vision, and only 41 percent of the electorate took part.

These examples of continuing communication breakdowns in our two cases draw attention to the need for more direct attention by both scholars and policy experts to the qualities of communication in contemporary politics. Democracy, after all, is not just about holding elections to organize governments; it is also about holding national conversations about what to do with those governments. When there are few good ideas on what to do with government, it should come as no surprise that governments often become objects of hostility or prizes sought by extremists.

In this book we have subscribed to the notion of democracy as a conversation or dialogue. We believe that democratic institutions must be arranged to facilitate open but politically disciplined debate. The goal of such communication should be to promote understanding of how issues fit into a broader social picture rather than, as is so often the case today, the emotional concerns of targeted individuals or the agendas of narrow interest groups. To find solutions to problems, a continued, vigorous, and issue-oriented conversation is necessary. Participation in the democratic dialogue is equally important, and if the communication channels are clogged or poorly integrated and noisy, as seems to be the case in many countries nowadays, democratic government itself may be imperiled (cf. Miller 1993; Rothstein et al. 1995). Our proposals for reforms are not written with the view that there is one ideal solution that can take care of every single problem. We do believe, however, that whatever the problems of modern societies are, government must have a part in solving them.

Notes

CHAPTER ONE

[1] Francis Fukuyama, "The End of History?" *The National Interest,* Summer 1989, pp. 3–18 (quotes on pp. 3 and 4). Fukuyama has since developed his ideas in a book, *The End of History and the Last Man.* London: Hamish-Hamilton, 1992.

[2] Alan Friedman, "In Europe's Jobs Crisis, Growth Is No Answer," *International Herald Tribune,* March 10, 1994, p. 1.

[3] BBC World News, July 21, 1995.

[4] Cf. Peter Gumbel, "Power Failure: Major Democracies Draw Widespread Vote of Waning Confidence," *Wall Street Journal Europe,* July 2–3, 1993, pp. 1, 10; James Walsh, "Where Have All the Leaders Gone?" *Time,* July 12, 1993, pp. 17–21.

[5] Charles Trueheart, "Stressing Jobs, Canada's Liberals Crush Tories," *International Herald Tribune,* October 27, 1993, pp. 1, 5; InfoFAX prepared by *The Globe and Mail* (Canada), December 14, 1993, p. 2/6.

[6] Japanese political analyst Shiego Hayasaka observed: "Traditionally about 80 percent of the Japanese people have identified with some political party, and 15 or 20 percent called themselves independent. But today, more than half the Japanese people refuse to align themselves with any political party. Most people just don't see any alternative that looks attractive." Quoted in T. R. Reid, "Japanese Voters Are Fed Up With Bleak Political Picture," *International Herald Tribune,* July 19, 1995, p. 6.

[7] See, e.g., Marguerite Johnson, "Italy: When Enough Is Enough," *Time,* April 19, 1993, p. 37; John Moody, "Italy: The Rise of a Demagogue," *Time,* January 11, 1993, pp. 16–17; Edward W. Desmond, "Japan: Draining the Political Swamp," *Time,* November 30, 1992, p. 51; James Walsh, "Isle of Despair," *Time,* pp. 22–27; "Rotten Politicians," *The Economist,* May 22, 1993, pp. 19–20; James O. Jackson, "Germany: Boom To Bust," *Time,* May 24, 1993, pp. 16–20; Gumbel, "Power Failure," pp. 1, 10.

[8] Surveys conducted by various national polling firms and government services from 1991 to 1993, and reported in "Democracies' Discontents," *The American Enterprise,* July/August, 1993, pp. 85–88. Stoors, Conn.: The Roper Center.

[9] Survey results reported in Richard Morin, "Myths and Messages in the Election Tea Leaves; One Thing Is Clear: The Republican Agenda Did Not Get a Mandate from the Voters," *The Washington Post National Weekly Edition*, November 21–27, 1994, p. 37.

[10] Small countries and economies, such as Sweden's, are especially vulnerable to these actions by managers and holders of private capital.

[11] David S. Broder, "Governing Isn't Impossible, Just Harder Than Before," *International Herald Tribune*, January 25, 1994, p. 6; E. J. Dionne Jr., "The Grumble Heard Around the World: The U.S. Is Not Alone in Voter Dissatisfaction," *The Washington Post National Weekly Edition*, July 13–19, 1992, p. 24.

[12] Quote from E. J. Dionne Jr., "The Grumble Heard Around the World," p. 24.

[13] Perhaps the best-known single monograph coming out of this tradition is Daniel Bell's *The End of Ideology: On the Exhaustion of Political Ideas in the Fifties*. Cambridge, Mass., and London: Harvard University Press, 1988. With a new afterword by the author. First published in 1960.

[14] See Craig R. Whitney, "Little Big Men: They're All Speaking Perot's Lines," *New York Times*, April 3, 1994, Sec. 4, pp. 1, 3.

[15] Quoted in Sidney Blumenthal, "The Candidate," *The New Yorker*, October 10, 1994, p. 55.

CHAPTER TWO

[1] Based on a sample of 1,001 adults in February, 1995, conducted by the Wirthlin Group. Reported in *Party Developments*, vol. 1, no. 3 (April 1995), p. 18.

[2] They note the factors of party strength, parliamentary system, the organization of the mass media, the regulation of campaigning and spending, and the residual importance of the intellectual dispositions of British political elites. We have framed our four factors in somewhat more general terms, permitting a broader range of comparisons.

[3] To some observers, the Democrats these days appear to be little more than a loose coalition of political entrepreneurs who find personal advantages in party membership (e.g., committee assignments in Congress and fund-raising help) but who have largely abandoned any interest in bringing large blocs of poor and minority constituents (and their ideas) into the party.

[4] For a good example of this, see the major difficulties the leadership of the white-collar union TCO had in handling the so-called wage-earner fund issue, analyzed in Micheletti (1985).

[5] Petersson et al. (1990), p. 187. The study does not analyze, however, whether these quantitative reductions also mean a qualitative change in the commission system's ability to function as a forum for consensus and compromise in the Swedish polity.

[6] Studies by Bennett (1989, 1990) suggest that the picture is a bit more complicated than this, reflecting once again the interactions among various regulatory mechanisms. For example, it appears that when national elites – particularly the political parties in Congress – are in conflict on an issue, the range of ideas in the news expands (measured both in terms of the range of sources cited in news stories and the debates on op-ed pages). Abortion is a case in which elite divisions correspond to a broad spectrum of grass-roots voices in the news and commentary. By contrast, fluctuating elite and congressional positions on Reagan-era Nicaragua and Central America policies corresponded to fluctuating media content as well.

[7] Everett Carl Ladd, "Campaign '88: What Are the 'Issues'?" *Christian Science Monitor,* June 3, 1988, p. 14.

CHAPTER THREE

[1] See Roosevelt's acceptance speech of 1932, along with the Democratic Party platform of that year.

[2] From George Bush's acceptance speech at the 1992 Republican National Convention, CNN, August 20, 1992.

[3] *Campaign Book of the Democratic Party: Candidates and Issues 1932.* Published by the Democratic National Committee, New York, 1932, p. 30.

[4] Fireside Chat of October 22, 1933 (p. 423).

[5] From p. 24 of the *Text-Book of the Republican Party: 1932.* Issued by the Republican National Committee.

[6] From *The Official Report of the Proceedings of the Democratic Convention.* Philadelphia, June 23–27, 1936, p. 340.

[7] The second Fireside Chat of 1934 (September 30), "We Are Moving Forward to Greater Freedom, to Greater Security for the Average Man."

[8] "Labor Day Greetings to the Workers of America," September 6, 1936, p. 330.

[9] Message of January 3, 1938, from Fred L. Israel, ed. *The State of the Union Messages of the Presidents: 1790–1966.* New York: Chelsea House, 1966, p. 2839.

[10] Message of January 3, 1936, from *The State of the Union Messages of the Presidents,* p. 2823.

[11] Acceptance Speech of July 26, 1952, from *Vital Speeches of the Day,* August 15, 1952 (vol. 18, no. 21), p. 646.

[12] Acceptance speech of July 15, 1960, from *Vital Speeches of the Day,* August 1, 1960 (vol. 26, no. 20), p. 611.

[13] Acceptance speech of August 27, 1964, from *Vital Speeches of the Day,* September 15, 1964 (vol. 30, no. 23), p. 710.

[14] Acceptance speech of July 14, 1972, from *Vital Speeches of the Day*, August 1, 1972 (vol. 38, no. 20), p. 612.

[15] Acceptance speech of August 8, 1968, from *Vital Speeches of the Day*, September 1, 1968 (vol. 34, no. 22), p. 676.

[16] Acceptance speech of August 15, 1980, from *Vital Speeches of the Day*, August 15, 1980 (vol. 46, no. 21), p. 646.

[17] Acceptance speech of June 12, 1936, from the *Official Report of the Twenty-First Republican Convention*, June 9–12, 1936. New York: Tenny Press, 1936, p. 249.

[18] Acceptance speech of August 18, 1988, from *Vital Speeches of the Day*, October 15, 1988 (vol. 60, no. 1), p. 5.

[19] GOP pollster Ed Goeas, *USA Today*, International Edition, August 15, 1992, p. 2A.

[20] *USA Today*, International Edition, August 5, 1992, p. 4A.

[21] John E. Yang, "Democrat Tailor-Makes a Talk to Westerners," *International Herald Tribune*, July 27, 1992, p. 3.

[22] C. Vann Woodward, "Made in the U.S.A.," *New York Review of Books*, July 16, 1992 (vol. 34, no. 19), p. 28.

[23] Acceptance speech of July 15, 1948, from *Vital Speeches of the Day*, August 1, 1948 (vol. 14, no. 20), p. 610.

[24] Acceptance speech of July 26, 1952, from *Vital Speeches of the Day*, August 15, 1952 (vol. 18, no. 21), p. 645.

[25] Acceptance speech of August 27, 1964, from *Vital Speeches of the Day*, September 15, 1964 (vol. 30, no. 23), p. 708.

[26] Based on a content analysis of references to the other party's positions in all the Democratic and Republican acceptance speeches from 1932 to 1988.

[27] *Ibid.*

[28] Acceptance speech of August 23, 1984, from *Vital Speeches of the Day*, September 15, 1984 (vol. 50, no. 23), p. 706.

CHAPTER FOUR

[1] The acronym for *Sveriges Socialdemokratiska Arbetareparti* is SAP.

[2] A related interpretation has been termed *the hegemony model*, which argues that consensus has indeed been a hallmark of Swedish politics but within a predominantly Social Democratic value structure (Heclo & Madsen 1987; Lane 1991; Tilton 1992).

[3] This is the conventional view in the literature. See, for instance, Hirdman 1988; Misgeld et al. 1992. For a rare counterview, see Södersten 1991.

[4] This point is further discussed in Chapter 6 of the book.

[5] This is not to say that conflicts have been absent or even rare in twentieth-century Swedish politics. But these conflicts, which seem to have become more common after 1970, still occur, we would argue, within a basically consensual political culture or climate that is heavily influenced by Social Democratic ideas and values (cf. Heclo & Madsen 1987; Hermansson 1993: Chs. 2, 9; Möller, 1993: 172–173, 189–191; Tilton 1992: 425–426).

[6] For a broad overview of how public language has changed in Sweden over the years, see Cederberg 1993 and Svensson 1993.

[7] This aspect is more fully examined in an interdisciplinary project on the language of the Swedish labor movement since the late nineteenth century (Johannesson et al. 1990).

[8] Prime Minister Carl Bildt in *The Parliamentary Record*, October 4, 1991 (vol. 92, no. 6), p. 14. Bildt's fellow conservative Bo Lundgren, soon to be minister of taxation, expressed similar hopes and views when he exclaimed shortly after the election, "Sweden has abandoned socialism!" (Elmbrant 1993: 287).

[9] Between 1920 and 1932, Sweden had no fewer than ten governments, the majority of them nonsocialist in outlook (Hadenius et al. 1991: 91–117).

[10] An even earlier proponent of the idea of the "good home" was Ellen Key, who introduced it around the turn of the century in progressive social and political circles (Larsson 1994: 91, 105–106).

[11] It is interesting that Kjellén, although he professed to be a conservative, held key ideas that overlapped with those later propagated by leading Social Democrats. One of those ideas was Kjellén's antiindividualism and his insistence on the whole being more important that its parts. He often stressed the primacy of the "interest of the state" and believed that the future belonged to the "power of the state" and not to the "right of the individual." Another joint theme was anticapitalism, which was evident in his encouragement of government intervention in the economy to protect the "national values" against the "dangers of a superior capitalism." Although Kjellén abhorred any hints of class language and did not advocate changes in the class structure or in the existing economic order, his whole approach was collectivist from start to finish (Elvander 1954: 25, 32–33). For Kjellén's contributions as a political scientist, see Falkemark 1992.

[12] The related concept of a *house* had been used already in the late nineteenth century, again primarily by conservative politicians. The term appeared in the famous 1865 debate on a major constitutional reform, as well as in an 1891 conservative manifesto calling for the creation of a common national *house* (Johannesson et al. 1992: 134, 165–166, 170–171).

[13] Quotations from Hansson's speech are from Tilton 1991: 126–129. The bulk of the speech is reprinted in Johannesson et al. 1992: 229–240.

[14] It is worth stressing here, however, that when the *folkhem* concept was conceived it had strong nationalistic overtones and did not entail any ideas of building a multicultural society (cf. Olsson & Gaunt 1990: 38).

[15] One writer goes as far as saying that the *folkhem* idea "gave birth to itself" (Hirdman 1989: 90).

[16] See the introduction to Hansson's speech in Johannesson et al. 1992: 226–229.

[17] Another leading Social Democrat who also had misgivings about using the *folkhem* label was Gustav Moller (Kristiansson 1989).

[18] In addition, the threat of Swedish farmers turning to fascism, as they had in other European countries during the Depression, was significantly reduced by the SAP–Agrarian agreement (Davidson 1989: 101f; Lindstrom 1985).

[19] The concept of a Swedish model is younger than the *folkhem* metaphor. The notion of a particular Swedish model was introduced to an American and international audience by Marquis Childs's famous book *Sweden the Middle Way* (1936). For an interesting account of the reception of the Childs book in the United States, see Curti 1968: 165–178. See also Stråth 1992: 205–206, footnote 29; and Isacson 1991: 16–17.

[20] We have looked at the following material: the main debates between the party leaders in the *Riksdag* following the opening of the new parliamentary season from 1929 to 1991 (the so-called *allmänpolitiska debatten* or *remissdebatten*); all the main speeches and articles by Per Albin Hansson from 1926 to 1946; a selection of articles and speeches by Arvid Lindman and Carl Ekman from 1928 to 1935; and the main speeches delivered by Per Albin Hansson, Tage Erlander, and Olof Palme at SAP's party congresses from 1928 to 1981. We thank our research assistants Paula Blomqvist, Pia Karlsson, and Dorothea Schweizer for their help in excerpting this vast material.

[21] There is some evidence, though, that he periodically used the word more frequently on the stump (Hallberg & Jonsson 1993: 44–45).

[22] Cf. Åberg 1986, who mistakenly believes that the rhetorical shift to the "strong society" in the 1950s represented a break with the ideas of the *folkhem*.

[23] The importance of economic growth had already been emphasized by Per Albin Hansson in his 1928 landmark speech (Larsson 1994: 111–112).

[24] Unless otherwise stated, the following section is built on Åsard 1979: 111–129. For quotations and references, refer to this source.

[25] A recent dissertation in political science by Kristina Boréus confirms that the influence of conservative and neoliberal thought grew considerably in Sweden from 1969 to 1989. The author argues, among other things, that there was a "neoliberal breakthrough" in the early 1980s and that the ideas most affected were those related to the economy and the public sector (Boréus, 1994: 7, passim).

[26] In an interview for the German daily *Berliner Zeitung* two months later, Bildt, now prime minister, contradicted himself somewhat by saying that such a model had never existed (Burke 1994: 52).

[27] The rules governing the old bicameral *Riksdag* are actually one of the main reasons the Social Democrats, despite fluctuating election results, managed to stay in power for forty-four consecutive years (1932–1976).

[28] Unless otherwise indicated, the following paragraphs are based on Åsard 1986.

[29] The gist of this proposal was that Sweden's large private companies would transfer annually a certain percentage of their profits to wage earners' funds. The system was collectivist in nature; the dividends earned on employee-owned capital were not to be given back in cash to the individual employee but used instead for various collective purposes, such as training for employee representatives on boards, research in the fields of work environment, job security, and so on (Åsard, 1986: 212).

[30] As exemplified, at least in part, by our case study of the 1990 Swedish tax reform (see Chapter 4).

[31] This development seems to substantiate the "fair weather" hypothesis, which says that the number of commission members from various interest groups increased in the postwar years, when the welfare state was being built, and decreased in the 1960s, when the major social welfare programs had been basically completed (Micheletti 1991: 154).

[32] Sweden's recent decision to join the European Union may provide interest groups with a new channel of influence. The country's membership in the EU will most probably mean a development toward a more significant role for court litigation and the judicial branch, something that various interest organizations are likely to use in furthering their agendas (Holmström 1994: 161–162).

CHAPTER FIVE

[1] Fairness implied two things: whether the rich would be taxed as heavily as the middle classes and whether the process of filing tax returns would be simplified for people who could not afford to hire lawyers and accountants. As Tulis (1987: 195) suggests, the rhetoric of fairness may have had much deeper cultural roots than economic ones.

[2] Reported in a *Time* cover story, "The Making of A Miracle," August 25, 1986, p. 12.

[3] Perhaps the biggest revolt of all was the silent one of widespread cheating on federal taxes. By the Treasury's own estimates, revenue losses resulting from tax evasion more than doubled between 1970 and 1981. *Time*, August 25, 1986, p. 12. A national poll commissioned by the Internal Revenue Service found that fully a third of Americans regarded cheating on taxes as perfectly acceptable,

another third had mixed feelings, and only one third regarded cheating as wrong. Cited in an opinion article by Floyd Haskell, *New York Times*, January 17, 1986, p. A31.

4 Among these calculations were the desire to avoid an early (and potentially losing) battle with special interests and with Congress, the reluctance to share the glory of tax reform with the Democrats, and a somewhat religious belief in a theory of supply-side economics whose advocates initially favored direct tax cuts over bracket adjustments and reform.

5 See, for example, the poll data analyzed in William Schneider, "Americans Still Wary on Tax Reform," *National Journal*, July 12, 1986 (vol. 18, no. 28), p. 1740.

6 No more than 1 to 2 percent named tax reform as the most important national problem in a series of ABC News/*Washington Post* surveys. Even after Reagan's nationally televised speech (discussed later) launching his rhetorical campaign, a *Newsweek* poll showed that respondents ranked tax reform last in importance among six issues. A CBS/*New York Times* poll showed tax reform ranking fourth in a list of five issues, far below budget deficits, arms control, and problems in Central America. See William Schneider, "Public Is Unready for Tax Reform Revolution," *National Journal*, June 15, 1985, pp. 1434–1435.

7 *Ibid.*, pp. 1435–1436. Stories circulated in the media about fabulous tax breaks received by corporations from 1981 to 1983 while most individuals netted only a few hundred dollars. One often cited example told how the highly profitable General Electric Corporation received $238 million in government rebates from the tax-cut bonanza under a program of "investment tax credits" designed to stimulate the renewal of factories and equipment. The news also reported that contrary to supply-side thinking, investment actually fell among the more than 200 top recipients of these tax credit "giveaways." *Washington Post*, February 3, 1985.

8 See David R. Francis, "Despite Critics, U.S. Tax Reform Plan Draws Widespread Favor," *Christian Science Monitor*, February 7, 1985, p. 21.

9 David S. Broder, "Tax Reform Is Possible," *Washington Post*, February 13, 1985, p. A23. More than 100 meetings were held with representatives of various interests, and the news contained pithy warnings that Baker would be "eaten alive" by special interests, and that "the first time he makes a concession a line will form a block long." An influential Washington columnist quipped, "At downtown restaurants, Reagan's proposal is dismissed as a wonderful employment program for special interest lobbyists."

10 Schneider, "Public Is Unready," pp. 1436–1437.

11 United Press International (UPI), September 26, 1985.

12 *U.S. News & World Report*, June 17, 1985, p. 26.

13 *Ibid.*, p. 27.

14 *Ibid.*, p. 27–28.

15 Bureau of National Affairs, *Daily Report for Executives*, September, 26, 1985, p. 65.

[16] *Los Angeles Times*, September 6, 1985, p. 1.

[17] Charlotte Saikowski, "Reagan Brings Tax Reform Campaign to a Close," *Christian Science Monitor*, October 11, 1985, p. 1.

[18] *Ibid.*

[19] UPI wire story "Tax Reform Mired in Uncertainty," November 2, 1985.

[20] One of the ironies of Reagan's rhetorical campaign is that it succeeded in shoring up his personal popularity even if it did not persuade people of his position on the issues. For example, White House pollster Richard Wirthlin showed personal popularity up as a result of the speeches, restoring some of the approval ratings lost owing to an unpopular trip to a German military cemetery and his battles with Congress over Central America and defense spending. *U.S. News & World Report*, June 17, 1985, p. 26ff.

[21] UPI wire story, February 25, 1985.

[22] *Ibid.*

[23] *National Journal*, June 8, 1985.

[24] UPI wire story, June 2, 1985.

[25] *Ibid.*

[26] *U.S. News & World Report*, June 17, 1985.

[27] *Ibid.*

[28] *National Journal*, June 8, 1985.

[29] *Ibid.*

[30] *Ibid.*

[31] All examples reported in *U.S. News & World Report*, February 25, 1985, p. 22ff.

[32] *Ibid.*

[33] Richard Gephardt quoted in UPI wire story, David E. Anderson, "'Brawl' Forseen Over Tax Reform," June 2, 1985, PM cycle.

[34] This is not to imply that the parties were models of internal unity, only that there was more effort to achieve party discipline on this issue than on many others. And, perhaps most important, this discipline extended to the development of rhetorical strategies.

[35] Anderson, "Brawl," June 2, 1985.

[36] *Ibid.*, p. 1ff.

[37] UPI financial wire, Joseph Mianoway, "Will Public Support Carry Tax Reform?" December 18, 1985.

[38] Polls suggested that most people expected a special interest victory, but it was hard to know whether that cynicism would translate into voter withdrawal or electoral backlash the following November.

[39] UPI financial wire, Joseph Mianoway, "Will Public Support Carry Tax Reform?" December 18, 1985.

40 *Ibid.* See also Tulis (1987: 193–196), who concluded that Reagan's major contribution was keeping the process moving even if not convincing many people that it was going the way they wanted it.

41 Floyd K. Haskell, "The Bottom Line of Real Tax Reform," *New York Times,* January 17, 1986, p. A31.

42 Evan Thomas, "Lights, Cameras, Tax Reform: Television's Eye Helps Keep the Lobbyists At Bay, For Now," *Time,* June 16, 1986, p. 16.

43 *Ibid.*

44 Earl Cheit, "Wrong Move at the Right Time," *Los Angeles Times,* September 7, 1986, pt. 4, p. 3.

45 *Time,* June 16, 1986, p. 16.

46 *Time,* August 25, 1986, p. 12.

47 *Ibid.*

48 Cheit, "Wrong Move."

49 UPI financial wire, Joseph Mianoway, "Tax Reform: The Good News and Bad News," September 18, 1986, PM cycle.

50 National survey conducted by *Money* magazine reported on the UPI financial wire, BC section, October 24, 1986.

51 John McEvory, "Tax Reform: A Lobbyist's Perspective," *The Bond Buyer,* October 14, 1985, p. 10.

52 Public expenditure at all levels of government in Sweden now amounts to roughly two thirds of the country's GNP (Heclo & Madsen 1987: 4).

53 People were generally unhappy with this. According to a survey in 1981, 83 percent thought the general level of taxes was too high, 15 percent felt it was about right, and almost no one thought it was too low (Hadenius 1986: 7).

54 The income tax commission consisted of seven members: three Social Democrats, one Communist, and one member from each of the three nonsocialist parties.

55 Not everyone was pleased with this "Americanization" of the Swedish tax system. Sten Johansson, a leading Social Democrat and a high-level official in the national bureaucracy, warned about the dangers of following the advice of the free-market economists. The effects of the U.S. reform, he stated, had not been what the economists predicted. Sten Johansson, "Lita inte på ekonomerna," *Dagens Nyheter,* December 17, 1989, p. 4.

56 The prime minister repeated this message throughout most of the campaign. Here we have used two speeches that were delivered in Fagersta on August 20 and in Stockholm on August 29, 1988. The call for "fairer taxes" is echoed in both speeches on pages 7 and 5, respectively. Source: The SAP.

57 In Sweden political commercials are not allowed in most of the electronic media (radio and television). This makes it all the more important the kind of coverage

campaigns get in the regular news and question-and-answer programs. In 1988 taxes figured prominently in television coverage, especially in the quiz programs with the party leaders (see Asp 1988; Bergstrom 1988; Gilljam & Holmberg 1990: Ch. 3).

[58] Åke Ekdahl, "Ingvar Carlsson: Ingen ny underbar natt," *Dagens Nyheter,* August 29, 1988, p. 8.

[59] For the "burned all bridges" quote, see Åke Ekdahl, "Fp slår tillbaka mot s: Nej till alla nya inviter," *Dagens Nyheter,* September 11, 1988, p. 8. For a good example of Westerberg's campaign rhetoric, see his speech in Medborgarhuset in Stockholm, September 7, 1988 (quote on pp. 7–8).

[60] Elvander 1989, p. 157; Elisabeth Crona, "Nytt skattesystem skall stoppa fifflet," *Svenska Dagbladet,* November 24, 1988, p. 8.

[61] Eva Stenberg, "Feldts skatteforslag: Andringar LO-krav," *Dagens Nyheter,* November 24, 1988, p. 14; Södersten et al. 1990: 14–16; Bo Sodersten, "En seger over populismen," *Dagens Nyheter,* April 18, 1990, p. 4 (quote).

[62] Dick Ljungberg, "Stig Malm nöjd: Helt nytt skattesystem," *Dagens Nyheter,* November 24, 1988, p. 14.

[63] Elisabeth Crona, "Nytt skattesystem skall stoppa fifflet," *Svenska Dagbladet,* November 24, 1988, p. 8. The idea of treating capital and personal incomes equally was one of the most surprising ingredients in the government's proposal (Elvander 1989: 162–163).

[64] *Vår bostad,* no. 1, 1990, p. 20.

[65] Erik Åsbrink, "Regeringens makt över matkulturen liten," *Svenska Dagbladet,* August 30, 1990, p. 2.

[66] Another factor was the government's austerity program, presented in the spring of 1989, in an effort to put an ailing economy on course. The measures proved to be immensely unpopular, leading to a confrontation between the Social Democratic party and the trade union movement. As the government's ratings began to drop, great concern was expressed among party officials around the country who urged more decisive action on the tax reform issue as one way of turning the tide. Monica Bjorklund and Elisabeth Crona, "Skattesamtalen – fem veckor i en slanggunga," *Svenska Dagbladet,* November 12, 1989, p. 12.

[67] Who should be favored and who should be discarded can sometimes be a tricky choice, but it is usually facilitated by the simple fact that some actors are more powerful – and thus more important allies – than others.

[68] The Moderates probably never had any intention of reaching an agreement with the Social Democrats. Still they made a point out of their withdrawal, saying that the "government had a lot of trouble getting rid of us." *Svenska Dagbladet,* November 12, 1989, p. 12.

[69] The Center Party also participated in the negotiations, but in the end its representatives chose to accept only parts of the final agreement and rejected others.

[70] The negotiation process is outlined in more detail in Björklund and Crona, *Svenska Dagbladet*, November 12, 1989, p. 12.

[71] For a summary of the income tax reform, see the government's law proposal to Parliament 1989/90, no. 110, pp. 1–5.

[72] See, for instance, Erik Åsbrink's speech in *The Parliamentary Record*, 1989/90, no. 140, p. 64.

[73] *Aktuellt*, Swedish Television, channel 1, November 7, 1989 (9:00 P.M. newscast).

[74] *Vår bostad*, no. 1, 1990, pp. 20–21.

[75] Dick Ljungberg, "Optimismen sjunker," *Dagens Nyheter*, June 11, 1991, p. 9. For an analysis of the Swedish tax reform, see also Hermansson 1993: 149–153, and Uddhammar 1993: 325–336.

CHAPTER SIX

[1] Robin Toner, "Bitter Tone of the '94 Campaign Elicits Worry on Public Debate," *New York Times*, November 13, 1994, pp. A1, 14.

[2] Boheman was speaker of the Swedish Parliament for many years and thus an attentive student of political speech making. He dryly notes, comparing eloquence in the early twentieth century with later periods, that it must have been easier to talk eloquently and passionately about problems connected with the necessity of democracy or socialism than with less grand matters such as budgets and taxes.

[3] Former Conservative Party chairman Ulf Adelsohn recounts an illuminating conversation he had in the summer of 1984 with the then Minister of Finance Kjell-Olof Feldt: "When I said that there are some things which we agree on, he [Feldt] said that 'we agree on quite a lot, but we are not allowed to show that'" (Adelsohn 1988: 239). See also Kjell-Olof Feldt, "Partierna är ense," *Dagens Nyheter*, July 16, 1991, p. 2. The only main issue still dividing the Swedish parties, Feldt believes, is the tax issue (i.e., whether to reduce taxes generally and substantially or to keep them at their present [high] level).

[4] One reason for this turn of events may have been that the 1988 election was the first one after the assassination of Prime Minister Olof Palme on February 28, 1986. The long-term effects of the assassination remain unclear, but there is no doubt that it affected the political climate and contributed to a calmer election debate.

[5] The Liberal Party leader Bengt Westerberg stressed the importance of tax cuts in every major speech during the campaign. See, for example, his speeches in Marstrand on July 23, 1988 (pp. 9–10), in Stockholm on August 14 (pp. 7–9), and in Gothenburg on September 13 (pp. 8–10). Source: *Folkpartiet* (the Liberal

Party). For an interesting account of the Social Democratic election strategy vis-à-vis the Liberals, see Feldt 1991: 370–373.

6 By adopting a strategy of silence, the Social Democrats also appealed to the powerful tradition of unity and cooperation in Swedish political culture. The strategy turned out to be effective in the short run, but as with much of the new rhetoric, its repeated use after the election quickly wore thin, contributing to the erosion of core support among the rank and file. The governing party's postelection flip-flops on a whole series of issues were so evident that they confounded opponents and supporters alike. The strategy is further described in Åke Ekdahl, "Passiviteten borjar vacka oro: Omstridd s-taktik," *Dagens Nyheter,* June 5, 1988, p. 15. A similar strategy was effectively used by George Bush in the 1988 U.S. presidential campaign.

7 Hans Bergstrom, *Televisionens val* (Stockholm: Näringslivets mediainstitut, report no. 8, 1988), p. 20; Gilljam and Holmberg 1990: 21–22. "Never before has a single issue dominated a Swedish election campaign like the Green issue did in 1988," write Bennulf and Holmberg (1990: 165).

8 Texts provided by the Social Democratic Party of speeches given in Fagersta, August 20, 1988 (quotes on p. 7), and in Stockholm, August 29, 1988, pp. 6–9. In one speech the prime minister even went so far as to put the environment ahead of the employment issue, traditionally the Social Democrats' leading campaign theme. Dick Ljungberg, "Ingvar Carlsson i Karlsborg: Miljon viktigare an jobb," *Dagens Nyheter,* August 9, 1988, p. 11.

9 The SAP's ratings had already started to drop dramatically during the winter and spring of 1989. Popular support dropped from over 44 percent in January 1989, to just 34 percent in January 1990. The party's core support (i.e., support from the "true believers") went down from 33 percent in 1988 to just 21 percent one year later (Holmberg 1990: 69–81). This was a market meltdown from which the party was not able to recover.

10 In the 1992 U.S. presidential campaign, candidate Bill Clinton had successfully used "America can do better" as one of his chief rhetorical weapons against the sitting Bush administration.

11 The analysis of the 1994 campaign is based primarily on Bengtsson and Nilsson 1994; Isaksson 1995; and a taped interview with SAP campaign coordinator Bo Krogvig, August 3, 1994.

12 Cf. Per Wendel, "Sossarna ser dig: USA:s framsta experter ska kartlägga de svenska valjarna," *Expressen,* August 10, 1994, pp. 10–11; Elisabeth Crona, "S-kampanj hamtar inspiration från USA," *Svenska Dagbladet,* March 15, 1994, p. 14.

13 Its electoral success notwithstanding, the SAP has been able to get an absolute majority of the vote only twice in national elections (1940 and 1968). Consequently, during most of its time in power, the party has had to rely on the support from other parties in Parliament, either to the left or to the right.

14 Such a historical compromise was by no means exclusive to Sweden. For example, New Zealand's first historical compromise was in its labor–employer agreements of the 1890s (Davidson 1989: 199, ftnt. 1).

15 For a more detailed description of the vast changes that took place from the 1930s to the 1960s and beyond, see Hadenius, Molin, & Wieslander 1991: 118–248.

16 The decline in the SAP blue collar base has continued to create problems for the party in subsequent elections.

17 Esping-Andersen, quoted in Davidson 1989: 223.

18 The Swedish model of public financing also extends to parties at the regional and local levels (see Gidlund 1983: Chs. 5–6; 1991; 1992: 107–109, 113–116).

19 For example, it has been estimated that the Association of Swedish Enterprises spent approximately 55 to 60 million Skr in the 1982 election campaign to fight the introduction of wage earner investment funds (Gidlund 1991: 46).

20 For a discussion of changes in the public language in Sweden after World War II, see Mårtensson and Svensson 1988: 94–97.

21 Again, the 1988 election appears to have been something of a watershed election. For the first time ever, less than half of the party leaders' appearances in that campaign took place in front of listening audiences (41 percent as opposed to 54 percent in 1985) (Esaiasson 1990: 442–445).

22 R. L. Berke, "Mixed Results for CBS Rule on Sound Bite," *New York Times*, July 11, 1992, p. 11.

23 Kevin Phillips, "The Silver Lining Behind All Those Clouds Over Clinton," *The Washington Post National Weekly Edition*, May 17–23, 1993, p. 23.

24 Kevin Phillips, "America, 1989: Brain-Dead Politics in a Transition," *International Herald Tribune*, October 4, 1989, p. 8.

25 Quoted in Robin Toner, "Image of Capitol Maligned by Outsiders, Insiders," *New York Times*, October 16, 1994, p. 18.

26 Charles Leonard, spokesperson for the Health Care Reform Project, quoted in Richard L. Berke, "Democrats See Voter Backlash Over President," *New York Times*, June 9, 1994, p. A12.

27 *Ibid.*

28 Richard Lacayo, "Off to the Races," *Time*, September 12, 1994, p. 39.

29 Richard L. Berke, "Pollster Advises Democrats: Don't Be Too Close to Clinton," *New York Times*, August 3, 1994, p. A1.

30 Berke, "Democrats See Voter Backlash."

31 William Schneider, remarks delivered at the conference on "The Clinton Presidency: Campaigning, Governing, and the Psychology of Leadership," held at the Graduate School and University Center, City University of New York, November 18–19, 1993. A video record of Schneider's remarks is available from Stanley Rensohn, the Ph.D. program in political science.

[32] Quoted in R. W. Apple, Jr., "Vote Against Crime Bill is Lesson in Clout," *New York Times*, August 17, 1994, pp. A1, A12.

[33] Quoted in Bill D. Moyers, "Johnson Preferred Integration to Disintegration," *International Herald Tribune*, November 15, 1988, p. 4.

[34] Data from the National Election Studies conducted by the University of Michigan record the following changes in party identification between 1952 and 1988: Democratic 47 to 35 percent; Independent 22 to 35 percent; Republican 27 to 30 percent.

CHAPTER SEVEN

[1] Electoral promises of finance reform have gone unfulfilled in each of five recent congresses, from the 100th (1987–1988) through the 104th (1995–1996). The dependency of individual politicians on vast sums of campaign money continually undermines even modest steps toward electoral responsibility. See Bennett (1996b: Ch. 4) for a historical overview.

[2] Many, of course, will rally around the symbol of free speech on this issue. However, the prohibition of political advertising on radio and television (the media in which it is subject to greatest abuse) has at least three precedents within the liberal democratic tradition. First, a number of relatively healthier Western democracies as diverse, for example, as England and Germany, all regulate political advertising and candidate access on the airwaves. Second, the United States has regulated various other forms of broadcast advertising deemed harmful to the national health – cigarettes, sexual services, and pornography, just to name a few. The deterioration of political life caused by candidate marketing on television and radio constitutes at least as great a public hazard as these already prohibited commodities. Finally, the free speech defense crumbles even if it is examined on strict constructionist terms. Almost nobody in public life subscribes to the absolute reading of the First Amendment clause that says "Congress shall pass *no* law [our emphasis]...."

[3] A promising development along these lines emerged in the 1992 presidential campaign with the addition of a debate in which candidates faced the audience directly and answered questions from ordinary people. Not only were the questions more varied, but people reported the debate as more useful than the familiar press panel format.

[4] As for the objection that no two news organizations would come up with the same national agenda, so much the better. If many societies thrive with an avowedly partisan press, surely the American people can live with media debates about national goals.

5 This goes back to an old tradition in Sweden which says that parties should basically be free from government intrusion. The fact that there have been so few instances of overt political corruption in the past has contributed to the remarkable lack of rules and regulations in this area.

6 Cf. Craig R. Whitney, "In 'New' Europe, Old Signs of Political Strain," *International Herald Tribune*, April 6, 1993, p. 5.

7 For a more elaborate discussion, see Chapter 1.

8 A *Time/*CNN poll taken from August 31 to September 1, 1994, as reported in *CNN Late Edition with Frank Sesno*, October 23, 1994. Cf. Kevin Phillips, "Fat City," *Time*, September 26, 1994, pp. 40–44.

9 Robin Toner, "Bitter Tone of the '94 Campaign Elicits Worry on Public Debate," *New York Times*, November 13, 1994, pp. A1, A14. Cf. E. J. Dionne, *Why Americans Hate Politics* (New York: Touchstone, 1992).

10 "Voters, Blame Thyselves," *The Economist*, October 29–4 November, 1994, p. 15.

11 *Ibid.*, pp. 15–16, 35–36, 47–48; Alan Friedman, "Austria's Man in a Hurry: Rightist Hopes to Get Top Job by '96," *International Herald Tribune*, October 12, 1994, pp. 1, 6; William Drozdiak, "Post-Fascist Leader in Italy is Soaring," *International Herald Tribune*, October 26, 1994, p. 7; William Drozdiak, "Far-Right Gains in Belgium and Austria Jar Mainstream Parties, *International Herald Tribune*, October 11, 1994, pp. 1, 8.

12 Most interesting of all is that Ingvar Carlsson, newly appointed prime minister, and some of his leading Social Democrats during the last stages of the campaign started to shift their arguments from those that were issue-oriented to a "trust me" argument. Again, we notice how difficult it is to mobilize stable public support for policies that are not backed up by appealing language and grand visions. This was a classic example of a failed communication strategy, one that almost resulted in a "no" vote and thus in a devastating blow to the reputation of the establishment politicians.

References

Åberg, Alf. 1986. "Nàr folkhemmet blev det starka samhallet," *Svenska Dagbladet*, February 26.

Adelsohn, Ulf. 1988. *Partiledare: Dagbok 1981–1986*. Malmo: Gedins.

Alexander, Herbert E. 1992. *Financing Politics: Money, Elections and Political Reforms*. 4th ed. Washington, D.C.: Congressional Quarterly Press.

Almond, Gabriel, and Sidney Verba. 1963. *The Civic Culture: Political Attitudes and Democracy in Five Nations*. Princeton, N.J.: Princeton University Press.

Anton, Thomas J. 1969. "Policy-making and Political Culture in Sweden." *Scandinavian Political Studies* 4:88–102.

———. 1980. *Administered Politics: Elite Political Culture in Sweden*. Boston: Martinus Nijhoff Publishing.

Arnold, Thurman W. 1935. *The Symbols of Government*. New Haven: Yale University Press.

———. 1937. *The Folklore of Capitalism*. New Haven: Yale University Press.

Arterton, F. Christopher. 1985. *Media Politics: The News Strategies of Presidential Campaigns*. Lexington, Mass.: Lexington Books.

Åsard, Erik. 1979. *Politik och ideologi: Artiklar och essayer i brännbara ämnen*. Stockholm: Liber.

———. 1985. *Kampen om löntagarfonderna: Fondutredningen från samtal till sammanbrott*. Stockholm: Norstedts.

———. 1986. "Industrial and Economic Democracy in Sweden: From Consensus to Confrontation." *European Journal of Political Research* 14:207-19.

———. 1989. "Election Campaigns in Sweden and the United States: Convergence or Divergence?" *American Studies in Scandinavia* 21:70–87.

———. 1990. "Politikens talekonst förfaller." *Tvarsnitt* 1:2–9.

———. 1991. "Svensk politik ar en fråga om sexårscykler." *Aftonbladet*. May 20.

Åsard, Erik, and W. Lance Bennett. 1990. "The Marketplace of Ideas in Sweden and the United States." Report to the *Riksbankens Jubileumsfond, Projektet "Politik och retorik" (DNR 86–277)*.

————. 1991. "The Shrinking Range of Ideas in the Political Marketplace: Candidate–Party Rhetoric in Swedish and American National Elections." Report to the *Riksbankens Jubileumsfond, Projektet "Politik och retorik" (DNR 86–277)*.

Asp, Kent. 1986. *Maktiga massmedier: Studier i politisk opinionsbildning*. Stockholm: Akademilitteratur.

————. 1988. *Sveriges Radios nyhetsbevakning av 1988 års val*. Gothenburg: Department of Political Science, Gothenburg University (mimeo).

————. 1995. *Kommersialiserade TV-nyheter-på gott och ont: En jamförande undersökning av Rapport TV2 och Nyheterna TV4*. Gothenburg: Department of Journalism and Mass Communication, Gothenburg University.

Bagdikian, Ben H. 1985. "The U.S. Media: Supermarket or Assembly Line?" *Journal of Communication* 35:97–109.

————. 1987. *The Media Monopoly*. 2d ed. Boston: Beacon Press.

Beam, David R., Timothy J. Conlan, and Margaret T. Wrightson. 1990. "Solving the Riddle of Tax Reform: Party Competition and the Politics of Ideas." *Political Science Quarterly* 105:193–217.

Bengtsson, Håkan A., and Tommy Nilsson. 1994. *Bakom Mona Sahlin: Ett reportage om Valhall, politiken, medierna, marknaden och valet*. Stockholm: Tiden.

Bennett, W. Lance. 1989. "Marginalizing the Majority: Conditioning Public Opinion to Accept Managerial Democracy," in Michael Margolis and Gary Mauser, eds., *Manipulating Public Opinion*. Belmont, Cal.: Brooks/Cole.

————. 1990. "Toward a Theory of Press–State Relations in the United States." *Journal of Communication* 40:103–125.

————. 1992. *The Governing Crisis: Media, Money, and Marketing in American Elections*. New York: St. Martin's Press.

————. 1996a. *News: The Politics of Illusion*. 3d ed. New York: Longman.

————. 1996b. *The Governing Crisis: Media, Money, and Marketing in American Elections*. 2d ed. New York: St. Martin's Press.

————. 1995. "The Cueless Public: Bill Clinton Meets the New American Voter in Campaign '92," in Stanley Renshon, ed., *The Clinton Presidency: Campaigning, Governing, and the Psychology of Leadership*. Boulder, Colo.: Westview Press.

Bennett, W. Lance, and Regina Lawrence. 1995. "News Icons and the Mainstreaming of Social Change." *Journal of Communication* 45:20–39.

Bennulf, Martin, and Soren Holmberg. 1990. "The Green Breakthrough in Sweden." *Scandinavian Political Studies* 13:2, 165–184.

Bergström, Hans. 1988. *Televisionens val*. Stockholm: Naringslivets mediainstitut. Report no. 8.

————. 1991. "Sweden's Politics and Party System at the Crossroads." *West European Politics*, no. 3:8–30.

Birnbaum, Jeffrey H., and Alan S. Murray. 1987. *Showdown at Gucci Gulch: Lawmakers, Lobbyists, and the Unlikely Triumph of Tax Reform.* New York: Vintage.

Blumler, Jay G., and Michael Gurevitch. 1975. "Towards a Comparative Framework for Political Communication Research," in Steven Chafee, ed., *Political Communication.* Beverly Hills: Sage: 165–193.

Blumler, Jay G., Dennis Kavanagh, and T. J. Nossiter. 1996. "Modern Communications vs. Traditional Politics in Britain: Unstable Marriage of Convenience," in Paolo Mancini and David L. Swanson, eds., *Politics, Media, and Modern Democracy.* Westport, Conn.: Praeger.

Boheman, Erik. 1970. *Tankar i en talmansstol.* Stockholm: Norstedts.

Boréus, Kristina. 1994. *Högervåg. Nyliberalism och kampen om språket i svensk offentlig debatt 1969–1989.* Stockholm: Tiden.

Brinkley, Alan. 1989. "The New Deal and the Idea of the State," in Steve Fraser and Gary Gerstle, eds., *The Rise and Fall of the New Deal Order, 1930–1980.* Princeton: Princeton University Press.

Burke, Al. 1994. "Borta bra men hemma värst," *Makt & Media* no. 3.

Burnham, Walter Dean. 1970. *Critical Elections and the Mainsprings of American Politics.* New York: Norton.

Carey, James W. 1989. *Communication As Culture.* Winchester, Mass.: Unwin Hyman.

Cederberg, Ann. 1993. *Stil och strategi i riksdagsretoriken: En undersökning av debattspråkets utveckling i den svenska tvåkammarriksdagen (1867–1970).* Uppsala, Sweden: Uppsala University, Department of Scandinavian Languages.

Childs, Marquis W. 1936. *Sweden the Middle Way.* London: Faber and Faber.

Curti, Merle. 1968. "Sweden in the American Social Mind of the 1930s," in J. Iverne Dowie and J. Thomas Tredway, eds., *The Immigration of Ideas: Studies in the North Atlantic Community.* Rock Island, Ill.: Augustana Historical Society.

Dahl, Robert. 1993. "The Ills of the System: Do We Need Basic Constitutional Reform?" *Dissent.* Fall:447–54.

Davidson, Alexander. 1989. *Two Models of Welfare: The Origin and Development of the Welfare State in Sweden and New Zealand, 1888–1988.* Stockholm: Almqvist & Wiksell.

Dewey, John. 1916. *Democracy and Education.* New York: Macmillan.

Dewey, Thomas E. 1940. *The Case Against the New Deal.* New York: Harper and Brothers.

Diamond, Edwin, and Steven Bates. 1992. *The Spot: The Rise of Political Advertising on Television.* Cambridge, Mass.: M.I.T. Press.

Domhoff, William. 1990. *The Power Elite and the State: How Policy is Made in America.* New York: Aldine de Gruyter.

Edelman, Murray. 1964. *The Symbolic Uses of Politics.* Urbana: University of Illinois Press.

———. 1974. *The Symbolic Uses of Politics.* 6th ed. Urbana, Chicago, & London: University of Illinois Press.

———. 1977. *Political Language: Words That Succeed and Policies That Fail.* New York: Academic Press.

———. 1988. *Constructing the Political Spectacle.* Chicago: University of Chicago Press.

Ekman, Carl. 1928a. "De senaste socialist- och hogerregeringarna i verklighetens ljus." Speech on July 8. In *Politiska dagsfrågor* no. 2. Stockholm.

———. 1928b. "Penningvalde, klassvalde, medborgarvälde." Speech on August 25 and 26. In *Politiska dagsfrågor* no. 9. Stockholm.

Elder, Neil, Alastair H. Thomas, and David Arter. 1988. *The Consensual Democracies? The Government and Politics of the Scandinavian States.* Oxford: Basil Blackwell.

Elliot, Maria. 1991. "Fortroendet for samhallsinstitutionerna," in Sören Holmberg and Lennart Weibull, eds., *Politiska opinioner: SOM-undersokningen 1990.* Gothenburg, Sweden: Departments of Political Science & Journalism and Mass Communication, Gothenburg University.

———. 1993. "Medborgerlig tillit och misstro: Om samhallsfortroende i kristider," in Sören Holmberg and Lennart Weibull, eds., *Perspektiv på krisen: SOM-undersökningen 1992.* Gothenburg, Sweden: Departments of Political Science & Journalism and Mass Communication, Gothenburg University.

Ellul, Jacques. 1965. *Propaganda.* New York: Vintage.

Elmbrant, Bjorn. 1993. *Så föll den svenska modellen.* Stockholm: T. Fischer.

Elvander, Nils. 1954. "Rudolf Kjellén och nationalsocialismen," *Statsvetenskaplig Tidskrift,* no. 1.

———. 1961. *Harald Hjärne och konservatismen.* Stockholm: Almqvist & Wiksell.

———. 1980. *Skandinavisk arbetarrorelse.* Stockholm: LiberForlag.

———. 1988. *Den svenska modellen: Loneförhandlingar och inkomstpolitik 1982–1986.* Stockholm: Allmänna forlaget.

———. 1989. "Från Wigforss till Feldt: Svensk skattepolitik 1947–1988," *Tiden* 3:157–165.

Entman, Robert. 1989. *Democracy Without Citizens: Media and the Decay of American Politics.* New York: Oxford University Press.

Erlander, Tage. 1954. *Människor i samverkan.* Stockholm: Tiden.

———. 1956a. *Framstegens politik.* Stockholm: Tiden.

———. 1956b. "Från klasskamp till folkhem," *Röster i Radio,* No. 35.

———. 1962. *Valfrihetens samhälle.* Stockholm: Tiden.

———. 1976. *Tage Erlander 1955–1960.* Stockholm: Tiden.

Esaiasson, Peter. 1990. *Svenska valkampanjer 1866–1988.* Stockholm: Allmänna forlaget.

Esping-Andersen, Gosta. 1985. *Politics Against Markets: The Social Democratic Road to Power.* Princeton: Princeton University Press.

Falkemark, Gunnar. 1992. "Rudolf Kjellén – vetenskapsman eller humbug?" in Gunnar Falkemark, ed., *Statsvetarporträtt: Svenska statsvetare under 350 år.* Stockholm: SNS.

Feldt, Kjell-Olof. 1991. *Alla dessa dagar ... I regeringen 1982–1990.* Stockholm: Norstedts.

Ferguson, Thomas. 1989. "Industrial Conflict and the Coming of the New Deal: The Triumph of Multinational Liberalism in America," in Steve Fraser and Gary Gerstle, eds., *The Rise and Fall of the New Deal Order, 1930–1980.* Princeton: Princeton University Press.

———. 1995. *Golden Rule: The Investment Theory of Party Competition and the Logic of Investment-Driven Political Systems.* Chicago: University of Chicago Press.

Ferguson, Thomas, and Joel Rogers. 1981. "The Reagan Victory: Corporate Coalitions in the 1980 Campaign," in Ferguson and Rogers, eds., *The Hidden Election: Politics and Economics in the 1980 Presidential Campaign,* pp. 3–64. New York: Pantheon Books.

———. 1986. *Right Turn: The Decline of the Democrats and the Future of American Politics.* New York: Hill & Wang.

Fishkin, James S. 1991. *Democracy and Deliberation: New Directions for Democratic Reform.* New Haven, Conn.: Yale University Press.

Frederick, J. George. 1933. *A Primer of "New Deal" Economics.* New York: The Business Bourse.

Fredriksson, Gunnar, Dieter Strand, and Bo Sodersten. 1970. *Per Albin-linjen: Tre ställningstaganden till en socialdemokratisk tradition.* Stockholm: Norstedts.

Gibbins, John R., ed. 1989. *Contemporary Political Culture: Politics in a Postmodern Age.* London: Sage.

Gidlund, Gullan M. 1983. *Partistöd.* Umeå: CWK Gleerup. Umeå Studies in Politics and Administration, No. 8.

———. 1991. "Public Investments in Swedish Democracy: Gambling With Gains and Losses," in Matti Wiberg, ed., *The Public Purse and Political Parties: Public Financing of Political Parties in Nordic Countries.* Jyvaskylä, Finland: The Finnish Political Science Association.

———. 1992. "From Popular Movement to Political Party: Development of the Social Democratic Labor Party Organization," in Klaus Misgeld, Karl Molin, and Klas Åmark, eds., *Creating Social Democracy: A Century of the Social Democratic Labor Party in Sweden.* University Park: The Pennsylvania State University Press.

Gilljam, Mikael, and Sören Holmberg. 1990. *Rött, blått, grönt: En bok om 1988 års riksdagsval.* Stockholm: Bonniers.

————. 1993. *Väljarna inför 90-talet*. Stockholm: Norstedts.

Ginsberg, Benjamin. 1986. *The Captive Public: How Mass Opinion Promotes State Power*. New York: Basic Books.

Ginsberg, Benjamin, and Martin Shefter. 1990. *Politics by Other Means: The Declining Importance of Elections in America*. New York: Basic Books.

Ginsburg, Norman. 1992. *Divisions of Welfare: A Critical Introduction to Comparative Social Policy*. London: Sage.

Gramsci, Antonio. 1987. *Selections from the Prison Notebooks*. Quinton Hoare and Geoffrey Smith, eds. New York: International Publishers.

Granberg, Donald, and Soren Holmberg. 1988. *The Political System Matters: Social Psychology and Voting Behavior in Sweden and the United States*. Cambridge: Cambridge University Press.

Green, David. 1987. *Shaping Political Consciousness: The Language of Politics in America from McKinley to Reagan*. Ithaca, N.Y.: Cornell University Press.

Greider, William. 1992. *Who Will Tell the People? The Betrayal of American Democracy*. New York: Touchstone.

Gronbeck, Bruce. 1990. "Electric Rhetoric: The Changing Forms of American Political Discourse," *Estratto da Vichiana* 1:144–159.

Gurevitch, Michael, and Jay G. Blumler. 1990. "Comparative Research: The Extending Frontier," in David L. Swanson and Dan Nimmo, eds., *New Directions in Political Communication: A Resource Book*, pp. 305–325. Newbury Park, Cal.: Sage.

Habermas, Jurgen. 1975. *Legitimation Crisis*. Boston: Beacon Press.

Hadenius, Axel. 1976. *Facklig organisationsutveckling: En studie av Landsorganisationen i Sverige*. Stockholm: Rabén & Sjögren.

————. 1986. *A Crisis of the Welfare State? Opinions about Taxes and Public Expenditure in Sweden*. Stockholm: Almqvist & Wiksell.

Hadenius, Stig. 1990a. "Regeringen och massmedierna 1840–1990," in *Att styra riket: regeringskansliet 1840–1990*. Stockholm: Allmanna Förlaget.

————. 1990b. *Vårt behov av press*. Stockholm: Dagspressen.

Hadenius, Stig, and Gustaf Anderberg. 1994. *Vem ager vad i svenska massmedier?* Stockholm: Department of Journalism, Media, and Communication, Stockholm University.

Hadenius, Stig, and Lennart Weibull. 1989. *Massmedier: En bok om press, radio och TV*. 4th ed. Stockholm: Bonniers.

Hadenius, Stig, Bjorn Molin, and Hans Wieslander. 1991. *Sverige efter 1900: En modern politisk historia*. Stockholm: Bonniers.

Hague, Rod, and Martin Harrop. 1982. *Comparative Government*. London and Basingstoke: Macmillan.

Hall, Peter A., ed. 1989. *The Political Power of Economic Ideas: Keynesianism Across Nations*. Princeton: Princeton University Press.

Hallberg, Mikael, and Tomas Jonsson. 1993. "'Allmånanda och självtukt': Per Albin Hanssons ideologiska förändring och folkhemsretorikens framvaxt." Uppsala, Sweden: Uppsala University: Department of Literature, Division of Rhetoric.

Hallin, Daniel C. 1985. "The American News Media: A Critical Theory Perspective," in J. Forrester, ed. *Critical Theory and Public Life*, pp. 121–146. Cambridge, Mass.: M.I.T. Press.

————. 1994. *We Keep America On Top of the World*. London: Routledge.

Hanson, Russell L. 1985. *The Democratic Imagination in America*. Princeton: Princeton University Press.

Hansson, Per Albin. 1935. *Demokrati: Tal och uppsatser*. Stockholm.

————. 1943. *Socialdemokratiska idéer och framtidsutsikter*. Stockholm.

Hansson, Sven Ove, and Anna L. Lodenius. 1988. *Operation högervridning*. Stockholm: Tiden.

Hårsmar, Mats. 1991. "Den ofullbordade tankereformen." *Tiden*, no. 5, 285–289.

Hartz, Louis. 1953. *The Liberal Tradition in America*. New York: Harcourt Brace Jovanovich.

————. 1955. *The Liberal Tradition in America: An Interpretation of American Political Thought Since the Revolution*. New York: Harcourt Brace Jovanovich.

Haskel, Barbara. 1987. "Paying for the Welfare State: Creating Political Durability." *Scandinavian Studies* 59:221–253.

Heckscher, Gunnar. 1984. *The Welfare State and Beyond: Success and Problems in Scandinavia*. Minneapolis: University of Minnesota Press.

Heclo, Hugh, and Henrik Madsen. 1987. *Policy and Politics in Sweden: Principled Pragmatism*. Philadelphia: Temple University Press.

Hedborg, Anna, and Rudolf Meidner. 1984. *Folkhemsmodellen*. Stockholm: Rabén & Sjögren.

Herbst, Susan. 1993. *Numbered Voices: How Opinion Polling Has Shaped American Politics*. Chicago: University of Chicago Press.

Herman, Edward S. 1985. "Diversity of News: 'Marginalizing' the Opposition." *Journal of Communication* 35:135–146.

Hermansson, Jörgen. 1993. *Politik som intressekamp: Parlamentariskt beslutsfattande och organiserade intressen i Sverige*. Stockholm: Norstedts.

Hershey, Marjorie R. 1989. "The Campaign and the Media," in Gerald Pomper, ed., *The Election of 1988: Reports and Interpretations*. Chatham, N.J.: Chatham House.

Hertsgaard, Mark. 1989. *On Bended Knee: The Press and the Reagan Presidency*. New York: Schocken Books.

Hirdman, Yvonne. 1988. *Vi bygger landet: Den svenska arbetarrörelsens historia från Per Götrek till Olof Palme*. Stockholm: Tiden.

————. 1989. *Att lägga livet till rätta – studier i svensk folkhemspolitik*. Stockholm: Carlssons.

Hofstadter, Richard C. 1973. *The American Political Tradition & the Men Who Made It.* New York: Vintage.

Holmberg, Soren. 1990. "Socialdemokraternas opinionsras 1989," in Soren Holmberg and Lennart Weibull, eds., *Medier och opinion i Sverige: SOM-undersökningen 1989.* Gothenburg, Sweden: Departments of Political Science & Journalism and Mass Communication, Gothenburg University.

Holmberg, Sóren, and Mikael Gilljam. 1987. *Valjare och val i Sverige.* Stockholm: Bonniers.

Holmstrom, Barry. 1994. "The Judicialization of Politics in Sweden." *International Political Science Review* 15, no. 2:153–64.

Huntington, Samuel P. 1984. "Will More Countries Become Democratic?" *Political Science Quarterly* 99:193–218.

Isacson, Maths. 1991. "Bruket och folkhemmet," *Häften för kritiska studier,* no. 2.

Isaksson, Anders. 1985. *Per Albin, vol. I: Vägen mot folkhemmet.* Stockholm: Wahlstróm & Widstrand.

————. 1990. *Per Albin, vol. II: Revolutionären.* Stockholm: Wahlstrom & Widstrand.

Iyengar, Shanto. 1992. *Is Anyone Responsible?* Chicago: University of Chicago Press.

Iyengar, Shanto, and Donald Kinder. 1987. *News That Matters.* Chicago: University of Chicago Press.

Jaccoby, Russell. 1987. *The Last Intellectuals: American Culture in the Age of Academe.* New York: Farrar, Strauss & Giroux.

Jamieson, Kathleen Hall. 1988. *Eloquence in an Electronic Age: The Transformation of Political Speechmaking.* New York: Oxford University Press.

————. 1992. *Dirty Politics: Deception, Distraction, and Democracy.* New York: Oxford University Press.

Jefferson, Thomas. 1939. *Thomas Jefferson on Democracy.* Saul K. Padover, ed. New York: New American Library.

Jerneck, Magnus, Anders Sannerstedt, and Mats Sjólin. 1988. "Internationalization and Parliamentary Decision-making: The Case of Sweden 1970–1985." *Scandinavian Political Studies* 11:169–194.

Johannesson, Kurt, Lena Johannesson, Olle Josephson, and Erik Åsard. 1990. "The Language of the Swedish Labor Movement: A Presentation of an Interdisciplinary Research Project." Stockholm: The Swedish Council for Research in the Humanities and Social Sciences (HSFR).

Johannesson, Kurt, Olle Josephson, and Erik Åsard, eds. 1992. *Svenska tal från Torgny lagman till Ingmar Bergman.* Stockholm: Norstedts.

Johansson, Jan. 1992. *Det statlig kommittéväsendet: Kunskap, kontroll, konsensus.* Dissertation, Stockholm University.

Josephson, Olle. 1991. "Diskussionsskolan 1886: Språkbruksmiljo, argumentation och stil i tidig arbetarrórelse." Uppsala, Sweden: Department of Literature, Uppsala University.

Katznelson, Ira. 1989. "Was the Great Society a Lost Opportunity?" in Steve Fraser and Gary Gerstle, eds., *The Rise and Fall of the New Deal Order, 1930–1980.* Princeton: Princeton University Press.

Kavanagh, Dennis. 1995. *Election Campaigning: The New Marketing of Politics.* London: Blackwell.

Kelly, M. 1993. "The Game." *The New York Times Magazine.* October 31: 64–103.

Kelman, Steven. 1981. *Regulating America, Regulating Sweden: A Comparative Study of Occupational Safety and Health Policy.* Cambridge, Mass.: M.I.T. Press.

———. 1988. "Why Public Ideas Matter," in Robert B. Reich, ed., *The Power of Public Ideas.* Cambridge, Mass.: Ballinger.

Keynes, John Maynard. 1964. *The General Theory of Employment, Interest and Money.* New York: Harcourt Brace Jovanovich.

Kingdon, John W. 1984. *Agendas, Alternatives, and Public Policies.* Boston: Little, Brown.

Korpi, Walter. 1983. *The Democratic Class Struggle.* London: Routledge & Kegan Paul.

Krasno, Jonathan S., and Donald Phillip Green. 1993. "Stop the Buck Here: The Case for Campaign Spending Limits." *The Brookings Review* 11, 2:17–21.

Kristiansson, Göran. 1989. "På tröskeln till folkhemmet." *Sydsvenska Dagbladet,* March 19.

Lane, Jan-Erik. 1991. "Interpretations of the Swedish Model." *West European Politics,* no. 3:1–7.

Larsson, Jan. 1994. *Hemmet vi ärvde: Om folkhemmet, identiteten och den gemensamma framtiden.* Stockholm: Arena.

Lasswell, Harold D. 1960. *Psychopathology and Politics.* New York: Viking Press.

Leff, Mark H. 1984. *The Limits of Symbolic Reform: The New Deal and Taxation, 1933–1939.* Cambridge: Cambridge University Press.

Leuchtenberg, William E. 1963. *Franklin D. Roosevelt and the New Deal: 1932–1940.* New York: Harper and Row.

Lewin, Leif. 1970. *Planhushållningsdebatten.* 3d ed. Stockholm: Almqvist & Wiksell.

———. 1975. "The Debate on Economic Planning in Sweden," in Steven Koblik, ed., *Sweden's Development from Poverty to Affluence, 1750–1970.* Minneapolis: University of Minnesota Press.

———. 1988. *Ideology and Strategy: A Century of Swedish Politics.* Cambridge: Cambridge University Press.

———. 1992. *Samhället och de organiserade intresserna.* Stockholm: Norstedts.

Lewin, Leif, Bo Jansson, and Dag Sorbom. 1972. *The Swedish Electorate 1887–1968.* Stockholm: Almqvist & Wiksell.

Lichtenstein, Nelson. 1989. "From Corporatism to Collective Bargaining: Organized Labor and the Eclipse of Social Democracy in the Postwar Era," in Steve Fraser and Gary Gerstle, eds., *The Rise and Fall of the New Deal Order, 1930–1980.* Princeton: Princeton University Press.

Lindgren, John. 1950. *Per Albin Hansson i svensk demokrati: Första delen 1892–1920.* Stockholm: Tiden.

Lindman, Arvid. 1928. *Det politiska läget just nu.* Speech in Lund on February 10. Stockholm: Allmänna valmansförbundet.

———. 1931. "Konservativ framstegspolitik." Speech on August 2.

———. 1935. "Levande konservatism." Speech on May 19.

Lindstrom, Rickard. 1952. *Per Albin Hansson.* Stockholm: Folket i Bilds forlag.

Lindström, Ulf. 1985. *Fascism in Scandinavia 1920–1940.* Stockholm: Almqvist & Wiksell.

Lippmann, Walter. 1922. *Public Opinion.* New York: Free Press.

Lipset, Seymour Martin. 1979. *The First New Nation: The United States in Historical and Comparative Perspective.* New York: Norton.

Lipset, Seymour Martin, and Stein Rokkan. 1967. *Party Systems and Voter Alignments: Cross-National Perspectives.* New York: Free Press.

Lipset, Seymour Martin, and W. Schneider. 1983. *The Confidence Gap: Business, Labor, and Government in the Public Mind.* New York: Free Press.

Ljunggren, Stig-Bjorn. 1992. *Folkhemskapitalismen: Högerns programutveckling under efterkrigstiden.* Stockholm: Tiden.

Locke, John. 1960. *Two Treatises of Government.* Peter Laslett, ed. New York: New American Library.

Lofgren, Orvar. 1993. "Materializing the Nation in Sweden and America." *Ethnos* nos. 3–4. Stockholm: Folkens Museum-Etnografiska.

Loomis, Robert. 1990. *The New American Politician: Ambition, Entrepreneurship, and the Changing Face of Political Life.* New York: Basic Books.

Louchheim, Katie, ed. 1983. *The Making of the New Deal: The Insiders Speak.* Cambridge, Mass.: Harvard University Press.

Lundquist, Lennart J. 1980. *The Hare and the Tortoise: Clean Air Policies in the United States and Sweden.* Ann Arbor: University of Michigan Press.

Malbin, Michael J. 1984. "Looking Back at the Future of Campaign Finance Reform: Interest Groups and American Elections," in M. J. Malbin, ed., *Money and Politics in the United States.* Chatham, N.J.: Chatham House.

Manheim, Jarol. 1991. *All of the People, All the Time.* Armonk, N.Y.: M. E. Sharpe.

Margolis, Michael, and Gary Mauser, eds. 1989. *Manipulating Public Opinion.* Belmont, Cal.: Brooks/Cole.

Mårtensson, Eva, and Jan Svensson. 1988. *Offentlighetsstruktur och språkförändring.* Lund, Sweden: Lund University, Department of Scandinavian Languages. Report no. 14.

Meijer, Hans. 1969. "Bureaucracy and Policy Formulation in Sweden." *Scandinavian Political Studies* vol. 4.

Merelman, Richard. 1991. *Partial Visions: Culture and Politics in Britain, Canada, and the United States.* Madison: University of Wisconsin Press.

Micheletti, Michele. 1985. *Organizing Interest and Organized Protest: Difficulties of Member Representation for the Swedish Central Organization of Salaried Employees (TCO).* Stockholm Studies in Politics, 29.

————. 1991. "Swedish Corporatism at a Crossroads: The Impact of New Politics and New Social Movements." *West European Politics* no. 3:144–65.

————. 1995. *Civil Society and State Relations in Sweden.* Aldershot, England: Avebury.

Mill, John S. 1966. *On Liberty.* London: Oxford University Press.

————. 1977. *Essays on Politics and Society,* J. M. Robson, ed. Toronto: University of Toronto Press.

Miller, A. H., and O. Listhaug. 1990. "Political Parties and Confidence in Government: A Comparison of Norway, Sweden and the United States." *British Journal of Political Science* 20, 3:357–386.

Miller, David. 1993. "Deliberative Democracy and Social Choice," in David Held, ed., *Prospects for Democracy: North, South, East, West.* Oxford: Polity Press.

Miller, T., and J. Pavlik. 1993. "Campaign Coverage by the Numbers," in The Freedom Forum Media Studies Center, *The Finish Line: Covering the Campaign's Final Days.* New York: Columbia University/Freedom Forum.

Milner, Henry. 1989. *Sweden: Social Democracy in Practice.* Oxford: Oxford University Press.

Misgeld, Klaus, Karl Molin, and Klas Åmark, eds. 1992. *Creating Social Democracy: A Century of the Social Democratic Labor Party in Sweden.* University Park: The Pennsylvania State University Press.

Möller, Tommy. 1993. "Forskning om svensk politisk historia 1945–1980," in Britta Lövgren, Tommy Möller, Torbjörn Nilsson, and Lars Pettersson, eds., *Svensk politisk historia: En kommenterad litteraturöversikt.* Uppsala: Swedish Science Press.

Neustadt, Richard E. 1990. *Presidential Power and the Modern Presidents: The Politics of Leadership from Roosevelt to Reagan.* New York: Free Press.

Nilsson, Göran B. 1975. "Swedish Liberalism at Mid-Nineteenth Century," in Steven Koblik, ed., *Sweden's Development from Poverty to Affluence, 1750–1970.* Minneapolis: University of Minnesota Press.

O'Shaughnessy, Nicholas J. 1990. *The Phenomenon of Political Marketing.* London: Macmillan.

Olson, Mancur. 1982. *The Rise and Decline of Nations: Economic Growth, Stagflation, and Social Rigidities.* New Haven and London: Yale University Press.

Olsson, Erik, and David Gaunt. 1990. "Ett folkhem för alla?" *Invandrare och minoriteter* nos. 5–6.

Osterberg, Eva. 1993. "Vardagens strava samförstånd: Bondepolitik i den svenska modellen från vasatid till frihetstid," in Gunnar Broberg, Ulla Wikander, and Klas Åmark, eds., *Tänka, tycka, tro: Svensk historia underifrån.* Stockholm: Ordfront.

Page, Benjamin. 1978. *Choices and Echoes in Presidential Elections.* Chicago: University of Chicago Press.

Page, Benjamin, and Robert Shapiro. 1992. *The Rational Public: Fifty Years of Trends in Americans' Policy Preferences.* Chicago: University of Chicago Press.

Patterson, Thomas E. 1993. *Out of Order.* New York: Alfred A. Knopf.

Petersson, Olof. 1993. *Svensk politik.* Stockholm: Publica.

Petersson, Olof, and Ingrid Carlberg. 1990. *Makten över tanken: En bok om det svenska massmediesamhället.* Stockholm: Carlssons.

Petersson, Olof, Yvonne Hirdman, Inga Persson, and Johan P. Olsen. 1990. *Demokrati och makt i Sverige: Maktutredningens huvudrapport.* Stockholm: SOU no. 44.

Phillips, Kevin. 1990. *The Politics of Rich and Poor: Wealth and the American Electorate in the Reagan Aftermath.* New York: Random House.

Pomper, Gerald, ed. 1989. *The Election of 1988.* Chatham, N.J.: Chatham House.

———, ed. 1993. *The Election of 1992.* Chatham, N.J.: Chatham House.

Pontusson, Jonas. 1987. "The Emergence of the Modern Swedish State," in Mark Kesselman and Joel Krieger, eds., *European Politics in Transition.* Lexington: Heath.

Premfors, Rune. 1983. "Governmental Commissions in Sweden," *American Behavioral Scientist* May/June, 26:623–642.

Ranney, Austin. 1983. *Channels of Power: The Impact of Television on American Politics.* New York: Basic Books.

Rodgers, Daniel T. 1987. *Contested Truths: Keywords in American Politics Since Independence.* New York: Basic Books.

Rogowski, Ronald. 1991. "Review of Peter A. Hall, ed., *The Political Power of Economic Ideas.*" *American Political Science Review* 85:999–1000.

Rothstein, Bo. 1986. *Den socialdemokratiska staten: Reformer och förvaltning inom svensk arbetsmarknads-och skolpolitik.* Lund, Sweden: Studentlitteratur.

———. 1992. *Den korporativa staten: Intresseorganisationer och statsförvaltning i svensk politik.* Stockholm: Norstedts.

Rothstein, Bo, Peter Esaiasson, Jorgen Hermansson, Michele Micheletti, and Olof Petersson. 1995. *Demokratirådets rapport 1995: Demokrati som dialog.* Stockholm: SNS.

Ruin, Olof. 1982. "Svensk politisk stil: att komma överens och tanka efter fore," in Lennart Arvedson, Ingemund Hagg, and Bengt Rydén, eds., *Land i olag: Samhällsorganisation under omprövning.* Stockholm: SNS.

———. 1986. *I välfärdsstatens tjänst: Tage Erlander 1946–1969.* Stockholm: Tiden.

Rustow, Dankwart. 1955. *The Politics of Compromise: A Study of Parties and Cabinet Governments in Sweden.* Princeton: Princeton University Press.

Sabato, Larry J. 1985. *PAC Power: Inside the World of Political Action Committees.* New York: Norton.

———. 1991. *Feeding Frenzy: How Attack Journalism has Transformed American Politics.* New York: Free Press.

Schattschneider, E. E. 1960. *The Semi Sovereign People.* Hinsdale, Ill.: Dryden Press.

Schlesinger, Arthur M., Jr. 1958. *The Coming of the New Deal.* London: Heinemann.

Schullerqvist, Bengt. 1992. *Från kosackval till kohandel: SAP:s väg till makten (1928–33).* Stockholm: Tiden.

Semetko, Holli, and Barkin, S. 1986. "Television and Election Agenda Setting." Paper presented at the Annual Meeting of the International Communication Association, Chicago.

Soderlind, Donald, and Olof Petersson. 1988. *Svensk förvaltningspolitik.* Uppsala, Sweden: Diskurs.

Södersten, Bo. 1991. *Kapitalismen byggde landet.* Stockholm: SNS.

Sodersten, Bo, Carl-Gustav Fernlund, Cecilia Gunne, Anders Kristofferson, and Ingemar Hansson. 1990. *Den stora reformen: Handbok om de nya skatterna.* Stockholm: SNS Förlag.

Spencer, Martin E. 1970. "Politics and Rhetorics." *Social Research* no. 4:597–623.

Steinmo, Sven. 1989. "Political Institutions and Tax Policy in the United States, Sweden, and Britain." *World Politics* 2:500–535.

Stone, Deborah A. 1988. *Policy Paradox and Political Reason.* Glenview, Ill.: Scott Foresman.

Stråth, Bo. 1992. *Folkhemmet mot Europa: Ett historiskt perspektiv på 90-talet.* Falun, Sweden: ScandBook AB.

Svensson, Jan. 1990. *Från debatt till utspel: Om språket i riksdagsanföranden från 1945 till 1985.* Lund, Sweden: Lund University, Department of Scandinavian Languages.

———. 1993. *Språk och offentlighet: Om språkbruksförändringar i den politiska offentligheten.* Lund, Sweden: Lund University Press.

Svensson, Torsten. 1994. *Socialdemokratins dominans: En studie av den svenska socialdemokratins partistrategi.* Stockholm: Norstedts.

Therborn, Göran. 1992. "A Unique Chapter in the History of Democracy: The Social Democracy in Sweden," in Klaus Misgeld, Karl Molin, and Klas Åmark, eds., *Creating Social Democracy: A Century of the Social Democratic Labor Party in Sweden.* University Park, Penn.: The Pennsylvania State University Press.

Tilton, Tim. 1991. *The Political Theory of Swedish Social Democracy: Through the Welfare State to Socialism.* Oxford: Clarendon Press.

————. 1992. "The Role of Ideology in Social Democratic Politics," in Klaus Misgeld, Karl Molin, and Klas Åmark, eds., *Creating Social Democracy: A Century of the Social Democratic Labor Party in Sweden.* University Park: The Pennsylvania State University Press.

Tingsten, Herbert. 1973. *The Swedish Social Democrats: Their Ideological Development.* Totowa, N.J.: Bedminster Press.

Tocqueville, Alexis de. 1969. *Democracy in America.* J. P. Mayer, ed. New York: Anchor Books.

Tragårdh, Lars. 1990. "Varieties of Volkish Ideologies: Sweden and Germany 1848–1933," in Bo Stråth, ed., *Language and the Construction of Class Identities: The Struggle for Discursive Power in Social Organisation: Scandinavia and Germany after 1800.* Gothenburg, Sweden: Gothenburg University Press.

————. 1992. "Svensk modell eller svensk kultur?" *Tvärsnitt* no. 2.

Tulis, Jeffrey K. 1987. *The Rhetorical Presidency.* Princeton, N.J.: Princeton University Press.

Uddhammar, Emil. 1993. *Partierna och den stora staten: En analys av statsteorier och svensk politik under 1900-talet.* Stockholm: City University Press.

Vedung, Evert. 1988. "The Swedish Five-Party Syndrome and the Environmentalists," in Kay Lawson and P. H. Merkl, eds., *When Parties Fail: Emerging Alternative Organizations.* Princeton, N.J.: Princeton University Press.

von Beyme, Klaus. 1992. "Den nordiska samhallsmodellens betydelse," in *Frihetens källa: Nordens betydelse för Europa.* Stockholm: Nordiska Rådet.

Wattenberg, Martin P. 1991. *The Rise of Candidate-Centered Politics: Presidential Elections of the 1980s.* Cambridge, Mass.: Harvard University Press.

Weir, Margaret, and Theda Skocpol. 1985. "State Structures and the Possibilities for 'Keynesian' Responses to the Great Depression in Sweden, Britain, and the United States," in P. Evans, D. Rueschemeyer, and T. Skocpol, eds., *Bringing the State Back In.* New York: Cambridge University Press.

Wertheimer, Fred. 1989. "Window of Opportunity: The Climate is Ripe for Ethics Reform." *Common Cause Magazine* July/August.

Westerståhl, Jorgen, and Folke Johansson. 1985. *Bilden av Sverige: Studier av nyheter och nyhetsideologier i TV, radio och dagspress.* Stockholm: SNS.

White, John Kenneth. 1995. "A Republican Realignment? Values and the 1994 Election." *Party Developments* 1, 3 (April 1995):1, 18–24.

Wildavsky, Aaron. 1987. "Choosing Preferences by Constructing Institutions: A Cultural Theory of Preference Formation." *American Political Science Review* 81:1, 3–21.

Witte, John. 1985. *The Politics and Development of the Federal Income Tax.* Madison: University of Wisconsin Press.

Wörlund, Ingemar. 1989. "The Election to the Swedish Riksdag 1988." *Scandinavian Political Studies* 12:1, 77–82.

Wright, Esmond. 1982. "How Relevant Is the New Deal?" *Encounter*, June–July; vol. 63, no. 6, p. 94.

Zaller, John. 1992. *The Nature and Origins of Mass Opinion*. New York: Cambridge University Press.

Index

For EU product safety concerns, contact us at Calle de José Abascal, 56–1°,
28003 Madrid, Spain or eugpsr@cambridge.org.

www.ingramcontent.com/pod-product-compliance
Ingram Content Group UK Ltd.
Pitfield, Milton Keynes, MK11 3LW, UK
UKHW020942270426
470322UK00029B/331